MW00442155

CONTEMPORARY LITERATURE AND THE STATE

Edited by Matthew Hart and Jim Hansen

CON
TEM
POR
ARY
LITERATURE

WINTER 2008 · VOLUME 49 · NUMBER 4

THE UNIVERSITY OF WISCONSIN PRESS

CONTEMPORARY LITERATURE

EDITORIAL OFFICE: *Department of English, 7141 Helen C. White Hall, 600 N. Park Street, University of Wisconsin, Madison, Wisconsin 53706.* Manuscripts are returned only if accompanied by a self-addressed envelope with sufficient first-class postage. The editors cannot review manuscripts that are simultaneously under consideration elsewhere and cannot assume responsibility for loss or damage of any work submitted. All details should conform to those recommended by the most recent edition of the *MLA Handbook.*

BUSINESS OFFICE: All correspondence about advertising, subscriptions, and allied matters should be sent to: *Journal Division, University of Wisconsin Press, 1930 Monroe Street, 3rd floor, Madison, Wisconsin 53711-2059.* Website: www.wisc.edu/wisconsinpress/journals

SUBSCRIPTION RATE: One year: $173 print and electronic; $161 electronic only (institutions); print and electronic $52; electronic only $45 (individuals only; must prepay); add $35 postage outside U.S. (no postage for electronic only).

Contemporary Literature (ISSN 0010-7484; E-ISSN 1548-9949) is published quarterly by the University of Wisconsin Press, 1930 Monroe Street, 3rd floor, Madison, WI 53711-2059. Website: www.wisc.edu/wisconsinpress/journals. Periodicals postage paid at Madison, WI and at additional mailing offices. POSTMASTER: Send address changes to *Contemporary Literature,* 1930 Monroe Street, 3rd floor, Madison, WI 53711-2059.

ONTENTS

MATTHEW HART
AND JIM HANSEN

Introduction: Contemporary Literature and the State

A writer's life is a highly vulnerable, almost naked activity. We don't have to weep about that. The writer makes his choice and is stuck with it. But it is true to say that you are open to all the winds, some of them icy indeed. You are out on your own, out on a limb. You find no shelter, no protection—unless you lie—in which case of course you have constructed your own protection and, it could be argued, become a politician.

Harold Pinter, "Art, Truth, and Politics"

It is only through being a member of the state that the individual himself has objectivity, truth, and ethical life.

G. W. F. Hegel, *Elements of a Philosophy of Right*

The passages quoted above represent the antinomy that this special issue of *Contemporary Literature* seeks to disrupt. If for Hegel the state is the necessary condition of political subjectivity—"It is the way of God with the world that the state exists," he is reported to have said—then for Harold Pinter the state too often serves as a mere shelter for lying politicians.[1] Speaking to the Swedish Academy in December 2005,

---

1. Our source for the Hegel quotation is the introduction to Tom Paulin's *Minotaur: Poetry and the Nation State*, which picks up several of the themes of our opening section (1). The authenticity of this dictum is debated. Walter Kaufmann explains that, despite its use by Hegel critics like Karl Popper, it derives from posthumous additions to *The Philosophy of Right*, based on lecture notes that might not be wholly reliable.

Contemporary Literature XLIX, 4   0010-7484; E-ISSN 1548-9949/08/0004-0491
© 2008 by the Board of Regents of the University of Wisconsin System

Pinter struck a theme out of George Orwell's journalism, seeming to divide art and politics into irreconcilable camps. As he explains in his Nobel Lecture, "Art, Truth, and Politics," he once believed that "a thing is not necessarily either true or false; it can be both true and false" (1). But in the context of the so-called war on terror, he now thinks these words require amendment. "I believe that these assertions still make sense," Pinter explains, "and do still apply to the exploration of reality through art. So as a writer I stand by them but as a citizen I cannot. As a citizen I must ask: What is true? What is false?" He warns us that political language does not share the same territory as the stylized interrogations of artistic practice, where one "stumble[s] upon the truth in the dark" of linguistic and aesthetic ambiguity (1). Politics, by contrast, is about "power and...the maintenance of that power. To maintain power it is essential that people remain in ignorance, that they live in ignorance of the truth, even the truth of their own lives" (3).

In his 1948 essay "Writers and Leviathan," Orwell likewise argued that in "an age of State control" writers must balance their duties as citizens against the imagination's need to resist "invasion" by politics (407–8). Adopting Thomas Hobbes's metaphor of the state as a "Leviathan"—a monstrous artificial man—Orwell argues that human beings have an obligation to take part in the messy and inherently compromised world of politics. For the special class of writers, however, this moral compunction goes hand-in-hand with the need to distinguish between "our political and our literary loyalties" (412). The fundamental nature of this opposition draws power from Orwell's sense that modern politics is unusually totalizing and irresistible: "War, Fascism, concentration camps, rubber truncheons, atomic bombs, etc. are what we daily think about, and therefore to a great extent what we write about, even when we do not name them openly. We cannot help this" (408). But a writer must keep some part of himself inviolate, so that "his writings...will always be the product of the saner self that stands aside, records the things that are done and admits their necessity, but refuses to be deceived as to their true nature" (414). For Orwell, as for Pinter, the state exists as a category of analysis in a largely negative sense. The state is overpowering, it demands conformity, and its power marks the failure of liberal principles of autonomy and free association.

It is questionable whether artists who use the ideologically charged medium of language can ever really separate, as Orwell desires, the realms of politics and literature. What's more, by reducing the relation between writers and Leviathan to a distinction between disinterested observation and necessary evils, Orwell acknowledges that he can't then discuss such subjects as state patronage of the arts (407). Angry at British and American militarism and imperialism, Pinter likewise tends to represent the state as a merely totalitarian regime blind to the slaughter of innocents and contemptuous of civil liberties—a rhetorical stratagem that implicitly occludes the state's long (if ambivalent) history as an agent of liberty, equality, and fraternity. As famously activist writers, Pinter and Orwell can hardly be accused of neglecting the collective dimensions of political struggle. Nevertheless, "Writers and Leviathan" and "Art, Truth, and Politics" finally favor the individual writer of conscience over the conformity implied by the state. In so doing they repeat a stance that is common among writers and intellectuals. Its roots perhaps lie in the poets' banishment from Plato's ideal republic; but it nevertheless received quintessential modern expression from Friedrich Nietzsche, who wrote in *Thus Spake Zarathustra* that a state is "the coldest of all cold monsters. Coldly lieth it also; and this lie creepeth from its mouth: 'I, the state, am the people'" (48). Motivated by the history of state violence against artists, and encouraged by an intellectual history in which artistic autonomy is opposed to institutionalized politics, authors like Pinter and Orwell distrust the cold monster and fear the synecdochical leap implied by the state's claim to represent the masses.

We don't write to belittle such fears. Indeed, by featuring dissident writers like the South African poet Jeremy Cronin and antifascists like Samuel Beckett, the contributors to this volume take them very seriously. We do, however, want to challenge the seeming necessity of the opposition between monolithic state and individual artist. As Bruce Robbins has argued in the context of debates about national guilt, it is sometimes difficult to break down the "supposed incommensurability of scale between moral individual and impersonal state." Yet such a relation does, in fact, exist: "The word we use to insist on the connection between those scales is *politics*"

(Robbins, "Comparative National Blaming" 152).[2] The essays in this volume therefore occupy the continuum between, for instance, Cronin's imprisonment by a tyrannical apartheid regime, the occluded literary history of the welfare state (the subject of recent books by Bruce Robbins and Michael Szalay), and the way fiction participates in the discursive examination of state failure—the topic of John Marx's essay on Chimamanda Ngozi Adichie's *Half of a Yellow Sun* (2006). Discussing a multinational range of texts from places as far apart as Yorkshire and Singapore, our contributors explore how and why the state model of government and citizenship remains important for writers and scholars in an age of "super mobility," where the movement of populations across the globe is more hectic than ever (Rutter et al. 6–11). Such questions have motivated our editorship of this special issue of *Contemporary Literature*, which we view not as an attempt to equate literature and politics but, rather, as a project that respects the complex semi-autonomy of those forms of human practice.[3] Though our contributors examine diverse textual and historical objects in sometimes dissimilar ways, they also refuse to see the state as a merely negative bugbear, purely affirmative category, or relic of bygone modernity.[4] The second section of this introduction therefore discusses two influential theoretical solutions to the perceived antinomy between the collective state and individuated subjectivity. Following a brief survey of the

---

2. Robbins's recent work on upward-mobility narratives and the welfare state is a perfect instance of work that takes place in the productive zone between negative and affirmative accounts of the state. For Robbins, one of the key lessons of the upward-mobility story is the way it restores our sense of how social class matters to real and imagined lives; but in reading narratives of the Progressive and New Deal eras, one cannot ignore the function of the state, which "cannot be seen as constituted *by* class identities and interests without also being seen as *constituting* class identities and interests" (Robbins, *Upward Mobility* 17). For discussion of Robbins alongside a wide range of new work on literature and the state, see Claybaugh.

3. In *Culture/Metaculture*, Francis Mulhern offers an important critique of how contemporary cultural studies strives "to institute culture as the authoritative subject of a discourse on social relations" at the expense of politics and the political (156).

4. Michael Szalay inveighs against this same dualism in criticizing "a politically safe reinvention of American radicalism, one in which the current academic left gets to discard two twinned versions of statism: the troubled legacy of Stalinism on the one hand, and the presumably hegemonic, mainstream liberalism of the New Deal on the other" (19). Szalay's brilliant rejoinder is to examine the aesthetic dimensions of social security projects that, in the words of Franklin D. Roosevelt, sought to "wipe out the line that divides the practical from the ideal" (qtd. in Szalay 9).

individual essays in the volume, we then consider the merits of the state as an analytical paradigm for literary studies in an age of globalization. These strands come together in a short reading of a recent novel by Mohsin Hamid.

Sovereignty and the Night Watchman

Philosophy and social thought provide an array of approaches through which to rethink the binary between state and individual subject. Perhaps the most famous of these is the micropolitical historicism of Michel Foucault, which begins by disentangling the state form of government from power in the abstract. In a 1976 lecture, Foucault argued that when it comes to political modernity, "we have to abandon the model of Leviathan...whose body is made up of citizens but whose soul is sovereignty" ("*Society*" 34). The transition into modernity under the aegis of the bourgeois liberal state involves the development of a new mechanism of power unsuited to the paradigm of unitary sovereignty. This modern form of "bio-power," as he would come to call it, "applies primarily to bodies and what they do rather than to the land and what it produces" (35). It is therefore not organized around territory, the law, or the body of the sovereign but around systems of surveillance and classification such as those found in human sciences like psychiatry, demography, or criminology. This "radically heterogeneous" power therefore depends not upon a "code of law" but upon "a code of normalization," such that its "jurisprudence...will be that of a clinical knowledge" (36, 38). In this context, Foucault declared in a 1977 interview that "for all the omnipotence of its apparatuses...the state can only operate on the basis of other, already-existing power relations. The state is superstructural in relation to a whole series of power networks that invest the body, sexuality, the family, kinship, knowledge, technology, and so forth" ("Truth and Power" 123).

Described this way, the state seems clumsily deficient for analyzing the political dimensions of the linguistic arts. After all, in the lists of human practices that deserve to be considered "radically heterogeneous," literary language-use surely occupies a prime spot. Against the theory of the state, then, we must surely prefer something like Foucault's "theory of domination, of dominations, rather than a theory of sovereignty" ("*Society*" 45). Yet even Foucault admits that, whereas the theory of sovereignty ought really to have been erased or overwritten by the emergence of disciplinary power, the sovereign state nevertheless retains meaning and authority, even in a modernity characterized by the rise of what Robbins calls "human rights individualism" ("Comparative National Blaming" 152). Foucault explains how, as the liberal democratic state emerged from the husk of the monarchical state, disciplinary modes of domination became the hegemonic form of power, even as they remained largely invisible. At the same time, however, the modern state inaugurated the democratization of law upon the basis of sovereignty, as we see in documents such as the American Declaration of Independence, where the claim of independence from Britain is inextricable from the defense of inalienable human liberties and the transference of the sovereign's representative function from the body of the monarch to the corporate body of "the people." This means that power is never entirely organized around disciplinary logics, for the discourse of sovereign individualism, and especially of human rights, acts as a brake upon the mechanics of discipline, with the authority of the state now finding expression in juridical codes and institutional norms. We are faced, then, with two antitheses that are "so heterogeneous that we can never reduce one to the other" but which nevertheless function as the limits between which modern politics is exercised and constituted. There is, first, "the principle of the sovereignty of the social body and the delegation of individual sovereignty to the State"; and then there is the "tight grid of disciplinary coercions that actually guarantees the cohesion of that social body" ("*Society*" 37). The solution to this antithesis is the "art of government," in which the management of the population through the new sciences of political economy and demography means that the object of politics changes from "the act of government itself" to the "welfare of the population" (Foucault, "Governmentality" 216–17).[5] As the modern state develops new forms of welfare provision and social policy, the dichotomy

---

5. See also, in this context, Foucault's investigation of the state's combined individualizing and totalizing power. In "'*Omnes et Singulatim*': Toward a Critique of Political Reason," he identifies a concept of "pastorship" that mitigates the contradiction between the tight grid of disciplinarity and the desire for autonomy that finds its juridical expression in the discourse of sovereign rights (298–325, esp. 324–25).

between sovereignty and disciplinarity is replaced by a three-way relation: "a triangle, sovereignty-discipline-government, which has as its primary target the population and as its essential mechanism the apparatuses of security" ("Governmentality" 219).

Thus while the state is weakened as an analytic paradigm by the way it presumes the unity of power, located in a representative body and in the idea that sovereignty extends over a territory, it remains fundamental to political modernity. As Eric Keenaghan shows in his essay for this volume, Foucault offers us a theory of power that productively avoids the state/individual dichotomy, allowing us to read an unusual political attitude like the American poet Robert Duncan's "queer anarchism" as a meaningful critique of liberalism and tyranny, not just an individualist reaction to the excesses of the Vietnam-era left. This does not mean, alas, that all our theoretical problems have been solved. Recent scholarship in international-relations theory, for instance, tends to insist that there are few real-world instances when a unitary mode of sovereign authority is dominant. Stephen D. Krasner, for one, describes four types of sovereignty that overlap and even contradict one another, thereby revealing how the arrangement of power within a given territory is only one matrix of political power at the state level: one must also consider inter- and transnational forms of sovereignty (5).[6] And while Krasner allows us to question the historical and spatial assumptions within Foucault's system, David Lloyd and Paul Thomas critique its philosophical underpinnings. In their investigation of how liberal theories of political representation depended upon a conservative notion of aesthetic education, they suggest that, despite Foucault's emphasis to the contrary, the "concept of an emergent governmentality requires not only disciplinary institutions themselves, but a certain *idea* of the state" (4). By concentrating on the arbitrary, the ad hoc, and disciplinary normalization, Foucault fails to articulate the synecdoche that is involved in

---

6. The four types of sovereignty are "domestic sovereignty," or "the organization of authority in a given state"; "interdependence sovereignty," or the right of a body to regulate phenomena, such as trade or immigration, across its borders; "international legal sovereignty," or the legal status of "a political entity in the international system"; and "Westphalian sovereignty," or the idea that foreign powers should be excluded from the nation-state territory (Krasner 7–11). Foucault focuses on the first of these types.

imagining a state in terms of representation, where a representative man—an ideal subject or legislator—stands in for the Leviathan and figuratively embodies what Lloyd and Thomas refer to as the very "*idea* of the state."

We turn to the transnational dimensions of this problem in a minute. For now, if Foucauldian microhistory doesn't quite satisfy the theoretical need to grasp the state in whole cloth, then Antonio Gramsci's work on hegemony and popular assent in the *Prison Notebooks* provides us with a model that looks at this "idea" of the state. In an entry entitled "Gendarme or Night-Watchman State, etc.," Gramsci observes the problematic of state power not only from the perspective of the Nietzschean dissident, but also from that of a dissident, heterodox Marxist. Here, Gramsci imagines the idea of an "ethical state," a state that can, at least in some sense, be celebrated as a "civil society" (75). Where Foucault's approach equates the formation of the subject with the ethical problematic of its normalization, Gramsci's thought holds the ethical and the political in tension. Rather than a unitary theory of the state, Gramsci develops a theory of a "regulated society" that includes a shift "from a phase in which state equals government to a phase in which state is identified with civil society" (75). In this process, there occurs "a transition phase of state as night watchman, that is, of a coercive organization that will protect the development of those elements of regulated society that are continually on the rise and, precisely because they are on the rise, will gradually reduce the state's authoritarian and coercive interventions" (75–76). For Gramsci, the coercive authority of the state cannot simply be countered by the individual, representative or otherwise. In fact, through a notion of representation or synecdoche—the principle, after all, of republican and liberal-democratic forms of government—the individual is already a version of either the authoritarian or the liberal state. What is called for, instead, is a theory that understands how hegemony is produced and asks which notions of representation produce assent in those governed by the state. Gramsci's method, as Timothy Brennan implies, shifts the terrain of political criticism away from the "immaterial desires and self-understandings" implied by Foucault's interest in disciplinary individuation and back toward more "material interests" that involve issues such as economy and labor (245). By focusing not only on the people governed by normative structures but also on how their assent is manufactured, reshaped, and reimagined, Gramsci offers us a way to think about state power that is nether wholly Hegelian—and so subject to the utopian impulses of Hegel's teleological idealism—nor merely piecemeal and so lacking an idea of the state. Gramsci's method offers us a critical strategy for viewing the state as neither a jackbooted extension of sovereignty nor a blindly utopian end point for all history. In opposition to a Foucauldian approach, which offers us a model of human interactions that eventually generate certain forms of governance, Gramsci makes the state a necessary precondition of human freedom. Reductively, then, we might say that where Foucault's method comprises a "bottom-up" approach to history, Gramsci's dialectical vision demands both the "bottom-up" and "top-down" approaches. In identifying how assent takes place, how hegemonic institutions are replicated and manipulated, we can better understand how to imagine other forms of governmentality, other forms of state power.

The goal of imagining alternative arrangements of power has been a lifelong project of the South African poet Jeremy Cronin, who is interviewed in the opening section of this volume by Andrew van der Vlies. Cronin first drew international attention in 1976, when he was jailed by the apartheid government for his work with the banned South African Communist Party. His first book of poems, *Inside* (1983), came out of this seven-year imprisonment—and not surprisingly, it has much to say about the use and abuse of power. In Van der Vlies's words, these poems represent "a political act of faith, a *demand* for a space for an imagined future community." As one of South Africa's leading Anglophone poets, Cronin continues to write poetry that he describes as "a place to keep the open-ended open." He refuses, however, to see poetry and politics as incommensurable. Indeed, they are the two pillars of his work, since his postapartheid life has been spent as a member of Parliament in the governing coalition of the African National Congress. As poet and acknowledged legislator, Cronin refuses to see politics as merely the art of the possible; he instead describes it as "a passionate struggle for the desirable" and talks of avoiding the consolations of individualism, ending one powerful answer with the Gramscian assertion, "I want to be part of a democratic hege-monic project, not a prophet in the wilderness."

Staying in South Africa, Rita Barnard's essay, "Tsotsis: On Law, the Outlaw, and the Postcolonial State," interprets the two versions of *Tsotsi*, Athol Fugard's 1980 novel and Gavin Hood's Oscar-winning 2005 movie adaptation. Barnard reads Fugard's *Tsotsi* as a kind of proto-*Bildungsroman*, a tale of outlaw life in which the possi-bility for progressive narrative development is almost wholly sup-pressed by the conditions of township life in a racist state. By contrast, Hood's celebrated film has a manifestly different orienta-tion to the state, an ideological shift that can be read in its whole-hearted embrace of the *Bildungsroman* genre. Mixing genre criticism with an analysis of South Africa's transition from settler-colonial state to "neoliberal punitive" polity, Barnard demonstrates the state's productivity as a lens for literary analysis, especially for post-colonial societies where ideas of national culture are often decidedly problematic.

The historicization of plot and form is also a key element of essays by John Marx and Matthew Hart. In "The Third English Civil War: David Peace's Occult History of Thatcherism," Hart provides the first extended essay on *GB84*, Peace's 2004 novel about the Thatcher-era miners' strike in Britain. Employing sociological and philosophi-cal work by Carl Schmitt and Chantal Mouffe alongside a discussion of Peace's attitude toward realism, Hart reads the "occult" style of *GB84* as a consequence of the existential dimensions of the strike—a life-and-death struggle that reflects a greater failure of liberal-demo-cratic politics. In "Failed State Fiction," Marx offers an implicit coun-terargument to Schmitt's critique of normative accounts of state power, an aspect of his political philosophy influentially adapted by Giorgio Agamben. Combining Foucault's concept of biopower with a theoretical framework that draws on mainstream social-scientific indices of civic dysfunction and collapse, Marx sketches a genealogy of fictions about state failure. This subgenre of the political and post-colonial novel not only shows how everyday life goes on amid the collapse of state services and sovereignty; it also demonstrates how authors use narrative fiction to challenge the agency and expertise of social scientists, relief workers, and government officials.

Hart's invocation of Schmitt and Marx's use of Foucault reflect the strength of the current interest in theories of "the political" and, especially, the "biopolitical"—the point at which governments exercise power through the facts of living and human reproduction. These terms are also important to the next two writers in our issue. In "Life, War, and Love: The Queer Anarchism of Robert Duncan's Poetic Action during the Vietnam War," Eric Keenaghan picks up the challenge of describing the American poet's beliefs in the 1960s and 1970s, when Duncan published his most aggressively political poems yet fell out with friends like Denise Levertov as a result of their antiwar activism. In order to explain this seeming paradox, Keenaghan looks to anarchism as a creed that doesn't just reject the ideas of state power fostered by Marxism and liberalism but also contains the seed of a "queer" redefinition of what counts as love and life. Jim Hansen's essay, "Samuel Beckett's *Catastrophe* and the Theater of Pure Means," sets Beckett's persistently negative theatrical experimentation against Agamben's highly influential conception of biopolitics. Rather than asking predictable questions about Beckett's various political commitments, Hansen proposes that we note how Beckett's dramatic pieces stage "theatricality" itself in order to draw attention to the failings of modern notions of the political. By reintroducing the Hegelian-Marxist conception of sublation into his analysis, Hansen implies that literature is, at best, a mode of mediation rather than a direct or immediate form of political action.

Our penultimate essay returns to the postcolonial context with which we began. Jini Kim Watson's "The Way Ahead: The Politics and Poetics of the Developmental Landscape" investigates state narratives of modernity via two Anglophone Singaporean poets, Edwin Thumboo and Arthur Yap. Locating a distilled "nationalist essense" in Thumboo's depiction of the urban landscapes of contemporary Singapore, Watson goes on to suggest that Yap's poetry reworks and rearticulates these landscapes so as to provide innovative ways to think about the spaces inhabited by those who are governed. In the end, Watson's essay, like Yap's poetry, affirms an open and potentially dissident version of the modern Asian state. Finally, in his specially commissioned afterword, "States of Time," Ian Baucom shifts the terrain of the debate by suggesting that the concept of temporality must remain central to any notion of governmentality, sovereignty, globalism, or hegemony. For Baucom, time finds its material signification in and as narrative. His far-reaching analysis discusses writers as diverse as John Milton and J. M. Coetzee, but his focus is always on the Hobbesian moment and on the concept of state sovereignty that it inaugurated. Claiming that modern Hobbesian conceptions of the state have imagined themselves outside of time itself—or, as Rita Barnard also notes, have rendered the time before the invention of the state unimaginable—Baucom finally argues that the state has made a kind of contract with its citizens "to guarantee that the unimaginable past will not invade the present and has been banished from the future." The labor of this collection, as Baucom asserts, is to complicate this contract, interrogate its ideologies, and listen to the past it tries to silence.

The State and the Globe

These descriptions suggest the state's importance as a lens through which to discuss writers' investigations of justice and authority. But what of the changing nature of political economy throughout the world? Can an apparently rooted and territorial concept like the state be reconciled with new approaches to transnational and world literature?

Conversations about globalization tend to combine a focus on newly transnational elements of political economy with the proposition that the national state is of declining importance as an object of cultural identification. Although there is much debate about the novelty or extent of globalization, theorists tend to agree that "economic globalization represents a major transformation in the territorial organization of economic activity and politico-economic power" (Sassen 1). Indeed, although the conversation surrounding the new capitalism became less utopian at the turn of the millennium—when a series of political and financial crises tested public confidence in global neoliberalism—even avowed opponents of globalization admit its transformative effects.[7] The Marxist historian

---

7. We refer to the pessimistic turn in popular discourse about economic globalization that followed upon the 1997 Asian financial crisis, the disruption of the 1999 World Trade Organization Ministerial Conference in Seattle by antiglobalization protesters, and the perennially stalled nature of the "Doha Round" (2001–present) of WTO negotiations between developed and less-developed countries.

Moishe Postone, for instance, has described the late twentieth century as bringing about "the end of the state-centric order," during which time "the global order was transformed from an international to a supranational one" (109). In Postone's analysis, a common thread links the collapse or deregulation of most socialist economies, the imposition of International Monetary Fund structural adjustment policies on governments in the so-called Global South, and the assault on welfare-state capitalism in Europe, North America, and Australasia. Together, these events comprise "the end of the phase of state-directed, nationally based development" (Postone 100).

For Postone, this development poses "huge conceptual difficulties for all those who viewed the state as an agent of positive change" (100). But it isn't finally clear that an increase in global economic connectedness necessarily portends a proportionate decrease in the analytic significance of the state. Saskia Sassen criticizes what she calls a "global-national duality," where world and state are "conceived as a mutually exclusive set of terrains where the national economy or state loses what the global economy gains" (6). Understood through this dualism, globalization becomes a zero-sum game in which salient aspects of the contemporary experience are missed. Sassen describes, for instance, how the managerial operations of transnational corporations are "disproportionately concentrated in the…highly developed countries" (10), so that much of the activity that drives the global economy, "including some of the most strategic functions necessary for globalization," remains grounded in nation-states of a familiarly powerful sort (14). For example, Sassen views the market deregulation that encourages the transnational movement of capital not as *prima facie* evidence of "loss of control by the state" but, rather, as an example of how governments have learned to handle "the juxtaposition of the interstate consensus to pursue globalization and the fact that national legal systems remain as the major, or crucial, instantiation through which guarantees of contract and property rights are enforced" (27). The justice of this view also appears to have been borne out by recent events. As we go to press, the United States has combined with European governments to coordinate the part-nationalization of banks and financial services companies. As the global economic system appears to totter under the weight of a systemic crisis in the availability of credit, the nation-state seems to have reemerged, not as the historical residue of transnational capitalism, but as the Keynesian banker of last resort.

We might criticize this language as too focused on elite economic experience or the contingencies of the present moment. Yet Sassen's case against global-national dualism is consistent with recent arguments by cultural theorists attuned to a different set of transnational subjects. In their work on "minor transnationalism," for example, the literary scholars Françoise Lionnet and Shu-Mei Shih have criticized the way that academic approaches to transnationalism tend to break down into a binaristic model that opposes the global to the local, consigns the former to the category of elite experience, and romanticizes locality as a site of resistance to the hegemonic order (6). For Lionnet and Shih, such undialectical thinking only crudely reflects the complex social and geographic realities of globalization. "What is lacking in the binary model of above-and-below, the utopic and dystopic, and the global and the local," they write, "is an awareness and recognition of the creative interventions that networks of minoritized cultures produce within and across national boundaries" (7).[8] In a similar vein, Aamir Mufti has described the relation between state-mediated "minority" experience and the political and economic "expansionism whose ultimate goal...is the global establishment of the market, and thus of the rule of equivalence (but not equality)" (3). If the global market involves the reshaping of diverse peoples and experiences into "equivalent 'values,' that is, citizens," then this global tale begins with the "well-known and well-understood story" that "'the nation' (of supposedly equal citizens) in the colonized world emerges out of the very socioeconomic processes that it comes to oppose" (3). Globalization and empire do not mean the dissolution of the state as a category of analysis; they rather denote its constitutive inflection by "foreign" geographies and developmental temporalities—whether local, global, or otherwise.

---

8. Moreover, theories of globalization risk marginalizing those with just claims to make on national governments and citizenries. Lionnet and Shih refer to the problems faced by undocumented migrants or refugees who lack the right kind of citizenship papers in contexts "when the nation-state remains the chief mechanism for dispersing and regulating power, status, and material resources" (8).

If the political economics of globalization do not imply the end of the state, how do we reconcile it with the idea of a world literature? The essays collected in this issue show the inadequacy of purely national categories for literary production and interpretation; at the same time, however, they demonstrate the importance of the state as a literary theme and critical optic. Two factors explain this apparent paradox. The first follows a logic familiar from Sassen's argument about global-national dualism. The second takes us back to an elementary—though sometimes overlooked—aspect of political theory.

First, the state and the world are not only commensurate: they are mutually productive. In *The World Republic of Letters* (1999; trans. 2004), Pascale Casanova criticizes "globalization" as a "neutralizing term…which suggests that the world political and economic system can be conceived as the generalization of a single and universally applicable model." She prefers, instead, the term "internationalization," which implies that it is "competition among its members that defines and unifies [world literary space] while at the same time marking its limits" (40). For Casanova, then, the very unity of global literature is predicated on the agonistic interrelation of its parts. Similarly, Lionnet and Shih's term "transnational" avoids the universality of the term "global." A transnational criticism, they suggest, goes through and across the state, as well as beyond or around it.

Second, state and nation are relatively autonomous concepts. The state form of government got a rare ideological fillip when Romantic nationalists like Johann Gottfried Herder sought to embed Nietzsche's "coldest of cold monsters" within the warm embrace of vernacular language and literature. But state and nation are not identical, and there is no good reason to assume that the "global" critique of nationality presumes an equivalent critique of the state. The idea of a state points to a political entity that, as Max Weber defined it, "(successfully) claims the *monopoly of the legitimate use of physical force* within a given territory" (78). The idea of a "nation," however, draws on concepts of consanguinity and folk heritage. With its etymological roots in the Latin for "birth" (*natus*), the political meaning of "nation" as indicating a group of citizens organized under a single government has only gradually supplanted the sense of a people unified by birth, customs, or language.

Or rather, the political meaning has not so much replaced the cultural as appropriated and redeployed it. As Weber remarks, modern states need to legitimize their monopoly on violence. This can be done through the influence of a charismatic leader, or through the body of "rationally created *rules*" we call the law (Weber 79). But legitimation can also be accomplished by using language and culture to provide a conceptual and emotional unity between state and people, a process that Weber describes as drawing upon "the authority of the 'eternal yesterday'" (78). In this way, the French state becomes the political home of those who belong to the ethnolinguistic family of France, Germany of the Germans, and so on.

These notions of ethnolinguistic consanguinity exercised extraordinary power during the institutionalization of literary studies in the Anglo-American academy, where scholarly fields, curricula, and departments are often still divided along national lines. They are, however, of declining significance today, when the contingent tie between language, literature, and nation is coming undone in the face of the global movement of peoples and books. In Rebecca L. Walkowitz's apt formulation, we live at a time when literary texts ask to be read through a proliferating number of literary-historical "objects" and "containers" (542–43). As Walkowitz writes about Caryl Phillips, "his books may seem like objects, but they are full of containers: comparative frameworks that impose new classifications and ask us to question what we know about the location of literature" (542). The state, the essays collected here suggest, remains one of those containers. It has been forced into new relations with a variety of local and global actors, to be sure; it even comes in nonnational garb. But whatever its appearance, the state and its agents have not left the scene. Contemporary literary production surely involves the crossing and confounding of national borders—if not in practice, then in imagination. But those borders—in practice, if not in imagination—are also policed by states with access to ever more panoptical forms of protection and control.

The Affairs of Others

The patterns we have so far outlined in general terms are realized with richly imaginative particularity in the second novel by Mohsin

Hamid, a writer of Pakistani birth, American education, British residence, and joint British-Pakistani citizenship. *The Reluctant Fundamentalist* (2007) is set in a Lahore marketplace on a single day in the recent past, from which perspective it narrates the events of several years on four continents. It is the monologue of a Pakistani university lecturer, Changez, who addresses his remarks to a silent and unnamed American of martial aspect—an off-duty soldier in the wrong place, perhaps, or a CIA agent sent to kill our narrator, whose videotaped harangues about U.S. foreign policy have begun to feature "in the occasional war-on-terror montage" (182).[9] Changez is a self-consciously transnational subject. The child of a shabby-genteel family, he initially leaves Lahore in search of the Subcontinental holy grail—an Ivy League education and a high-paying job with coveted H–1B visa status.[10] After graduating from Princeton, where he discreetly holds down three jobs to supplement his scholarship, Changez is taken on by an elite New York financial services corporation that—after bankrolling a summer of island-hopping in Greece—sends him to Chile and the Philippines to determine the value of companies before their inevitable takeover or downsizing. He initially enjoys life in Manhattan, pursuing a romance with Erica, a beautiful novelist manqué from the Upper East Side, and reveling in the coexistence of Wall Street's cathedrals to high finance and the Pak-Punjab Deli: "I was, in four and a half years, never an American; I was *immediately* a New Yorker" (33). As he assimilates to the corporate elite, Changez even succumbs to the postpolitical language he later detests as the taint of market-led imperialism: "On that day, I did not think of myself as a Pakistani, but as an Underwood Samson trainee" (34).

The Reluctant Fundamentalist is concerned with subjects like cross-cultural romance, transnational capitalism, and the limits of cosmopolitan space. The topicality of its themes has moreover combined

---

9. The monologue structure of *The Reluctant Fundamentalist* is an overt homage to Albert Camus's 1956 novel *The Fall* (Hamid, "Critical Outtakes").

10. The "H–1B" is a nonimmigrant U.S. visa granted to university-educated foreign workers in fields such as academia, banking, and information technology. Its coveted nature is attested to by the fact that the entire 2007–8 quota of sixty-five thousand visas was exhausted on the very first day they were offered ("Labor").

with the global market for Anglophone South Asian fiction to ensure its translation into twenty languages, securing a readership in countries as diverse as China, Turkey, and Finland. This is an instance, however, where the text's adventures in world literary space provide more room for optimism than the novel itself. Hamid holds no brief for painless cultural translation or hybridization; he rather explores how the force of events drives individual men and imperial states alike into a mutual destruction—a nightmare of imperial conflict in which, as in Beirut or Berlin in decades past, armed Americans haunt countries that are not quite enemies but hardly friends.

The key event in this narrative is Al-Qaeda's September 2001 attacks on New York. Changez witnesses the carnage on TV from his Manila hotel room, and his first reaction, before being overcome with shame, is one of satisfaction: "I stared as one—and then the other—of the twin towers of New York's World Trade Center collapsed. And then I *smiled*. Yes, despicable as it may sound, my initial reaction was to be remarkably pleased.... I was caught up in the *symbolism* of it all, the fact that someone had so visibly brought America to her knees" (72–73). *Schadenfreude* has a price, however, and for a Muslim male like Changez it comes quickly. Returning to the U.S., he is challenged by an immigration agent, who quashes any hope that membership in the corporate elite trumps race or citizenship: "'What is the purpose of your trip to the United States?' she asked me. 'I live here,' I replied. 'That is *not* what I asked you, sir,' she said" (75). Soon after, he has to confront public racism, a traumatized girlfriend, and the suspicion of his colleagues. Beloved Manhattan is festooned with flags, transformed into an island fortress.

From this point on, Changez fights a losing battle to separate cosmopolitan New York from the chauvinism and imperial self-interest he associates with the U.S. wars in Afghanistan and Iraq. In this context, his postpolitical self-image crumbles. In Chile, the gently erudite manager of a failing publishing house compares him to the foreign-born janissaries of the Ottoman Empire: "They were ferocious and utterly loyal: they had fought to erase their own civilizations, so they had nothing else to turn to" (151). As before, the point is driven home when Changez crosses the border between international airspace and the sovereign territory of the U.S. homeland:

I was struck by how traditional your empire appeared. Armed sentries manned the check post at which I sought entry; being of a suspect race I was quarantined and subjected to additional inspection; once admitted I hired a charioteer who belonged to a serf class lacking the requisite permission to abide legally and forced therefore to accept work at lower pay; I myself was a form of indentured servant whose right to remain was dependent upon the continued benevolence of my employer.

(157)

Such passages speak to the ways in which global villages like New York remain subject to the exceptional power of the state; they don't, however, tell us what sort of "reluctant fundamentalist" Changez will become. In fact, Hamid's title contains an irony because, while Changez is indeed slow to oppose American might, as a secular Muslim he is no religious fundamentalist. (The true fundamentalists are the employees of Underwood Samson, whose relentless focus on the global bottom line is the secular complement to Al-Qaeda's dreams of a new caliphate.)[11] At the end of the novel, Changez has returned to Lahore and has allied himself with jihad-inclined students. Still, his commitment, such as it is, is not to a religion but to the fundamentals of shame and anger: anger at American indifference to the victims of U.S. military reprisals, shame for Pakistan's place in the world; anger at the death of his immigrant dream and shame for his complicity in American empire. The politics that emerges from these emotions is basically nationalist. Changez speaks of the time when Pakistan was not "burdened by debt, dependent on foreign aid" and falls into a first-person plural that is the polar opposite of his earlier claim to corporate citizenship: "*We* built the Royal Mosque and the Shalimar Gardens in this city, and *we* built the Lahore Fort with its mighty walls.... when your country

---

11. In the nervous period after 9/11, Changez clings to his work as an economic analyst in language that clarifies its status as a secular fundamentalism, complete with immanent revelation and messianic teleology: "I was never better at the pursuit of fundamentals than I was at that time, analyzing data as though my life depended on it. Our creed was one which valued above all else maximum productivity, and such a creed was for me doubly reassuring because it was quantifiable—and hence *knowable*—in a period of great uncertainty, and because it remained utterly convinced of the possibility of progress while others longed for a sort of *classical* period that had come and gone, if it had ever existed at all" (116–17).

was still a collection of thirteen small colonies, gnawing away at the edge of a continent" (102–3). For all this, however, his nationalism contains no ethnopoetics of Pakistani difference. Indeed, Changez is critical of how, in the wake of 9/11, America gave itself over "to a dangerous nostalgia," a black-and-white image of a Technicolor world: "What your fellow countrymen longed for was unclear to me—a time of unquestioned dominance? of safety? of moral certainty? I did not know—but that they were scrambling to don the costumes of another era was apparent" (115). This element of his politics is figuratively confirmed, meanwhile, by the fate of his lover. Traumatized by the 9/11 attacks into a recurrence of her adolescent depression, Erica gradually succumbs to grief for a long-dead boyfriend. Like the cosmopolitan city that disappears into the body of American empire, she becomes more and more distant, wasting away before finally vanishing from the hospital. Erica's story therefore forms a loose allegory within Changez's autobiography, her suicidal melancholia representing America's collective retreat into "myths of [its] own difference" (168).[12] National difference, Erica's story implies, risks becoming mere nostalgia—a tragic failure to face the present as it is.

If it is neither religious nor ethnopoetic, how then to describe Changez's nationalism? The short answer is that it is *political*— political because it is predicated on an agonistic relation between two states, the U.S. and Pakistan, and on the judgment that the American response to 9/11 has only worsened Pakistani underdevelopment and insecurity. Hamid gives us reason to doubt the moral effects of this judgment—Changez resorts to evasive courtroom clichés, for instance, when discussing his complicity with terrorists—but *The Reluctant Fundamentalist* leaves no room for us to reject the ex-janissary as a merely atavistic effusion, a symptom of "Islamofascism" or worse. Rather, Hamid wants us to take Changez seriously. This is partly because—like Pinter—he shares Changez's resentment of America's "constant interference in the affairs of others" (156). More importantly, it is because Changez's story is

---

12. James Lasdun points out how the lovers' names confirm this allegorical relation: "It dawns on you that Erica is America (Am-Erica) . . . while the narrator himself stands for the country's consequent inability to accept, uh, changez." The allegory is less clumsy than Lasdun makes it sound.

about the resurgence of inter-national politics from within the carapace of globalization and the postpolitical. This is why it is so important that Changez journeys from a life of unipolar cosmopolitanism—a life in which America represents global modernity, a city in which a brown-skinned man appears for a while to move as freely as the dollar—into a world of armed belligerents, fortified borders, and agonistic nationalisms. The post–9/11 world, Hamid implies, is full of new terrors and opportunities; but it is also a familiar world of imperial states and nationalist insurgencies, where the work of language and politics goes on—uncertainly, unflinchingly.

Acknowledgments

This issue represents the collaborative work of many people. Thank you, first and always, to our families. Thanks also to Rebecca Walkowitz, Tom Schaub, and Mary Mekemson at *Contemporary Literature*, who responded positively and constructively at every stage of this project's development. Like all editors, we owe a debt of gratitude to those unsung heroes, our anonymous peer reviewers; and to our contributors for producing such fine essays and for putting up with our editorial deadlines and suggestions. Special thanks to Rita Barnard for putting us in contact with Andrew van der Vlies (and thus Jeremy Cronin) and to Amanda Claybaugh for connecting us with John Marx. We owe a particular debt of gratitude to Ian Baucom, who read the whole issue in draft before writing his afterword, thereby earning himself a short deadline and a hard word limit.

Our colleagues at the University of Illinois, and elsewhere, have been invaluable sounding boards. We are grateful for the encouragement and wisdom provided by Amanda Claybaugh, Jed Esty, Lauren M. E. Goodlad, Andy Hoberek, Lawrence Jones, Michael Rothberg, Andrea Stevens, Philip Stern, and Joe Valente. Our initial thinking was stimulated by the Unit for Criticism and Interpretive Theory conference, "States of Welfare," organized by Michael Rothberg and Lauren Goodlad at the University of Illinois in March 2006. Thanks, finally, to the institutions that supported us in numerous ways. Matt Hart wrote the proposal while a fellow of the Society for the Humanities at Cornell University. The introduction was written while Matt was on leave courtesy of the University of Illinois Campus Research Board. The initial germ for the collection came from two events we coordinated at the 2005 and 2006 conventions of the Modernist Studies Association. Thanks to the participants in our panel on sovereignty, in which Jim presented an early version of his Beckett essay, and our seminar on modernism and the state. A section of Matt's paper on David Peace was presented at the 2007 "Millennial Fictions" conference sponsored by Brunel University and the London Network for Modern Fiction Studies. All these trips were made possible by the generous support of the Scholars' Travel Fund at the University of Illinois.

WORKS CITED

Brennan, Timothy. *Wars of Position: The Cultural Politics of Left and Right*. New York: Columbia UP, 2006.

Casanova, Pascale. *The World Republic of Letters*. Trans. M. B. DeBevoise. Cambridge, MA: Harvard UP, 2004.

Claybaugh, Amanda. "Government Is Good." *Minnesota Review* 70 (2008). 20 Dec. 2008 <http://www.theminnesotareview.org/journal/ns70/claybaugh.shtml>.

Faubion, James B., ed. *Power: Essential Works of Foucault, 1954–1984*. Trans. Robert Hurley et al. Vol. 3. New York: New P, 2000.

Foucault, Michel. "Governmentality." Faubion 201–22.

———. "*'Omnes et Singulatim'*: Toward a Critique of Political Reason." Faubion 298–325.

———. *"Society Must Be Defended": Lectures at the Collège de France, 1975–1976*. Ed. Mauro Bertani and Alessandro Fontana. Trans. David Macey. New York: Picador, 2003.

———. "Truth and Power." Faubion 111–33.

Gramsci, Antonio. *Prison Notebooks*. Trans. Joseph A. Buttigieg. Vol. 3. New York: Columbia UP, 2007.

Hamid, Mohsin. "Critical Outtakes: Mohsin Hamid on Camus, Immigration, and Love." Interview. Conducted by John Freeman. *Critical Mass: The Blog of the National Book Critics Circle Directors* 30 Mar. 2007. 7 Apr. 2008 <http://bookcriticscircle.blogspot.com/2007/03/critical-outakes-mohsin-hamid-on-camus.html>.

———. *The Reluctant Fundamentalist*. Orlando, FL: Harcourt, 2007.

Hegel, G. W. F. *Elements of the Philosophy of Right*. Ed. Allen W. Wood. Trans. H. B. Nisbet. Cambridge: Cambridge UP, 1991.

Kaufmann, Walter. "The Hegel Myth and Its Method." 1959. 17 May 2008 <http://www.marxists.org/reference/subject/philosophy/works/us/kaufmann.htm>.

Krasner, Stephen D. "Problematic Sovereignty." *Problematic Sovereignty: Contested Rules and Political Possibilities*. Ed. Stephen D. Krasner. New York: Columbia UP, 2001. 1–23.

"Labor. U.S. Gets H–1B Applications." *Washington Post* 4 Apr. 2007. *Lexis-Nexis Academic*. University Library at University of Illinois, Urbana-Champaign. 20 May 2008 <http://www.lexisnexis.com/>.

Lasdun, James. "The Empire Strikes Back." Rev. of *The Reluctant Fundamentalist*, by Mohsin Hamid. *Guardian* 3 Mar. 2007. 13 May 2008 <http://books.guardian.co.uk/review/story/0,,2025106,00.html>.

Lionnet, Françoise, and Shu-Mei Shih. "Thinking Through the Minor, Transnationally." *Minor Transnationalism*. Ed. Françoise Lionnet and Shu-Mei Shih. Durham, NC: Duke UP, 2005. 1–26.

Lloyd, David, and Paul Thomas. *Culture and the State*. New York: Routledge, 1998.

Mufti, Aamir. *Enlightenment in the Colony: The Jewish Question and the Crisis of Postcolonial Culture*. Princeton, NJ: Princeton UP, 2007.

Mulhern, Francis. *Culture/Metaculture*. New York: Routledge, 2000.

Nietzsche, Friedrich. *Thus Spoke Zarathustra*. Trans. Walter Kaufmann. New York: Viking, 1954.

Orwell, George. "Writers and Leviathan." *In Front of Your Nose: Collected Essays, Journalism, and Letters, 1945–1950*. Vol. 4. Ed. Sonia Orwell and Ian Angus. Boston: Godine/Nonpareil, 2000.

Paulin, Tom. *Minotaur: Poetry and the Nation State*. Cambridge, MA: Harvard UP, 1992.

Pinter, Harold. "Art, Truth, and Politics." Nobel Lecture. 7 Dec. 2005. *Nobelprize.org*. 31 Mar. 2008 <http://nobelprize.org/nobel_prizes/literature/laureates/2005/pinter-lecture-e.html>.

Postone, Moishe. "History and Helplessness: Mass Mobilization and Contemporary Forms of Anticapitalism." *Public Culture* 18.1 (2006): 93–110.

Robbins, Bruce. "Comparative National Blaming: W. G. Sebald on the Bombing of Germany." *Forgiveness, Mercy, and Clemency*. Ed. Austin Sarat and Nasser Hussain. Stanford, CA: Stanford UP, 2007. 138–55.

———. *Upward Mobility and the Common Good: Toward a Literary History of the Welfare State*. Princeton, NJ: Princeton UP, 2007.

Rutter, Jill, Maria Latorre, and Dhananjayan Sriskandarajah. *Beyond Naturalisation: Citizenship Policy in an Age of Super Mobility*. London: Institute for Public Policy Research, 2008.

Sassen, Saskia. *Losing Control? Sovereignty in an Age of Globalization*. New York: Columbia UP, 1996.

Szalay, Michael. *New Deal Modernism: American Literature and the Invention of the Welfare State*. Durham, NC: Duke UP, 2000.

Walkowitz, Rebecca L. "The Location of Literature: The Transnational Book and the Migrant Writer." *Immigrant Fictions: Contemporary Literature in an Age of Globalization*. Ed. Rebecca L. .Walkowitz. Spec. issue of *Contemporary Literature* 47 (2006): 546–69.

Weber, Max. *From Max Weber: Essays in Sociology*. Ed. and trans. H. H. Gerth and C. Wright Mills. London: Routledge, 1991.

JEREMY CRONIN

an interview with

JEREMY CRONIN

Conducted by Andrew van der Vlies

The work of South African poet Jeremy Cronin illustrates uncommonly well the difficulties and dangers of writing in, and in relation to, the institutions of the state— in particular, states in which freedom of expression can be taken neither for granted nor at face value. Cronin was incarcerated for political activity against the apartheid state, and his early poetry attests—in theme and form—to the tenacity with which literary discourse is able to confront the limitations put upon public expression and the private sphere by a totalitarian state. The erstwhile cadre in the freedom struggle is today a leading parliamentarian and high-ranking member of the ruling party in postapartheid, democratic South Africa. Cronin's poetry now finds new ways of engaging with the state, attesting to the tensions in the relationship between an aspirational developmental state and its expectant subjects in an age of global neoliberalism—an age in which the state is an increasingly less powerful agent, though never one without power to intervene in the lives of its citizens.

Born in 1949 in Durban, Cronin was raised in a middle-class white family in Simonstown, on the Cape peninsula south of Cape Town, and in Rondebosch, a white Cape Town suburb, where he attended a Catholic high school. He served his military conscription in the Navy (headquartered in Simonstown), in a period before the large-scale campaigns against military service, and entered the University of Cape Town as an undergraduate student (of philosophy, with English and French) in 1968. He soon became involved in radical student politics at the historically overwhelmingly white

Contemporary Literature XLIX, 4   0010-7484; E-ISSN 1548-9949/08/0004-0515
© 2008 by the Board of Regents of the University of Wisconsin System

university and, his political conscience heightened by involvement in student protests, was recruited into an underground cell of the South African Communist Party (SACP), which had been banned by the apartheid government in 1950. Cronin studied in France between 1972 and 1974, completing a master's thesis on Jean-Jacques Rousseau under the cosupervision of Pierre Macherey and Etienne Balibar. He has spoken to Helena Sheehan about being particularly influenced by a kind of Sartrean existential Marxism during this period. Returning to teach philosophy at the University of Cape Town (where he coedited a volume entitled *Ideologies of Politics*), Cronin continued to work covertly for the SACP, among other activities producing and distributing an underground newspaper. It was for this illegal activity that he was convicted—he pleaded guilty—of conspiring to further the aims of the banned liberation organizations. (For the apartheid state, seventeen editions of the proscribed organ constituted, in effect, seventeen acts of sabotage.) He served seven years in prison. Six months into his sentence, his first wife, Anne-Marie, died suddenly of a brain tumor from which Cronin had not known she was suffering.

Cronin began composing poetry while in detention awaiting trial. Many of these poems, along with those written secretly in the notorious Pretoria Maximum Security prison, smuggled out or memorized to be written down and revised after his release, were published in 1983 as *Inside*, in progressive South African publisher Ravan Press's groundbreaking Staffrider series. An expanded edition was published in Britain, by Jonathan Cape, in 1987. The collection's title refers to Cronin's incarceration, while alluding to his poems' status as acts of solidarity with those political prisoners then languishing inside apartheid jails, as well as to the poet's own interiority (there is a moving sequence of poems exploring the poet's childhood memories and on the subject of his wife's death). The opening poem, "Poem-Shrike," effects an imaginative escape for words, as the poet launches a metaphorical paper missile over the prison walls, a statement of his intention and capacity to render brutalized bodies—and language—dignified. *Inside* proclaimed the arrival of a powerful voice of witness and invention whose ability to render extraordinary the details of ordinary lives, and whose adeptness at capturing the polyphony of South Africans' vernacular speech, constituted not merely verisimilitude but a political act of faith, a *demand* for a space for an imagined future community, and also its *enunciation*, the verbal and psychic enactment of what Rita Barnard, writing in *Research in African Literatures,* calls a "utopian national consciousness."

In a sequence entitled "Venture to the Interior," Cronin embarks on an archaeology of language and belonging, testing sounds in what the poem "Cave-Site" calls the cavity of his "mouth or / cave-site of word," to explore the politics of naming in a multiply colonized country. The literal inside of his mouth serves, as Brian Macaskill observes (in an essay in Derek Attridge and Rosemary Jolly's 1998 collection, *Writing South Africa*), as a potent "metonym for historical and geological formations of paleographic interiority." This demands that the poet, as representative of an imagined, liberated South Africa, begins—in the words of what is arguably Cronin's most anthologized poem ("To learn how to speak")—"To learn how to speak / With the voices of the land, / To parse the speech in its rivers, /.... / To visit the places of occlusion."

Inside engaged, too, with the fractured nature of subjectivity for inhabitants of a country that was itself, as a popular trope in liberation literature had it, a (racially segregated) prison. In "Removed from the city," Cronin muses on his experience of a divided city and addresses another writer concerned with the relationship between the individual and the polity:

> Poet, I too have tasted the city,
> your polyglot, cosmopolite, mankind city!
> On escalators I have felt the thrum simultaneous
> I was ascending, that one descending,
> that person also was me.
> Yet Walt Whitman this unity is not yet won.
> Our essence the aggregate of social relations, I live divided
> from my city: my city
> not yet
>   diversely one.

In this city not yet diversely one—Cape Town, to which he returned on his release—Cronin continued to work for the political liberation of his country, this time in the newly formed United Democratic Front (UDF). He served between 1983 and 1987 as a political education officer for the movement in the Western Cape, as well as editing its national theoretical journal, *Isizwe* (The Nation). The authorities sought actively to break up the UDF, however, and Cronin narrowly escaped arrest during the states of emergency enforced between 1985 and 1987, which gave the state's security organs extensive powers of arrest and detention. Having had to operate under false names, and evading capture twice, Cronin was urged to leave the country in September 1987. With his partner and their three-month-old son, he began a period of exile in London, later working for the African National Congress (ANC) office in Lusaka, Zambia, where he also became a member of the SACP's Politburo.

Cronin was among the first exiles to return to South Africa after the ANC and SACP were unbanned in 1990. He has served on the ANC's Central Committee since 1991 and was involved directly in the multiparty negotiations that led to the adoption of the interim constitution and to the first multiracial democratic elections in April 1994. These, of course, resulted in the inauguration of ANC leader Nelson Mandela as president of the Republic of South Africa. Based in Johannesburg for most of the 1990s, Cronin worked as a party functionary and was heavily involved in worker education. The poems in his second collection, *Even the Dead: Poems, Parables and a Jeremiad* (1997), address the turbulent mid-1980s, exile, return, and acclimatization to the new challenges facing the nation—and the state—in the 1990s. Many of the poems also reflect the fact that, after his release from prison, Cronin had begun to be called upon to perform his poems at the liberation movement's rallies and at mass funeral gatherings, contexts in which he was able to draw on South Africa's rich heritage of performance poetics, and which allowed him to incorporate features associated with oral literatures into his own practice. These included, he told Barbara Harlow in 2001, "[r]epetition, parallelism, call-and-response possibilities, a strong narrative" and were not merely "stylistic features, but necessary for the poetics of communication."

Even the Dead also offers ironic readings of some of the myths of the new nation, diagnosing collective amnesia as among the most pressing dangers to the social democracy for which Cronin had fought. These lapses included what the collection's title poem calls "upwardly mobile amnesia / Affirmative action amnesia /.../ (syntagmatic amnesia—an elite for the whole) //...winning-nation amnesia," and so on, all eliding the fact that the country's wealth remained—and still largely remains—concentrated in the hands of the (mostly white) few. The collection's title poem ends with a quotation from Walter Benjamin that warns, "In every era the attempt must be made anew to wrest tradition away from a conformism that is about to overwhelm it." If the achievement of Cronin's writing in the context of the struggle to overthrow the apartheid state was to create, in the space of poetry, what he calls in this interview "an alternative hegemonic power," then in the new dispensation Cronin came to envisage his writing continuing the same "aspirant trajectory towards trying to build a sense of a collective 'us'"—a writing which offered engaged, intelligent critique in service of what he calls "a democratic hegemonic project."

Cronin entered Parliament as an ANC member in 1999 and is currently chair of the parliamentary standing committee on transport. He is also deputy general secretary of the SACP, which continues to be part of the complex tripartite governing alliance, with the ANC (there was historically considerable overlap at the leadership level in the membership of both organizations) and the country's main trades union congress. In this capacity, Cronin has long been a leading voice in opposing the increasingly neoliberal macroeconomic policies that Thabo Mbeki's presidency, in particular, pursued. The ANC government's attempt to engage with the demands of capitalist globalization in a manner conducive to encouraging foreign investment has led to a shift away from its former conception of the state as redistributor of wealth and steward of developmental economics, to one in which it seemed, to its critics, that it acted merely as a manager, a technocrat, mediating between labor and the markets, and in no way driving the redistribution of resources. In 1996, Cronin coauthored (with Blade Nzimande) a stinging Communist Party critique of this tendency entitled "We Need Transformation, Not a Balancing Act" (published in the SACP's mouthpiece, *The African Communist*), which concluded ironically that the ANC's discussion paper *The State and Social Transformation* might more accurately have been called "The State and Social Accommodation." Since this interview was conducted, Cronin and the SACP emerged as among the most vocal supporters of Jacob Zuma, former deputy president of the country, who defeated Mbeki in elections at the ANC's national gathering in Polokwane in December 2007 to become the ANC's president. Mbeki resigned as president of South Africa in September 2008, and Zuma is widely expected to assume the office after the 2009 general elections.

Cronin's most recent collection, *More than a Casual Contact* (2006), attests to his concern to make poetry speak to these new conditions. It explores, as one might expect, the demands placed on the poet as politician and—as poems like "To discuss issues through other issues" makes amusingly, movingly, and devastatingly clear—the politician as poet: "'We saw you in parliament on TV last night,' friends say with a disapproving look. 'But are you still at least . . .' (here come capital letters) '. . . WRITING?'" ("Where to begin?"). The collection bears testimony to Cronin's belief, expressed in this interview, that poetry ought to aspire to be both a "thoughtful science of the probable and a passionate struggle for the desirable," and to his poetry's ongoing, necessary exploration of the space of and for poetry, in and in relation to South Africa's twenty-first-century state.

This interview was conducted by email between June and October 2007. The final text was edited lightly, by both parties, to read more like a transcribed conversation. Comments about the events of 2008 were added in late September 2008. I am extremely grateful to Jeremy Cronin for his generosity and willingness to undertake this project, and to Rita Barnard and Matt Hart for making it possible.

Q.   The first poem—"Where to begin?"—in your latest collection, *More than a Casual Contact*, seems like a good place to start because it stages usefully the question of the poet's own history and identity, his historical complicity, and his literary and intellectual points of contact, as an open-ended question: "Is poetry the irruption of the suppressed? Or is it a holding onto the faith?" the poem asks; "Why separate poetry from what poetry is not?" How does Jeremy Cronin, poet, answer these questions? Would Jeremy Cronin, ANC member of Parliament and South African Communist Party deputy general secretary, answer them differently?

A.   I guess the poet, at least this poet, would answer that poetry is both the irruption of the suppressed and a holding on to the faith; and that the anxiety about defining poetry, by delineating it from what it is not, is misplaced. Which is why, I suppose, this particular poem—"Where to begin?"—dreams of a shopping list falling in love with Pablo Neruda's poetry. Poetry is a place to keep the open-ended open.

Would the politician agree? Yes. But would the politician say it in the same ways as the poet? Not entirely. For me, there is certainly considerable cross-fertilization. An idea that begins in a poem finds its way into a parliamentary speech. A metaphor that seemed to work in a trade union discussion gets feet and runs off into a poem.

But we are dealing with different contexts, audiences, expectations, possibilities. Roman Jakobson says that all lyrical poetry is ultimately reducible to one single thought: "I love you." Most political discourse, however contemplative, is ultimately traveling elsewhere, which, if reduced to another single thought, might be: "Now is the time!"

Poetry and politics necessarily have their own rhetorical strategies and resources. But there is no Chinese wall between them. As a politician I want to resist the sterilization of politics into merely the art of the possible. I believe it should also seek to be a thoughtful science of the probable, and a passionate struggle for the desirable.

Q.   How, then, do you feel your concern with what poetry is, does, or might do, as well as with what threatens it, may have changed over the past thirty years—specifically in relation to your idea of a public polity, whether that is "the people," "South Africans (of all ethnicities, affiliations, languages)," or "the nation"?

A.   Recently I had a session with University of Cape Town creative-writing graduate students. I was invited to intersperse the reading of poems with a freewheeling interaction with students and staff. As often happens on these occasions, I was asked a question that I fumbled. I've been trying to answer it in my head ever since.

"Why," I was asked, "in the concluding lines of the title poem of your last collection do you say, 'All the more reason to keep faith / To struggle / To stay / To stay on / To be gentle / To all of those, who / Somehow, more or less / (That's all of us) // Survive'?" The poem in question ("After more than a casual contact") has as an underlying context the AIDS pandemic sweeping our country, and a tragic denialism in the face of it from some of our leading politicians. Why, the student wanted to know, was I so generously inclusive? Why refer to "ALL of us," when surely, as a Marxist, I would want to draw a firm line between friend and foe, victim and oppressor, AIDS activist and AIDS denialist?

It's a troubling question. Having tossed it around in my head for months now, I realize that many—possibly all—of my poems enact a movement towards some kind of restorative if imaginary unity, whether personal, social, physical...even linguistic (by way of giving things back their names). Of course I don't really believe in nominalism, that each thing has its pregiven name. Nor do I believe in the utopian construction of a unified society that glosses over real contradictions. But this play within poetry can at least have some purpose.

Poetry doesn't change the world, but it might make changing the world imaginable. You won't transform society through magical incantation, but a performed poem might forge, for a moment, a sense of community. Or a quietly read poem on the page tested on the lips of a reader might help to construct a capacitating subjective place for that reader. That sense of community, or that discursively constructed subjective positioning, reinforced by many other things, of course, might become a significant social reality.

Q. So in part you'd want to assert the right to defend the humanizing capacity of the poem, of the space of the poem?

A. Yes, and at a personal level, poetry and other writing played this role for me in the depths of the apartheid years. After some years of underground activism, when I was finally arrested by the apartheid security police, for instance, there were several resources that helped me survive solitary confinement and interrogation. One resource was the many harrowing accounts of Nazi detention and torture, or of similar brutality by French colonial interrogators. My underground handlers had compelled me to read all of this material before deploying me. Recognizing the disorienting impact of isolation, the familiar attempts by interrogators to build dependency upon them, the good cop–bad cop routine, in short, the universal grammar of my situation was somehow a consolation. I was able to be a critical Brechtian spectator looking in from the outside, and not just a victim in the center.

But poetry was another resource. I found myself, for instance, for a brief time in the same police cells in which the important antiapartheid poet Dennis Brutus had once been held. He had named the walls, the bars, the space, in lines that I had previously read. The place had been blessed with meaning. It was miserable, but somehow more endurable.

On a larger, less personal scale, the role of poetry in the midst of, and often barely distinguishable from, other oral performances (funeral orations, political speeches, songs, chanted marches, call-and-response slogans) was central to the South African resistance struggle. This was particularly the case in the nearly two decades of rolling, semi-insurrectionary struggle from the mid-1970s that eventually propelled the 1994 democratic breakthrough. Lee Hirsch's 2002 Emmy-winning documentary, *Amandla! A Revolution in Four-Part Harmony*, movingly makes the case for the centrality of song, in particular, within the South African revolutionary struggle. For an oppressed and largely unarmed majority, facing the most powerful army and police force on the continent, counterhegemonic power lay in building collective unity. The slogan "Amandla!" (Zulu for "Power!"), called out by a speaker at a mass meeting, and its choral response from the gathered congregation, "Ngawethu!" ("Is ours!"), is what linguists, I think, call a performative utterance. Like the "I do" in a wedding ceremony, the utterance is constitutive of the reality itself. Thousands of people responding in unison "Is ours!" start to cohere, collectively empowering themselves in the utterance.

Q.   But are there not also dangers in this? Are these aesthetic strategies not available to all manner of demagogic agendas, including reactionary ones?

A.   Yes. And that is why, in the present South African situation, it is particularly important to reconsider many things in the light of the new reality. The ANC-led movement is no longer a persecuted formation; it is in power, at least in political power. Walter Benjamin writes somewhere that fascism systematically introduces aesthetics into political life. It marshals art into what he describes as "the production of ritual values." He suggests that we should respond to fascism's rendering politics aesthetic by politicizing aesthetics.

I certainly do not think that we are on the brink of fascism, not even remotely. But the dangers of the aesthetic, including poetry, now being pressed into the service of a lulling complacency, a ritualistic sentimentalism that loses the zip and edge of the collective self-emancipatory struggles of the previous period, are very real. The aesthetic runs the danger of becoming anesthetic.

Q.   Which is why that poem, the closing lines of which prompted the troubling question during that UCT seminar, includes barely veiled critiques of AIDS-denialism ("Living with a disappointment / not without a cure") and the ANC government's neoliberal economic policies ("Mass action becoming / transaction // Liberation / liberalisation").

A.   And which is why I don't find it possible to write poetry in exactly the same way now as in an earlier period. For instance, one of my first proto-poems in prison in the late 1970s was the simple and laconic recitation to myself, over and over, of the standard South African Broadcasting Corporation's weather forecast of the time. "... Port Shepstone to the Tugela Mouth... the Tugela Mouth to Kosi Bay ..." I'd fill in weather details as the mood took me. Using the bare resources of breath, tongue, gum, word, I was able to make geography in the theater of my mouth. Much of my earlier poetry owes, I think, something to this kind of sensibility. The largely implicit context is of violent dislocation, but that's off-stage, as it were. The poems themselves tend to be focused on rebuilding a sense of solidarity, of reconnecting a disrupted world, with whatever minimal resources to hand.

Q.   Whereas the imperative now is—what?—to perform a different kind of interventionist, critical aesthetics?

A.   At present I am inclined to make my poems much more actively disruptive within themselves, to foreground contradiction and paradox, to enact interruption, to celebrate the parenthetical, to make manifest the unresolved. In the first post-1994 decade of democracy in South Africa, public discourse was overwhelmed with the notions of harmony and self-congratulatory contentment. We had achieved a "political miracle," we were a "rainbow nation," we had finally "rejoined the family of nations," we were "a winning nation," internationally we could "punch above our weight," we were at the cutting edge of a global "third wave of democracy," our own achievement heralded an "imminent African renaissance." Of course, there is much to be proud of in the South African democratic transition. The public discourses of the time were certainly flatter-ing to all of us in the new political elite (myself included). But the tendencies towards excessive contentment and therefore closure have been even more helpful to the old, the well-entrenched eco-nomic elite in the mining houses and financial institutions, the very entities that helped to shape a century of racial segregation and apartheid. They were perfectly happy with a message that said the black majority has got the vote now, *uhuru* (independence) is upon us, the struggle is over, *a luta discontinua!*

To my discomfort, some of my own earlier poetry, written in the spirit of a counterhegemonic project, risked being anthologized into the discourse of this shallow, postcolonial triumphalism. A poem like "To learn how to speak / With the voices of the land . . .," which I performed frequently in the 1980s, and which was intended as a relatively defiant expression of unity in diversity (in opposition to apartheid's diversity in unequal diversity), is all too easily decon-textualized in the present.

However, the present also has other dangers and temptations. Many South African intellectuals, novelists and poets among them, have slipped into the individualistic comfort zone of "speaking truth to power." I say "comfort zone" because the political power reality to which the truth is supposedly spoken is a relatively benign and often disorganized power reality. Recently I was asked to partic-ipate in a television series on dissident artists from around the world. I declined: I like to think of myself as being critical, but I don't think of myself as a South African dissident—although that's exactly how some of my ideological opponents within the broader ANC would be happy to label me and other like-minded left activists.

During the apartheid period we were not endeavoring to speak truth to power, as if we were petitioners. We were trying to contribute, in small ways, including through poetry, to forging an alternative hegemonic power. Surely the struggle, then and especially now, is not so much to speak truth to power as to make truth powerful and, the hardest of all, power truthful. That, I suppose, is a belated and still provisional response to the University of Cape Town student who asked me the perplexing question that I failed to answer at the time. I think that the strategies deployed in my post-1994 poetry are somewhat different to those in the preceding period, but there is still the same ultimate, aspirant trajectory towards trying to build a sense of a collective "us" in my poems. I want to be part of a democratic hegemonic project, not a prophet in the wilderness.

Q.   I want to return to the issue of your identity as poet *and* politician and ask you about some of the spaces that bring into focus your own negotiation of public and private concerns (as a writer, as a citizen, as a member of Parliament, as author of both policy documents and poetry). Cars, in particular, provide you with powerful images of ambivalence ("Being of the street and / Not of it, just passing through," as you put it in "End of the century—which is why wipers," part 9). You return to them time and again in *Even the Dead* and *More than a Casual Contact*. Objects of a love-hate relationship ("I dislike this over-reliance on cars. I cherish this time inside of my car" ["Where to begin?"]), they afford time for reflection but also immunity from the dangers of the street, real or imagined.

Cars also have rearview mirrors: one can look behind while traveling forward. You deploy this image in "Switchback," in particular, to engage with your preoccupation with Benjamin, whose angel of history comes "[d]rifting into" the "rear-view mirror," though she is "Out of breath, blurred, no longer able / To sustain a story" ("Switchback"), and her imagined message is a chilling indictment of opportunism, ill-judged reformism, the kind of amnesia other of your poems have in their sights—perhaps none more trenchantly than the final, title poem of *Even the Dead*, which opens and closes with quotations from Benjamin to the effect that, in any era, conformism (or the complacency to which you referred earlier) will threaten to overwhelm and transform radical achievement.

A few questions follow from these observations. Could you comment on your need to negotiate your sense of an ambivalent placement between public and private (in all spheres)? Might you say something more about the spaces that you figure in your poems? And could you gloss your engagement with Benjamin, and the productive image of the angel of history, in your current concerns with the role of poetry, the demands of history, and the identity of the nation?

A.   Pablo Neruda says somewhere that lyrical poetry is born in the tension between solitude and solidarity. Perhaps this is the fascination of Baudelaire's poet as *flâneur*, engaged in random meandering through a cityscape, a loner in a crowd that sweeps past. Benjamin, amongst others, has written about this defining experience of modernity, and many poets, among them Frank O'Hara and the New York school, have explored it. But for me the *flâneur* has also had a personal, South African resonance. In the first place, in being a white South African, in the midst of cities in which there is a black majority, there has been an inevitable sense of belonging and not belonging. This was much stronger in my younger years.

But there have been other personal resonances. In one of my earlier poems I borrowed an O'Hara title ("A Step Away from Them") and lifted its penultimate line—"But my heart's in my packet...." In my own poem, the autobiographical *flâneur* is more of a pseudo-*flâneur*, and the "step away from them" has another, a clandestine meaning as I pretend to wander aimlessly through the streets of Cape Town, recalling earlier years when, indeed, I aspired to be the genuine article: "trying to be Baudelaire, I'd maunder / round town watching women's legs, but now / I've only / eyes for postboxes and / my heart's in my packet: it's / one thousand / illegal pamphlets to be mailed."

In much of my later poetry, traveling by car features centrally and ambivalently, as you have noted. In some of the poems the car and driver have, I suppose, now become the *flâneur*. But there are other themes at play. One of the great myths of the dominant discourse that prevailed after our 1994 democratic breakthrough in South Africa was the idea that a "prodigal" South Africa (we all started to assume collectively the guilt and the partial previous isolation of the apartheid minority regime!) had now rejoined the "family" of nations. All that was now supposedly required was that we follow the Washington consensus signposts to the necessary on-ramp of belt-tightening, privatization, and liberalization, which, in no time, would deliver us onto the freeway of boundless growth.... I'd used this kind of metaphor in trade union meetings, and it seemed to work, and so I pursued it further in some of the poetry.

Cars have rearview mirrors, as you've noted, but they also have windscreen wipers. There is a Chinese proverb that says, "When the finger points at the full moon, the fool looks at the finger." Sometimes there's wisdom in the fool's distraction. I like the idea of foregrounding the windscreen wiper to disrupt the illusory, headlong vista of boundless globalizing growth.

Q. You observed in "Three reasons for a mixed, umrabulo, round-the-corner poetry" that there was a shift in public discourse in South Africa (in a popular sense of the urgency of change) in the mid-1980s, "[f]rom lyric to epic." What genre do you think, then, is most appropriate to the current state of public discourse and private engagement with the political in contemporary South Africa?

A. The claim that I make in the opening poem of "Even the Dead," that somewhere between 1984 and 1986 "There was a shift out there / From lyric to epic," was rather rash. I notice that I qualified the claim in the poem, but insufficiently, with the caveat that I was "(Speaking from my own limited, personal experience, of course)." It's obviously a far too generalizing claim to map genres on to periods, especially relatively brief periods. Besides, I think the more specific shift in my writing occurs post-1994, and it is less towards the narrative and more towards the epigrammatic disruption of narrative—hence my fascination with the *rubber-thump, rubber-thump* disruptive insistence of windscreen wipers.

Q. If I can pick up on your sense of the purpose of this "epigrammatic disruption" of all-too-easy narratives, and also refer to the suggestion in your poem "Heron's Place" that poetry is the least commodified of the arts, perhaps I can ask you about audience, your sense of how your audience—for your published work, but also for your poems in performance—may have changed. How important has audience been for your writing (as opposed to performance)?

A.   A sense of audience has always been important for me. When I write a poem, or when I go back to an old poem, I try to listen to it with the ear of someone else, perhaps an audience, real or imagined. One audience whose feedback and engagement I have always appreciated is the relatively small circle of fellow South African poets, critics, and academics teaching poetry. But I have also always wanted to write a poetry that is generally accessible to a wider audience.

In this I have not always succeeded, of course. The failing is not just personal; there are many objective challenges. There are, for instance, eleven official languages in South Africa, and while English is the major *lingua franca*, writing poetry in English is not necessarily an advantage. Afrikaner nationalism, with all of its reactionary tendencies and faults, was centrally a cultural and language-based movement, and poetry was (and still is) cherished amongst a broader Afrikaans-language public. This has never been the case with the often pseudo-cosmopolitan, white, English-speaking community into which I was born. Major English-language South African writers—like the two Nobel laureates, Nadine Gordimer and John Coetzee—tend to be much better known outside of South Africa and tend to write, one suspects, with a European or North American audience in mind. For me, oral performances, particularly in contexts which are not narrowly poetical (a trade union meeting, or a political conference, for instance), have been a very important means for reaching a wider, more diverse audience.

Q.   What about the problems attendant on "educating" new audiences, or competing with the new languages, the new discourses of contemporary cultural formations?

A.   Well, over the years I have also done many classroom poetry readings in schools around the country. In the 1980s these readings were invariably associated with student political struggles and heightened periods of mobilization. Now things have shifted along. Last week [in August 2007], for instance, I was in the rural town of George, where teachers from the South African Democratic Teachers Union had organized final-year students from six surrounding township schools. Over several years now, at least one of my poems has been set in the national matriculation syllabus, and for some reason (perhaps because it is conveniently short), it often appears in the examination paper itself. So these school events involve a captive audience. I am not deluding myself that the majority of learners are present for the sheer love of poetry, or that, as I step into the venue, I have an extensive and passionate school readership; I try to respect these realities. I have heard that the British poet Adrian Mitchell refuses permission on principle for any of his poems to be published in anthologies that will be used for school examination purposes. I can understand that, but in a South African situation such a refusal would be elitist in its own way. I have never written (has anyone ever written?) poetry with the objective of having it prescribed in the school syllabus....However, school examinations have brought with them another audience, a new examination for me. I value these interactions with school students; they provide a poet and the poems with a reality check.

Over the recent period there has been a certain predictability about these engagements. There are the usual preliminaries. We meet briefly in the staff room before proceeding to the school hall. Many of the teachers are not first-language English speakers themselves. They are operating in underresourced and overwhelmed township public schools. I am here at their invitation and they express excessive appreciation for my presence. Over a cup of tea they complain about "the new generation." They say the students just want to "enjoy their freedom" without showing "any awareness for the generations who actually fought for that freedom." We then proceed to the venue for the poetry reading....I am introduced in glowing terms to the audience from a potted CV. It includes my birthdate, 1949. There are mocking gasps. (Perhaps 1949 is so far back, I may as well be dead? Does this have anything to do with tumbling life expectancy rates in our country as a result of the HIV/AIDS pandemic? Who says these seventeen- and eighteen-year-olds are not themselves in the front line of a new struggle?)

After reading some poems, including *the* poem from the syllabus, I open up for discussion. "Can you make money from writing poetry?" I am always asked. (South Africa currently has a 37 percent unemployment rate. Amongst black youth it often surpasses the 60 percent level.) "What does 'perpetrate' mean?" (I've used the word in the set-work poem.) "Do you regret committing the crimes that got you into jail?" (This question comes from an alert black student who also asks me more directly poetical questions about the use of repetition and irony. Although I listen carefully for it, sadly I don't detect any sense of irony in her initial question.)

"Do any of you write poetry?" I ask in turn. Several hands go up, and some students come forward to perform their own poems. Two do a rap performance. The poems are about family hardships, child abuse, drunken adults, youth drug addiction, and the need for caring, for empathy with others. And now the hour and a half is over.... The fifty-something poet will leave. His poem, itself now thirty years old, older than the wife it was once written about, written in prison out of psychic necessity to deal with her death, the poem stays behind in the dog-eared textbooks of the students. This, for me, is also what poetry is about: it must take its chances as an ordinary citizen in dialogue along the rough edges of life.

Q.   You mentioned earlier how a poem may expand a metaphor (first given an outing in the context of a political meeting and then used in a poem, and vice versa); do poems grow differently for you now that you are a politician in the ruling coalition than they did when you were in opposition/resistance? I wonder whether, or how, you might feel the presence—the nuisance? the threat?—of the (voice of the) "State" in your work (a "cheeky" question, I acknowledge).

A.   I am now in government, so to speak, but it is a potentially interesting if complex end of government. As a parliamentarian I am not (or shouldn't be) part of the state bureaucracy in the full sense of the word. Cabinets and state departments have their necessary hierarchies and confidentialities. One of the responsibilities of an MP is to cut across these hierarchies and opaque departmental silos. We should be prepared, in the public interest, to summons a minister or departmental director-general to account publicly in Parliament, on the one hand, or to burrow down into a department and interact with middle-ranking and local-level civil servants. The latter, like public sector workers (not least schoolteachers), are often able to provide a more accurate picture of what is happening or, frequently, not happening. MPs have a poetic license. We should be prepared to use it.

Q.   A fortuitous turn of phrase ("poetic license")! But do national responsibilities imperil aesthetic freedoms?

A.   As a member of the ANC parliamentary caucus, I am, of course, bound by caucus discipline. Even if I don't always agree with the caucus line, I don't have a problem with the principle of party discipline. This is especially relevant in the South African Parliament where we are elected on a 100 percent proportional representation system. Voters vote for party lists and not individuals, and I am not aware of anyone in particular (except perhaps my mother) who happened to vote ANC because I was on its list! But there is, indeed, a challenge here. For obvious reasons that I've already alluded to, a great premium is placed on unity and loyalty within the culture of the ANC-led liberation movement. In the days of illegality and repression, carefree individualism could be a deadly indulgence. Unity and loyalty are still important. But national liberation movements, pre- and postindependence, also have a problematic habit of identifying themselves as "the nation." There are numerous examples crystallized in once-popular slogans: "CPP is Ghana, Ghana is CPP"; "SWAPO is the Nation, the Nation is SWAPO"; "the Kenyan African National Union is the Mother and Father of the Nation."

I have never heard anyone quite say these things of the ANC, but there are strong inclinations in this direction. To be politically outside of the ANC is still often characterized as being part of the "enemy" forces. To differ with the majority line within the ANC is sometimes to risk being accused of "siding" with the "enemy." Lenin was fond of quoting [Carl von] Clausewitz's maxim, "War is politics by other means." But Lenin (even Lenin) never claimed that politics is war by other means. He quite correctly insisted on the primacy of a political understanding of war. Politicizing the military is one thing; the converse is quite another. Unfortunately, militarizing politics (at least discursively, by regarding all opposition as the enemy) is a natural but ruinous habit in political formations, particularly those that have waged armed struggles.

Q.   Do you foresee the possibility of a space developing soon for robust critical engagements with the party line? You seem to experience no anxieties about your own constructive criticisms of government policy—in poetry, or in your frequent contributions to the opinion pages of South African newspapers, not to mention in SACP policy and discussion documents. But you do, in a sense, occupy a position *within* the ranks of leadership from which criticism is, paradoxically, perhaps more easily accepted than it is from *without*.

A.   I know that in South Africa, many black intellectuals, in particular, have recently battled with the inner dilemma of disagreeing with the ANC government. There is a sense of betraying their own, of feeding the racial stereotype that black majority governments "are bound to fail." The present vice chancellor of the University of Cape Town, a fine novelist and essayist, Njabulo Ndebele, wrote in 2003, "I increasingly experience the need to transgress but feel anguished by the thought that my transgressions, committed in the belief that they represent a process of democratic self-actualization, could be mistaken for the outmoded oppositions of old." I would venture to say that increasingly among a wide range of black intellectuals and others, this sense of anguish is no longer so strong. Both from within the ANC-led movement and in other quarters, not least among a feisty new generation of black journalists and columnists, there are robust critical voices that are prepared to oppose government on many issues without being oppositionist for its own sake.

I have never quite shared Ndebele's sense of anguish. Being simultaneously a member of both the ANC and its allied SACP (we are an interesting and, internationally, probably unique political alliance with overlapping memberships) has provided me with organizational spaces that are neither oppositionist nor monolithically univocal. Nelson Mandela, after I had unintentionally and unknowingly irritated him, and not for the first time, once told a comrade that he was convinced I had a "split personality"—good on some days, not good at all on others. In mitigation, I would argue that a bipolar disorder is a necessary attribute in our post-(or is it neo-?) colonial reality in which, to paraphrase Gramsci, we are living in a time when the old is dying and the new is still struggling to be born.

But my bipolar disorder also takes refuge in poetry. Some of my poetry is definitely born of a frustrated voice that is unable to express itself forthrightly on a parliamentary podium. This has particularly been the case with the challenge of HIV/AIDS denialism. You asked whether I had a problem with the danger of the voice of the state surfacing in my own writing. You said this was a "cheeky" question. Well, this is a cheeky response: the voice of government does surface, explicitly if ironically, in at least one recent poem. In "Clarification" I assume the voice of a government spokesperson on a national news bulletin and begin to wonder whether there is any empirical proof for the existence of "government," whether it has ever been isolated in laboratory conditions, and whether we can be sure that its hypothetical, and very "Eurocentric" subcategory, "cabinet" exists. (I hope that Nelson Mandela won't object to this one.)

There is, I believe, a continuity rather than a disjuncture between the underlying sensibility in both my political and poetical endeavors. Part of this continuity lies in trying to take on the dangers of "totalitarianism"—which is incipient not just in the Marxist or the third-world national liberation movement legacies but also where we might least expect to find it, in liberalism. Particularly in the 1990s, the crushingly dominant hegemony of neoliberalism proclaimed that history had ended, the East was supposedly becoming the West with a new wave of postcommunist democracies and...well, nobody quite remembered the other, more enduring global fissure, North/South. (I have actually heard prominent black voices in South Africa say "we in the West.") Market totalitarianism prevailed. Democracy was reduced to "rules of the game," which amounted to electoral alternation between indistinguishable center-left and center-right parties. And statecraft became technocratic management. There were no real choices to be made. In this totalitarian scheme of things, the ability to admit difference, the capacity to imagine that not everything was a "win-win" situation, disappeared. There was profound global denialism about vast and often deepening crises, especially in the South.

Politics was depoliticized in the 1990s. Difference was denied. We were all global consumers and clients. The fact that millions of third-world peoples were profoundly marginalized, alienated, and impoverished by "globalization" was repressed. When the repressed returned in person (of course in a myriad of political forms, some of them extremely reactionary), the inability to conceptualize this reality *politically* persisted. Denied in the first moment, it was then thought of in "civilizational" (the "clash of civilizations") or even apocalyptic terms (the "axis of evil") in the second. Because these latter explanations are essentially nonpolitical, in fact racist and delusional, they cannot ground a strategically intelligent politics, even from the point of view of imperialist circles.

Q.   The Truth and Reconciliation Commission had begun but not yet concluded its hearings when *Even the Dead* was published. Several poems in *More than a Casual Contact* engage with issues of (public) memory, and the need for discourses appropriate to acts of remembering, of challenging those different forms of amnesia diagnosed in "Even the Dead" as infecting the new body politic. They suggest, however, that some conceptions of poetry might not be entirely able to withstand the pressures: "If poem be attempt to soothe / The ache of the gap between / A thing and its name, then this / Is anti-poem, is ache, is gap" ("The letter bomber seeks amnesty"); "in the inquest court, no such thing / as pure poetry" ("In a pool of water . . ."). Are you less optimistic now than you have been before about the possibilities, the strengths, of poetry—or the place from which the poet is able to speak?

A.   Your reading of "The letter bomber seeks amnesty" is legitimate but caught me by surprise. I certainly do not claim any privileged paternity rights over the meanings of my poems. But what I had intended by the "this" in "then this / Is anti-poem, is ache, is gap" is not the poem itself but the pseudo-confession being made by the apartheid security policeman's amnesty application to the Truth and Reconciliation Commission. I spent several days in this particular amnesty hearing. The ex–security operative in question had helped to prepare and mail a letter bomb to an address in Angola. The bomb killed Jeannette Schoon and her six-year old daughter, Katryn. I had known Jeannette at university; we were contemporaries. A sinister feature of the amnesty appeal was the fact that the appellant, Major Craig Williamson, had been a family friend and even a houseguest of the Schoons while acting as an apartheid police informant. I have used passages from Williamson's submission to the TRC in my poem. His submission was a sustained rhetorical sleight of hand: the tone was monotonous, minute and irrelevant details were recounted at length, the tragic event got lost in the narrative, everything moved towards anticlimax, subjects became objects, verbs were passive, the perpetrator a victim.

Q.   Fair enough, although I think the ambiguity of "this" in that poem adds to its poignancy. I suppose it made me think about Theodor Adorno's suggestion that (lyric) poetry seemed impossible after Auschwitz; it seemed apt that poetry grappling with the violence done to language, let alone to human bodies, is willing to explore its own necessary—perhaps inevitable—failure.

A question now about metaphor and ethics via one on animals, which feature frequently in your work, becoming (or providing an occasion for) complex metaphors exploring the nature of poetry, or reflecting on history or identity. I'm thinking, amongst others, of poems like "Poem-Shrike," "Chameleon," "Kwikkie," "Penguins," even "Heron's place." Would you reflect on your engagement with the "otherness" of nonhuman animals, but also on the way in which you engage politics and politicians through metaphor—I have in mind, in particular, the poem "To discuss other issues through other issues"—specifically metaphors which are also observed things and circle back to metapoetic commentary?

A.   The animal and natural world as a metaphorical reference point is, in the first place, a means to connect with and explore the resources of older African traditions. In several poems, most obviously a prison poem like "A Tale of Why Tortoise Carries His Hut upon His Back," I directly reference this tradition. In the very next poem ("Chameleon") from the same prison collection, *Inside*, I am evoking a tradition of praise poetry that was usually directed at great warrior heroes and tribal chiefs, but sometimes there were praises for the more everyday, a favorite bull, perhaps. So why not a chameleon? There are also important white South African literary traditions that evoke landscape and a local natural world, in both English and Afrikaans—the muscular romanticism of Roy Campbell or Douglas Livingstone, the tightly observed natural settings in Nadine Gordimer's lyrical prose, the often erotically charged landscapes of Breyten Breytenbach or Antjie Krog. I have certainly been influenced by all of these.

Clearly, part of what is at play in my evocation of a South African natural reality is an attempt to establish a sense of South Africanness—not just, in fact hopefully not at all, in folkloric references to the veld and the like but more by way of celebrating the layers of human settlement left behind in diverse namings and honorings of places, plants, and animals that are still around us.

At present there are sharp political disputes in the South African media and on radio phone-in programs about names. Local ANC-led municipalities have been renaming towns, streets, airports. Where the imposed names they are changing are offensive, as they often are, this is especially understandable. Like the case of Triomf (Afrikaans for "triumph"), a white, apartheid-era suburb that was arrogantly built in the 1960s upon the ruins of a formerly vibrant black community—Sophiatown—whose homes had been demolished and the residents forcibly removed to distant townships. Many South African places have two or more names, a colonial name and, beneath it, a still-preserved earlier name that a majority of people often use, regardless of what the road signs might say. Durban has always been eThekwini for the majority of its inhabitants. As a poet, I am less interested in what is official, nor am I in pursuit of what is supposedly authentically original. I am much more fascinated by the polyphonic layering of names, languages, cultures that has sedimented around the natural landmarks and the wildlife of our country, where contradictions are kept in play.

Q. Perhaps, as we edge towards a conclusion, I can ask how you feel your poetry and your idea of the place with which it engages, South Africa as a "nation" (albeit a place of "polyphonic layering" and productive contradictions), have changed since the mid-1980s, especially since the publication of *Even the Dead*, and perhaps since the publication of *More than a Casual Contact*.

A. I am not sure if my idea of South Africa as a "nation" has changed radically through this period. But I am certainly more conscious of the need to assert the mixed, the creole, the open-ended reality of South African "nationhood." In this respect, the ANC is a fascinating national liberation movement. It was formed in 1912, in the immediate aftermath of the post–Anglo-Boer War settlement. That 1910 settlement established South Africa as a formal political entity for the first time. But it excluded from citizenship rights the majority of inhabitants within the new national space. The founders of the ANC appreciated that this exclusion had something to do with the fragmentation of the indigenous black majority into "balkanized" tribes. The founding project of the ANC was, therefore, to build a new overarching unity, a shared sense of Africanness. In its early writings and slogans, the ANC roundly condemned the "demon of racism." Interestingly, it was not referring to white racism—a more obvious target—but to the "demon" of tribalism. The ANC founders were proselytizing, mission-school–educated Westernizers. For them, national identity was not something that was going to be recovered by a return to the source, to a pristine African origin. It was a modernizing project. In fact, the project was, to some extent, proto-postmodernist. National "identity" was not something given: Xhosas, Zulus, Sothos, Tswanas, Shangaans, Vendas were, in a sense, not yet Africans, and building a sense of unity would have to be a collective project that required construction, organization, discursive practices, political activism. It was always less about national "identity" and more about national unity, and a necessary affirmation of diversity within that unity.

The nonracial generosity of Nelson Mandela is justly celebrated internationally, but it is not just a personal trait. It is very much anchored in the confidence of an overwhelming majority, in a sense of dignity and of unbroken if diverse cultural continuity, and, above all, in a decades-long struggle tradition of forging national unity out of diversity. Which is to say, the generous and dominant nonracism of the black majority in our country should not be taken for granted; it was not something preordained. It is a political achievement, and a remarkable one, given the brutal history of centuries of colonial dispossession and racist white-minority rule.

However, having said this, it is important to note a relatively new ideological current in South Africa, associated with an emergent black economic and ruling elite. There is a move into identity politics, an inclination to establish an essentialist African identity. It is a current that succeeded in becoming relatively dominant for at least a decade in the post-1994 democratic state. It remains influential, although it is now substantially challenged from within the broad ANC-led movement.

Much of the ideology of this current has been borrowed from the United States; it is essentially a discourse of representative redistribution. Transformation came to mean...rather the elite redistribution of some racialized power (whether in the boardrooms or national sports teams). Representative individuals from formerly disadvantaged groups became the beneficiaries. Informing this politics are three buttressing paradigms: an individualistic, liberal rights politics (individuals are entitled to a slice of the action); an identity politics that posits relatively fixed and pregiven identities ("blackness" or "Africanness"); and a paradigm of democratic transformation that tends to reduce democracy to representation, what, in poetics, we would call "metonymy," a part for the whole. In the new South Africa, a small number of representatives have staked a claim to enjoy new powers, privileges, and personal wealth on behalf of the historically disadvantaged majority. It easily becomes a discourse of racialized self-righteousness. Newly enriched multimillionaires justify their ongoing benefit from "black economic empowerment" deals by maintaining an equals sign between themselves and the historically (and still presently) disadvantaged majority. Only the insistence on a fixed and supposedly unchanging black identity will allow this.

It is in this context that I have tried to explore further the questions of mixedness, the carnivalesque, polyphony, Colouredness, the creole, multiple identities—themes that have been present in my poetry for some time. My home city, Cape Town, is unique in South Africa in that around half of its population is, to use South African parlance, "Coloured," neither of distinctly European settler nor of indigenous African (including Khoisan) origin, but a blend of these and, importantly, also of diverse East Asian, Madagascan, and Angolan origins—the result of over a century and a half of slavery at the Cape. Cape Town is not always a popular city among many in the new South African elite, partly, I suspect, because its mixedness starkly challenges the cornerstone assumption of fixed racial identities. Anyhow, all of the above is the immediate context for some of my recent Cape Town work, like "A poem for Basil Mannenberg Coetzee's left shoulder."

Q. I'm glad you refer to this poem; it seems like a good place to conclude, being a jazzlike hybrid performance, both elegy and defiant celebration, memorializing a community's sense of resilience in its ability to elude definition, to subvert "naming," past and present. Perhaps you could tell me something about its genesis, and about how you see it fitting into writing of and about Cape Town's—if not South Africa's—racial and cultural politics.

A. Basil Mannenberg Coetzee was an iconic tenor saxophonist in Cape Town. His signature tune, "Mannenberg," named for a particularly tough Coloured ghetto on the outskirts of the city, was always played to great acclaim in the 1980s in political mobilizational drives (along with scratchy recordings of Bob Marley's "Buffalo Soldier"). "Mannenberg" is one of the classics of Cape jazz, a style that evokes many local sounds—Malay choirs, carnival troupes, church brass bands, the muezzin's evening call to prayer, the dried-kelp horn of fish vendors, eighteenth-century Dutch sailors' chanteys, and much more. My own poem evolved eclectically out of sketches and notes I have been making over the last twenty years. The white, working-class municipal swimming-pool attendant who was always high on marijuana and who liked to tell me his "philosophy of life" is there. The community organizer who, in the 1980s, was always urging us to get our "arses into gear," and who then went on to be South Africa's High Commissioner in London, is there. So is the trade-union organizer who avidly read Lenin and had detailed plans for a citywide insurrection that never quite happened. (The insurrection was going to be based on Coloured garment workers in factories with rather non-Leninist names—Fun Frills, Tiny Tots, Parklane Lingerie. How could a poet not fall in love with the creative energies and incongruities of all of that?) The poem, and others like it, is, I hope, a celebration of popular creativity and struggle…a struggle that has not ended.

RITA BARNARD

Tsotsis: On Law, the Outlaw, and the Postcolonial State

Awuyodubula, awuyopansula, awuyokhuthuza, uyodlwengula . . .
Ha, dubula mbayimbayi! Ma libhubha liyabhubha . . .
Namhlanj 'uthint'ezidl'inhlok'uthint'uBhambatha
Awu, Tsots'usuze kaBhambatha namhlanje
Uthini? Hhe, awufun'ukuza ngala?
Awu, klev'usuze kaBhambatha namhlanje!

Zola, "Bhambatha" (from the *Tsotsi* sound track)

It is hardly in our power to change the form of the state and impossible to abolish it because, vis-à-vis the state, we are, precisely, powerless. In the myth of the founding of the state as set down by Thomas Hobbes, our descent into powerlessness was voluntary: in order to escape the violence of internecine warfare without end (reprisal upon reprisal, vengeance upon vengeance, the vendetta), we individually and severally yielded up to the state the right to use physical force (right is might, might is right), thereby entering the realm (the protection) of the law. Those who chose and choose to stay outside the compact become outlaw.

J. M. Coetzee, *Diary of a Bad Year*

· 1 ·

From its very first page and arguably throughout, J. M. Coetzee's multivoiced, multigeneric *Diary of a Bad Year* stages a debate about the origins of the state and its function in contemporary society.

This essay was written with the support of the University of Pennsylvania Research Foundation and a Weiler Faculty Fellowship. Thanks are due to Audrey Mbeje and

That this topic should engage Coetzee (or, rather, the Coetzee-like narrator and his antagonist) is hardly surprising. In the post–9/11 world, the state—never an easy matter to define—is at once vulnerable and powerful. It is vulnerable not only because its regulatory, protective, and redistributive functions have been stripped in accord with neoliberal economic doctrines, but also because it seems to be facing a new kind of adversary. Its security is no longer perceived to be challenged by other states, but rather by individuals, by outlaws, raiders, terrorists: people who have no interest in playing by its rules. Yet the contemporary state appears in some ways more powerful than before (or more willing to display its power) because the emergence of these outlaws provides it with a justification for overriding civil liberties and sanctioning cruelties in a way that, in Coetzee's (or Señor C's) "strong opinion," brings dishonor to us all (139–45). "The line between minimal government and fascism lite," as Jean Comaroff and John L. Comaroff wryly observe, "is very thin indeed" ("Figuring Crime" 229). The state compels our attention today precisely because of its alarming contradictions.

Coetzee's vision of the state as the power—the bandits—to whom "we" choose to cede our freedom is not as novel or as "African" as it might appear to those in favor of the new managerial dispensation (94–95). It accords in many ways with Philip Abrams's seminal essay "Notes on the Difficulty of Studying the State," which presents the state as "the device in terms of which subjection is legitimated... present[ing] politically institutionalized power to us in a form that is at once integrated and isolated and by satisfying both these conditions... creat[ing]... an acceptable basis for acquiescence" (68). But it is characteristic of the novelist that the temporality—the plot structure, if you will—of our subjection should be of interest. When exactly did we voluntarily accede to the

MariannaVisser for help with the isiZulu, and to Gavin Steingo and Lesley Marx for indispensable insights. The rap lyrics in the epigraph can be loosely rendered as follows: "Just go shoot, go dance (the tsotsi dance), go steal, go rape . . . Yea, shoot, big gun! If the world ends, it ends . . . / Today you've fucked with the guys who'll eat you for breakfast / You've run into the Bhambatha gang / Yo, Tsotsi, you've come to the Bhambathas today / What are you saying, hey? / You don't want to come over here? / Yo, clever boy, you've come to the Bhambathas today."

rule of the state? Can we imagine an alternative to it? The safest answer is that we cannot: we are, as Coetzee declares, "born subject" (4). For it is the state that defines us, gives us identity and personhood, not least in the form of certificates of birth and death. The origins of the state are therefore *sensu stricto* unimaginable—by "us," that is. We cannot reverse the narrative of our acquiescence and think entirely outside the structures of the state: "The option is not open to us to change our minds," says Coetzee, "to decide that the monopoly on the exercise of force held by the state, codified in law, is not what we wanted after all, that we would prefer to go back to a state of nature" (4). But we can, of course, imagine the unimaginable, as Coetzee likes to do, by creating fables and stories about the origins of the state. Akira Kurosawa's film *The Seven Samurai*, the story of a band of warriors who protect a village against bandits and then offer to remain as permanent protectors, Coetzee suggests, is one such fable—a wonderfully optimistic one, in his view, since the villagers choose to decline the offer and the samurai obligingly retreat.

Coetzee's enterprise in these early sections of *Diary of a Bad Year* is reminiscent, in its somewhat contradictory impulses, of Louis Althusser's essay "Ideology and Ideological State Apparatuses." Like Coetzee, Althusser knows that we are always already subject; there is, properly speaking, no primal scene of subjectivization. Yet he stages, famously, his "little theoretical theater" (174) in which the policeman hails a person on the street and that person obediently turns around in response to the officer's "Hey, you there!"—thus accepting his submission to and naming by the law. I have argued elsewhere that the scene is something of a testimony to the theoretical power of fiction and the degree to which our concept of individuality is derived from narrative forms (Barnard, *"Smell of Apples"* 213). But the point I wish to make here is that identity, the formal-abstract "personhood" of human rights law, is dependent on that equally formal-abstract entity that is the state.[1] The state, moreover,

---

1. This point is made in relation to the twinned "enabling fictions" of the *Bildungsroman* and human rights law in Joseph Slaughter's book *Human Rights, Inc.*, to which the present essay is indebted throughout. Slaughter cites Hannah Arendt's observation about the stateless: "It seems that a man who is nothing but a man has lost the very qualities which make it possible for other people to treat him as a fellow man" (12).

is just as much an ideological and cultural and even, to a degree, an imaginary matter as the person. Its ostensible coherence, its sense of purpose, and its morality are all theoretical constructs, and its origins, as we have seen, are best (perhaps *only*) to be grasped in fictional, even mythic form.

Yet the state has perhaps seemed to be too much of a *thing*, a *fact* of political life, to strike students of literature as a particularly useful concept. In contemporary criticism, though the term "nation-state" often features, it tends to be the nation (and, lately, of course, its irrelevance and transcendence) that compels attention, sparks debate, and provides the obvious analytical optic. That this should be so is no accident: literary studies, after all, were until recently organized around the emergence of national cultures. We have also been the beneficiaries over the past two decades of compelling theorizations of the nation, most notably, of course, Benedict Anderson's definition of it as an imagined community, whose spatial and temporal preconditions are established by (or at least echoed in) the chronotopes and structures—the "meanwhile" effects—of the realist novel. In South African literary and cultural studies, the state tends to emerge in discussions of censorship, banning, and exile of writers; but the idea of the nation has generally seemed far more pertinent than that of the state.[2] Indeed, the very idea of "South African literature" in English emerged, at least since the mid-1970s, as a challenge

---

Coetzee similarly implies that without the state we are not persons: "Animals do not have identity papers," he drily points out, and people "who condemn themselves to living outside the state" share their fate (8).

2. There are, of course, many Foucauldian studies of literature (a classic example is D. A. Miller's *The Novel and the Police*) in which the state is present but radically dereified, dispersed into a myriad capillary forms of governance and surveillance. I am deemphasizing such studies here, because I am intrigued by Jean Comaroff and John L. Comaroff's argument that the Foucauldian understanding of the state may no longer be valid today. Foucault presumes, after all, the capacity of an increasingly powerful state to regulate and survey everyday existence and to enforce punishment—something that cannot be taken for granted as the state divests itself from many of its formerly grand disciplinary institutions, like education, mental health care, security provision, and so forth. This situation is particularly evident in the contemporary postcolony, where the state is constantly in danger of being overwhelmed by various forms of disorder and therefore still needs to centralize its authority and stage it in very theatrical ways ("Criminal Obsessions" 822–24).

to the official, ethnocentric—even tribal—notions of the relation of cultural production and nationness. All of the major South African writers under apartheid, as Salman Rushdie once noted, "set themselves against the official definition of the nation. Rescuing, perhaps, the true nation from those who held it captive" (22).

Yet it is essential to bear in mind that, despite the existence and display of national trappings—the flag, the anthem, the Springbok rugby team, and so forth—a sense of a nation that could include all of the country's inhabitants became viable only in the late 1980s and early 1990s with the demise of apartheid. (And it is an open question how long the postapartheid dream of a "rainbow nation" will prove sustainable.) Like all African (post)colonies, South Africa lacks what Jean Comaroff and John L. Comaroff call "hyphen-nation": the intimate nexus of nation and state never did and probably never will exist in such an endemically policultural society. For this reason alone, the state, rather than the nation, may emerge as the more vital and enduring framework for cultural analysis, especially if we trace its impact not only in the obvious legal restrictions imposed on literary creativity, but in the more implicit and also more wide-ranging effects on literary themes and forms. The latter would include such fertile, enduring, and popular genres as the gangster story (in which the fate of state power is dramatized through the figures of the outlaw and the police) and the *Bildungsroman* (which—in its affirmative form, at least—proposes a narrative resolution to the tensions between the anarchic predispositions of the individual and the conformist demands of the state).[3]

For this to shift to occur, however, it would be necessary for literary scholars to come to a better understanding of the complex and even contradictory character of the state in its colonial, apartheid, and postapartheid guises. We need to be aware, for example, of the argument, launched by scholars like Mahmood Mamdani and John Comaroff, about the historically bifurcated nature of the colonial African state—a structure that undermines colonial governments'

---

3. We may, in the context of this essay, think of the *Bildungsroman* as the cultural form that makes the obligatory seem desirable, that makes our interpellation as citizens seem like a choice.

claims to universality or modernity, and that continues to exert its dubious legacy in the persistence of customary law, even under new, progressive constitutions.[4] History textbooks (or at least the ones I studied years ago) tend to draw a broad distinction between "direct" and "indirect" rule: the former a mode of governance practiced in French Africa colonies and the latter in British ones. But the truth is that both forms were deployed in British colonial Africa, and in apartheid South Africa as well. Direct rule (or "concentrated despotism") was exerted in the cities, while indirect rule (or "decentralized despotism") held sway in the countryside, native reserves, and later the Bantustans (Mamdani 17–19). While white settlers were citizens in the full sense of the word, entitled to the rights and protections of the modern state, black South Africans were interpellated in two different and, indeed, antithetical ways, depending on their geographical location. In the cities, they directly confronted a racist centralized bureaucracy. They were converted into serialized individuals, in the sense that they were issued birth certificates and passes, their marriages and divorces were recorded, and their properties and taxes were regulated. But while subject to the laws of the state, they were resolutely barred from its privileges and from rights-bearing citizenship. In the countryside and tribal reserves, where daily governance was yielded to native authorities, black South Africans were treated not as *citizens* but as racialized *subjects*, denizens of a collective and thoroughly antimodern ethnoscape,

---

4. On contemporary tensions between customary law and South Africa's liberal constitution, based on universal personhood and individual rights, see, for example, the Comaroffs' "Criminal Justice." I should note that Mamdani's book has often been criticized for ignoring many specificities about South African society in its polemical effort to work against the rather persistent orthodoxy of South African exceptionalism (see, for example, Thornton). Yet *Citizen and Subject* continues to strike me as a suggestive work, not least (for our present purposes) in the way it insists—as does John Comaroff's masterful "Reflections on the Colonial State"—that in order to fully understand African colonialism and apartheid it may prove more useful to focus on the state than, say, on the political economy. (See Comaroff, "Reflections" 324; and Mamdani 59.) Far from locking one in rigid binaries, Mamdani's emphasis on the migrant, the figure of the city-in-the-country and the "country-in-the-city," seems rather compatible with more recent calls for attention to the "entanglements" of South African history—to the ways in which rigid oppositions (like those of the bifurcated state) are often traversed in daily practice (Nuttall 337–38).

who were incorporated into state-enforced systems of customary law. Migrants, the aporetic figures in the system, remained suspended in what Mamdani calls a juridical limbo—as "a class *in* civil society, but not *of* civil society" (19, 218).

It is therefore no wonder that the "Jim Comes to Joburg" story, which strives to provide a narrative account of this contradictory subject position, proved to be one of the most important and enduring genres of South African writing, one in which we can readily trace the generic legacy of the bifurcated state. These fictions (dating, roughly, from the teens to the early seventies) concern the journey of a black protagonist from the country to the city. Though their narrative drive partakes of the dynamism of urban, industrial modernity in which the youthful central character is swept up, the "Jim Comes to Joburg" story never really becomes what in any European nation-state it surely would have been: a *Bildungsroman*. This is not because the authors who contributed to this genre lacked the interest in or the literary talent for representing interiority and "character development." Rather, the sociopolitical conditions for closure that pertain in the affirmative *Bildungsroman* were lacking: it is neither possible nor desirable (whether from the point of view of the individual or that of the colonial state) for the protagonist to become a fully developed "person." For to do so, for the process of *Bildung* to come to term, the protagonist must be capable of exercising the rights enabled by a particular sociopolitical formation and, at the same time, be willing to submit "freely" to its norms. The movement toward modernity traced in the "Jim Comes to Joburg" plot thus never really becomes a movement toward maturity; the African city never becomes a site of emancipation. Hence the tendency of these novels to remain entrapped in the tropes of the picaresque (where closure can be almost endlessly deferred) or, alternatively, to turn toward the tragic (where death provides a convenient ending) or to a conservative and urbophobic version of the pastoral (where the protagonist returns, finally, to his "proper place" in the country).

If the "Jim Comes to Joburg" story provides us with insights into the characteristically bifurcated structure of the British colonial state and vice versa, I would like to focus my attention in the rest of this essay on a text that enables us to read the impact of the apartheid state and its increasingly neoliberal successor in similar fashion.

This text—and I am using the singular form provocatively and advisedly—is Athol Fugard's novel *Tsotsi* (written around 1959, at the time of the infamous demolition of the vibrant freehold township of Sophiatown) and its 2005 remake as a successful feature film by director and screenwriter Gavin Hood. Fugard's novel, composed during a miserable period of his life when he was working for the Native Commissioner's office in Johannesburg and saw the cruel effects of the pass laws at firsthand, cannot strictly speaking be treated as the "original" incarnation of the story. Fugard never saw fit to publish his "novel (à la Beckett)," which he considered a failure (*Notebooks* 51). In fact, the problems he saw in it persuaded him to abandon fiction and turn resolutely to the medium of drama.[5] The manuscript only emerged some twenty years later, when Sheila and Athol Fugard donated their papers to the newly founded National English Literary Museum in Grahamstown. It was then extensively edited by the prolific writer and literary historian Stephen Gray (whose role in the creation of *Tsotsi* is insufficiently acknowledged) and published by the Johannesburg firm Ad Donker. Fugard claims never actually to have read the novel (Miller). Even before it became a film, in other words, *Tsotsi* was a text that straddled historical moments—that of its writing (a moment when the triumphal apartheid state was setting its policies of forced removal in motion) and that of its publication and first reception (a moment when, in the wake of the 1976 Soweto rebellion, a new phase of political and cultural resistance was gathering steam).[6] It seems fair, therefore, to consider the film, which updates the novel in extremely revealing ways, as the latest historical staging of a quasi-mythic plot, a staging

---

5. My hunch has always been that Fugard must have sensed the imaginative, linguistic, and ethical difficulty of trying to express the inner life of an oppressed black character in English prose. (His comments to the *Mail & Guardian*'s Andie Miller confirm as much and reveal that he often had to deal, in the course of his career, with the charge of authorial appropriation—especially in the U.S.) It would then make sense for him to turn to the more obviously dialogic form of theater, where words are always cited and performed, and where textual ownership, authority, and the task of witness is shared between the playwright and his actors (who were, of course, frequently black).

6. The novel, Gray thought at the time, could serve as a kind of stand-in for the rich literature about black urban life in the 1950s, most of which was then banned, leaving a vast gap in the canon of an emergent oppositional South African literary tradition (Miller).

that vividly captures the differences between apartheid's racist police state and its successor—a postcolonial polity whose legitimacy, despite the "miracle" of the transition to democracy, is far from secure. Rooted in the paradoxes of a punitive neoliberal ethos, the film version of *Tsotsi* dramatizes (in ways that give it a highly exportable emotional appeal) the lead-up to the irreversible moment of voluntary submission to the state—to that mythic moment of choice I discussed earlier in relation to Coetzee and Althusser.

· 2 ·

Fugard's novel *Tsotsi* is, in essence, a meditation on the sociopolitical preconditions for coherent subjectivity and narration. It shares something of the metatextual dimension of his theatrical masterpieces of the sixties and seventies, and it foreshadows the materialist radicalism of their treatment of the dialectic of subjectivity and space. As we learn from his compelling *Notebooks, 1960–1977*, Fugard always conceived of individual subjectivity not as something given but as an effect of memory. A unified self is for him a fictional construct retrospectively glued together from otherwise hopelessly fragmentary sensory perceptions and experiences (*Notebooks* 102). This idea lies at the heart of his austere masterpiece *Boesman and Lena* (1968), a play that is simultaneously legible as a stripped existential drama and as a profound protest against the geographical injustices perpetrated under the Groups Areas Act. The two characters named in the title are doomed to a life of vagrancy by the apartheid government. Their latest pitiful shack, we learn, has been bulldozed right before the action of the play begins. Lacking any home, Lena, in particular, feels herself to be deprived of any memory and therefore of any coherent sense of identity. In an effort to reach beyond the immediate here and now, she repeatedly tries to recall, in correct order, the names of the scruffy places through which she has wandered. Her effort is thwarted by violence—not only that of the state but (perhaps first and foremost) that of her abusive partner Boesman's fist in her face. Boesman, by contrast, has no desire to narrate or claim a self. His identity can, he feels, be summarized in an almost untranslatable expression of disgust: "*Sies!*" (187). Defined as white man's rubbish and living in rubbish—discarded cardboard and corrugated iron—his life story would be only a source of shame. The chief obstacle to selfhood in this text—and in all of Fugard's *oeuvre*—is what he terms "the violence of immediacy" (*Notebooks* 125). The poor and oppressed, in other words, are deprived of *mediation*—both the material mediation of adequate shelter and the cognitive mediation of narration and retrospect.[7] "Anything can get at us," laments a choral voice in *Tsotsi*, "fleas and flies in summer, rain through the roof in winter, and the cold too and things like policemen and death. It's the siege of our life, man" (115).

As this quotation suggests, Fugard's early novel already presents a coherent identity as a kind of sociopolitical and cognitive privilege. *Tsotsi* concerns a vicious gangster who has no name (the word "tsotsi" means simply "thug"), no memory, and no identity. He cannot, as a key passage would have it, "assemble himself into any coherent shape":

> [I]n front of a mirror [he] had not been able to put together the eyes, and the nose, and the mouth and the chin, and make a man with meaning. His own features in his own eyes had been as meaningless as a handful of stones picked up at random in the street outside his room. He allowed himself no thought of himself... and his name was the name, in a way, of all men.
>
> (19)

Tsotsi operates, moreover, in a world of fragmentation: the white city's backyard of rubbish and ruins, where the "essentials and excesses" of lives are "measured... in the smallest units of the white man's money" (71). The narrative nevertheless traces the character's redemption or, more exactly, his second birth as a person capable of development. The agent of this change is a baby, who is shoved into his arms one dark night by a woman Tsotsi was planning to rape. Through his identification with and caring for the baby, Tsotsi eventually gets a sense of what empathy, mercy, and decency (a key word in the novel, just as "dignity" is in other works by Fugard) might mean. He also gradually pieces together a series of disconnected images (a dog, a spider, the smell of wet newspapers) into a coherent narrative of his childhood. He recollects the traumatic loss of his

---

7. For a fuller discussion of this idea, see Barnard, *Apartheid and Beyond* 100–105.

mother, who is taken away by the police in a pass raid, as well as his own subsequent life with a band of orphans who sleep in big drain-pipes near a river, from which he graduates into a life of crime. In the final paragraphs of the novel, he recalls his given name and, for the first time, reciprocates the greetings of other men. But the ending is also bleakly and melodramatically ironic. The very moment when Tsotsi can finally say "My name is David Madondo" (166) is the moment of his death: he is crushed by the government bulldozers that have come to demolish the ruins where he has hidden the baby. Fugard's *Tsotsi*, then, is a novel of the most minimal *Bildung* possible—and in this lies its profound reproach to apartheid's injustices.

It is useful, in fact, to consider this work—the first South African novel with a black protagonist to fully engage with the tradition of the *Bildungsroman*—in relation to recent theories of the genre. In his important essay on Olive Schreiner's *Story of an African Farm*, Jed Esty argues that the colonial *Bildungsroman* formally expresses the way in which the progressive elements of the European bour-geoisie's project of modernization began in the late nineteenth cen-tury to capitulate to the regressive logic of racialism. The expansive geography of imperialism, moreover, meant that "national-historic time," the chronotope best suited for the traditional *Bildungsroman*, no longer seemed to be the sole or the obvious spatiotemporal framework for narration. Thus, especially in the colonial novel, the dynamic plot of education and social mobility—the kind of story in which the emerging fates of the individual and the nation can be fused—ceases to be imaginable. What we have, instead, are fictions in which narrative progress is blocked and time seems strangely stagnant, bereft of its traditionally progressive dynamic: we have, in a word, *modernism* with its grotesquely distorted temporalities.

Despite its (post)colonial interests, Esty's historical framework is fairly Eurocentric (as his intense polemical engagement with Franco Moretti virtually ensures), and he focuses, perhaps unduly, on the nation, rather than the state.[8] Yet one can readily see how his formal

---

8. Esty argues that Moretti leaves unexplored the symbolic function of the nation, which gives a "finished" form, a historically meaningful shape, to modern societies in the same way that adulthood in the *Bildungsroman* tradition gives a finished form to the mod-ern subject ("Virginia Woolf's Colony" 74).

logic might apply, *mutatis mutandis*, to a twentieth-century South African novel like *Tsotsi*—a (very late) modernist work, whose various forms of experimentation with time can be understood as registering the specific impact of the retrogressive apartheid state.[9] To be sure, the agents of the state are not the focus of narrative attention: this is no cops-and-robbers story. But these agents are a persistent and threatening presence, whether in the shape of prowling police cars, the bulldozers of the "slum clearance men," or the rubber stamps of an absurd bureaucracy (6).[10] The state severely delimits the characters' social options and mobility. A profoundly ironic passage describes the "big choice" of things one can do at night in the impoverished township, where illegal shebeens offer the only available public space:

> You could drink with the men or you could drink with the girls. You could drink alone if it was that sort of day and that sort of world, you could sit alone in a chair in a corner and drag out the one tot to last all night and no one would give a damn one way or another why your mother was dead or your woman gone. You could drink with a picture on the wall or no picture at all. You could drink comfortable in a club easy, or sitting on a wooden bench, you could even drink standing up in a backyard.
>
> (14)

Most importantly, the effect of the state's denial of full human development is marked in the novel's style and temporality. Fugard's prose style brilliantly captures what Coetzee once described as apartheid's "viscous, sluggish chronicity" (*Doubling* 209) in long, loping, quasi-Faulknerian sentences.[11] This lack of any progressive

---

9. The theme of time is omnipresent, even at times in the mode of black comedy. A migrant named Gumboot Dlamini, whose hopeful quest is cut short by Tsotsi's murderous gang, is renamed by a laconic grave-digger as (the generic) "Friday night" who is buried on "Saturday afternoon" (49).

10. The absurdity is, again, rendered in terms of the distortion of standard chronologies. In one of the novel's fascinating subplots, Boston, the only educated member of Tsotsi's gang, sets himself up in the illegal business of providing pass applicants with signatures of "previous employers," without which they can never hope to get a first or future employer (146).

11. Coetzee's reflections on the temporality of apartheid are strikingly relevant here: "Time in South Africa has been extraordinarily static for most of my life . . . I was born in 1940; I was eight when the party of Afrikaner Christian nationalism came to power and

dynamic is evident also in the banal, disconnected imagery of town-ship life, whether it be "the dust of the men who had passed, a child without a game and a dog with a flea," or a gramophone that "repeat[s] unheeded the meaningless phrase of its last groove" (25). The pointless drifting or the insignificant actions of the gangsters waiting for nightfall (yawning, stretching, and scratching) are recorded with slow, almost suspended deliberation, as are the Beckettian non sequiturs of their darkly comic conversations. The principle of repetition even determines the novel's stark descrip-tions of the modern city:

> It was a world which must have had as its model the plaything precision of a child's blocks. The streets, crosslaid in the faultless squaring of a grill, were completely untenanted.... The black squares of double doors, side entrances, high barred windows...chequered the night with another vari-ant of the severe pattern. The street lamps, spaced at unvarying intervals along the edges of the pavements, added a final, strict rhythm to the monotony of the night...
>
> (88)

The novel's ruling temporality, in short, is one of recurrence and habit. "I will do exactly the same as I always do," we find Tsotsi thinking at the beginning of the novel, before "clos[ing] his mind and [thinking] about nothing" (16).

The grim, often labyrinthine urban spaces evoked in the novel serve as an objective correlative of sorts to Tsotsi's pathological psyche. His threatening presence in the township is represented from the start as something that blocks the community's capacity for protest and progress: the appearance of his gang, as we see in one of those endless sentences in the novel's first pages, dispels the community's twilight moment of respite and recollection and

---

set about stopping or even turning back the clock. Its programs involved a radically dis-continuous intervention into time, normal (in the sense of being the norm) in colonial societies. It also aimed at instituting a sluggish no-time in which an already anachronistic order of patriarchal clans and tribal despotisms would be frozen in place. This is the polit-ical order in which I grew up. And the culture in which I was educated—a culture look-ing, when it looked anywhere, nostalgically back to Little England—did nothing to quicken time" (*Doubling* 209). For an example of Fugard's Faulknerian sentences—too long to quote—see the description of the gang's effect on the community on pp. 8–9.

ruptures not only its collective feelings of anger and loss, but even its "count[ing] the days past and hop[ing] for tomorrow" (9). Habitual violence is also his mechanism for repressing his own traumatic memories, and therefore his ability to develop. Though other characters see him as a (sinister) young man, he is in a more profound sense outside of time: "he remember[s] no yesterdays and tomorrow existed only when it was the present, living moment. He was as old as that moment" (19). If, as Hayden White suggests, the "growth and development of narrative capability" have "something to do with...the legal system...the form in which the subject encounters most immediately the social system in which he is enjoined to achieve a full humanity" (14), Tsotsi's law-lessness goes hand-in-hand with his denial of these progressive principles. His ruinous "inward maze" (88) is what is left when one is bereft (and robs others) of narrative and developmental capacity.

It is interesting, therefore, that the catalyst that eventually gives the plot its largely retrospective dynamic—the baby who is thrust into Tsotsi's arms—is in a certain sense also out of time: it is described as "lined and wrinkled with an age beyond years" (34). Yet precisely because of its strange condensation of extreme youth and extreme age, the baby expresses the very principle of *Bildung*: "This small, almost ancient, very useless and abandoned thing," Tsotsi thinks at one point, "was the beginning of a man...[it] would one day straighten out, smooth and shape itself into manhood" (40). The baby forces Tsotsi to think of himself as a person with an origin—a mother, in particular—and therefore also, potentially, a telos. The same can be said of Morris Tshabalala, the crippled beg-gar, whom Tsotsi encounters midway through the novel and selects as his victim-for-the-night. Like the baby ("older than anything [Tsotsi] had seen in his life" [34]), the legless cripple, who thinks, bitterly, that "half a man" might get older quicker than "a full one" (60), is a grotesque emblem of distorted temporality. Together they impel Tsotsi to examine his own stalled psyche, to look inward, and, eventually, to recollect the continuous story—the "silk thread" (128)—of his origins: his mother's singing, the enormous khaki-coated shadows who burst into his home and dragged her off, his father's violent outburst in the face of this loss, and his own descent into an existential nothingness that (like Boesman's) is kept at bay only by violence.

One might say, in sum, that Fugard's *Tsotsi* is not so much a *Bildungsroman*—not even what Joseph Slaughter would call a "dissensual" one—as a kind of proto-*Bildungsroman*.[12] Forced into the temporality of repetition by the retrograde apartheid state and its cruel destruction of black urban modernity, Tsotsi/David Madondo can develop only to the point where the usual kind of novelistic maturation—the kind that conventionally fuses the emergence of self and society—might begin. Though the melodrama of Tsotsi's death in the ruins of Sophiatown risks being so ironic as to be corny, it is in a sense the only closing gesture possible. The subjective conditions for affirmative *Bildung* have come into existence by the end of the novel, but they are rendered null and void by the objective conditions of the apartheid state, which is presented throughout the text as the agent of reification, grotesque deformation, and temporal suspension.

· 3 ·

Fugard's *Tsotsi*, as I noted above, was not published in its day and was considered of scant interest by its author. (Even now, critical commentary on the novel remains slight.) By contrast, Gavin Hood's cinematic recasting of the novel was an instant national and international hit, winning—among other prizes—the 2006 Oscar for Best Foreign Language Film. The different reception history of the two versions of the story can be explained not so much by the translation from prose to film (not all films, after all, are global successes), but by the ideological effects of the updating of the plot—by the changed relationship, if you will, of the story to the state. These effects may be summarized, for now, as follows: while the "original" *Tsotsi* has a metafictional and critical edge, the film version is quite unproblematically (or I guess I would prefer to say

---

12. For Slaughter's definition of the "dissensual *Bildungsroman*," see chapter 3 of *Human Rights, Inc.*, especially pp. 181–85.

problematically) a *Bildungsroman*.[13] It is, in the director's rather banal formula, "a universal coming of age story that transcends race" (De Bruyn), and it serves the standard "feel-good" pedagogical function that such stories have come to serve in today's global cultural marketplace—that of developing the "full humanity" of the international audience, who are treated to a *soupçon* of difference reassuringly tempered by the same.[14]

If Fugard's job at the Native Commissioner's Office in Johannesburg shaped the form and the subject matter of his novel, Gavin Hood's early career is similarly relevant to his cinematic reinterpretation of the story. He was originally trained as a lawyer, and his abiding interests in the law—fairly conservative ones, I would argue—leave a mark on his directorial and screenwriting oeuvre. Two of his films, in fact, are based on legal cases. His 1999 film *A Reasonable Man* (concerning a Zulu herdboy who commits a murder while under the impression that the victim is a *tokoloshe*, or evil spirit) offers a timely exploration of the ways in which South Africa's new liberal constitution comes up against custom and customary law.[15] Even more interesting, for our purposes, is his first feature film, *The Storekeeper*. This silent melodrama concerns a rural storekeeper who sets a trap for a robber, accidentally kills a little girl, and is duly arrested at the end of the film. Its theme, in other words, is the danger of vigilantism ("what happens when we take the law in our own hands," as Hood puts it), and it concludes with a

---

13. I know, of course, that a film is not a novel; but I use the term *Bildungsroman*, as Slaughter does, to indicate not only a literary but a "life" genre—a technology for producing normative forms of modern personhood (see, for example, "*Clef à Roman*" 6 and *Human Rights* 304–16). I consider the affirmative *Bildungsroman* form problematic here, not only because of its international marketability, which I will touch on shortly, but also because of the intriguing work done by theorists like Abdoumaliq Simone and Achille Mbembe, who have spoken of the new performative subjectivities—the "mitotic identities"—that arise from the very effort of surviving in Africa's informal settlements, identities which may demand wholly different forms of narrative expression (Mbembe 5; Simone 173–87).

14. The director suggests as much in his 2005 interview with *Cinéaste* (47), as I will discuss later on. See chapter 5 and the "Codicil" to Slaughter's *Human Rights, Inc.* for a full discussion of the *Bildungsroman*'s traditional and contemporary function for its readership.

15. For a brief discussion of the film in relation to the Mbombelwa case (about a "man who mistook his neighbor for a bat"), see Comaroff and Comaroff, "Criminal Justice" 195.

decisive reaffirmation of the official forces of law and order and the state's monopoly over the means of coercion.[16] The film version of *Tsotsi*, likewise, is resolutely on the side of law and order. Indeed, it is interesting to note how frequently Hood resorts, in both his director's commentary and in his interviews about the film, to what has become a standard conversational item for South Africans craving more effective policing: the crime anecdote. (He tells us that his mother was twice carjacked at gunpoint, that he and his father were both mugged, etcetera ["Interview" 46].)[17]

Now, one cannot deny that *Tsotsi* is, in many ways, an impressive piece of filmmaking that takes commercial and artistic risks.[18] The director decided to work with untried—and extremely young—actors in the major roles, to shoot the film on location in the squatter camps, and to do the dialogue in *tsotsitaal*, a hybrid mix of Afrikaans, Sotho, Tswana, and Zulu spoken in the townships around Johannesburg. Hood deploys an ensemble of carefully considered techniques—including a very still rather than handheld camera, an alternation of intense close-ups and wide-angle shots, and an expressive color-coding of costumes and sets—to express

---

16. See the director's commentary on the DVD of *Tsotsi*. It is interesting that Hood seems aware that *Tsotsi* and *The Storekeeper* are linked, but he sees the matter in technical terms, as having to do with stripping dialogue to a bare minimum. Hood, whose interviews and commentaries are a curious blend of the insightful and the banal, thinks that his legal background helped him to present "both sides" in *Tsotsi* ("Interview" 47), a view I would contest, given the film's overall narrative drive toward the incorporation of the outlaw and its sentimental foregrounding of "family values."

17. The best true crime story surrounding *Tsotsi*, however, concerns the cinematographer Lance Gewer, who, while driving with a female companion, was carjacked by three men. His companion, perhaps in shock, asked one of the muggers if he had seen the film *Tsotsi*. He replied that he had seen it and then said, "That is why I am so sorry to do this to you. I saw *Tsotsi* and it is a good film. My heart is sore for you. Please forgive me for doing this" ("Cinematographer"). On the meaning of proliferating crime anecdotes and the production of a culture of "vicarious victimhood," see Comaroff and Comaroff, "Figuring Crime" 233.

18. A particularly laudable decision was the one not to use voice-over. This technique would have implied a kind of retrospective self-sponsorship more characteristic of *Bildungsromane* of emerging intellectuals. For more on this kind of narrative, see Slaughter's fourth chapter, "Compulsory Development," and also Jameson 203. Fugard's Tsotsi—illiterate, barely articulate, devoid of memory—is not undergoing an intellectual's apprenticeship (to say the least): "Decency—books and words!" he declares early in the novel. "I wipe my backside with books and words" (19).

interiority with minimal dialogue and to distinguish the film from such "third world" classics as *The Battle of Algiers* and *City of God* (Archibald 44). The film's abiding conception of human psychology, however, is rather middlebrow and conventional. Hood even implies in one of his interviews that Tsotsi's criminality is a mask, which has to be "peel[ed] off," so that the basically "decent kid" underneath can stand forth (De Bruyn). This notion of subjectivity is, of course, vastly more simplistic than that of Fugard's novel, where sociogeographical contingencies—the exposure of the poor to the state's various forms of "direct rule"—negate the possibility of a quintessential but repressed inner self.

The screenplay also modifies Fugard's plot in ways that are both inventive and disconcerting. First of all, Tsotsi does not have the baby thrust at him by a troubled mother. Instead, he perpetrates a nasty carjacking, shoots the vehicle's owner (who is a wealthy black woman), and discovers, as he makes his escape from her affluent suburb, a baby in the backseat. Though the film traces the gangster's redemption through memory along lines similar to the novel's (there are a number of flashbacks in which a younger actor plays the traumatized David Madondo), there are certain major differences—not least of which is the focus on the baby's parents, whose plight makes it impossible for us to think of the baby in purely emblematic terms. That these victims should be black, moreover, is hugely significant. The film studiously declines to racialize (or even politicize) the vast distinction between rich and poor, even though this distinction is extremely marked by the *mise-en-scène*—in the contrast between the dilapidated township shacks and the very luxurious (and stylishly Afrocentric) suburban home.[19] No one who has seen the film can fail to note the heartrending contrast between Tsotsi's old abode, the row of stacked drainpipes where the street children—played by actual AIDS orphans—must live, and the opulent bedroom of the stolen child, decorated with colorful murals of African sunrises and replete with stuffed toys. The

---

19. While it is in a sense true that Hood has "repoliticized" *Tsotsi*, as he claims to have done ("Interview" 46), the distinction between rich and poor is not the site of this repoliticization. That occurs, as I will show, in relation to the police and the modified denouement.

recollected traumatic event, moreover, is not the result of the agents of the state: the young David loses his mother to AIDS and flees from his sick and drunken father's uncomprehending rage. The protest posters proclaiming "WE WON'T MOVE" (140), which are part of the grim landscape of Fugard's novel, are duly replaced in the film with health-education banners declaring "WE ARE ALL AFFECTED BY HIV/AIDS." The appropriate sentiment of the contemporary South African public sphere, it would seem, is no longer anger or indignation but a generalized, Oprahesque empathy for fellow sufferers.[20]

While Hood clearly understands the power of Fugard's indirect treatment of the effects of the apartheid state in his novel, he seems to misunderstand the degree to which his own version of the story continues to be about the state and not really about the AIDS epidemic—the putative new "elephant in the room," as he puts it in the *Cinéaste* interview (45). The film seems concerned, above all, to dramatize the legitimacy of the postapartheid state and, in Joseph Slaughter's apt formulation, to "domesticate the impulse of the revolutionary plot of rebellion into the less spectacular, reformatory plot of human personality development" (*Human Rights* 91). This project is most clearly evident in the updating of Fugard's ironic ending. Hood ended up shooting three versions: one where Tsotsi dies in a shoot-out with police, one in which he escapes, and one in which he hands over the baby and surrenders to the authorities. Though all of these can be viewed on the DVD of the film (as a bonus for buyers), it is clear that the final option, the one that was chosen, is really the only one that fits the logic of the film. And it is certainly the one most interesting to us as students of the *Bildungsroman* and of the relationship between culture and the state. The moment of closure is, after all, the moment in which there should, notionally at least, be some accommodation between the protagonist and the social order. And this is indeed—and rather depressingly—the case. If Tsotsi is to become human, the selected ending implies, it is only by ignoring the discrepancies between rich and poor, so vividly

---

20. For a discussion of affect in relation to South African culture and society, see my essay on Oprah's Book Club and the "globalization of suffering."

evident in the film's domestic spaces, and by acceding to the pre-scriptive universality of family and family values. (It is significant, as other commentators have also noted, that the father of the child addresses Tsotsi as "brother.")[21] Althusser's theoretical drama of interpellation and subjectivization comes to mind here: Tsotsi, as it were, becomes part of humanity only by responding to the police-man's "Hey, you there!"—or, more exactly, his *"Bek'izandla zakho phezu kwekhanda lakho!"* ("Put your hands above your head!")—by gesturing his surrender, thus accepting his identity as criminal (the liability of all rights-bearing citizens, if you will), rather than outlaw.

But what is in it for Tsotsi, one might ask? What's the difference in terms of the achievement of full human potentiality between an individuated criminal (or eventual prisoner) and the generic "tsotsi" with which we start out? The difference is the infinitesimal space of development permitted once the neoliberal state (which promises freedom from fear, but not freedom from want) asserts itself in the form of the rule of law. If we think about it this way, the ending of *Tsotsi* is about as unsatisfactory as political allegory as is the hokey reconciliation at the end of Fritz Lang's *Metropolis*, with its insistence that the heart must mediate between brains and brawn, even though the structure of the dystopian city remains the same.

Except, except for the fabulous sound track. The music played at the end of the film almost irresistibly guides the audience's affec-tive response: it more or less forces us to take the meaning of the story affirmatively—and it surely has a great deal to do with the film's success as an export product. As the credits roll, we hear the song "Bhambatha" as performed by Zola, the nationally and inter-nationally known kwaito singer, who has a bit part as an older gangster in the film.[22] The name "Bhambatha," we should note, has historical resonances: the Bhambatha uprising of 1906 was one of

---

21. Lesley Marx, for instance, observes that the word "brother . . . carries all the weight of the family of which Tsotsi has been deprived and suggests the other history that might have been his, but will now belong to the baby, the gift he has returned" (24). We may here play with the idea that this moment correlates with the paternal recognition scene in that ur-*Bildungsroman*, Goethe's *Wilhelm Meister*.

22. Kwaito is a South African version of rap. The word derives from the Afrikaans "kwaai," which means "angry" but can also be colloquially rendered as "awesome."

the last instances of armed resistance against the British colonial government in South Africa. But here "Bhambatha" is clearly the name of a gang. The song presents the usual gangster raplike celebration of violence and, even more significantly for our purposes, seems to invite the addressee to join their badass *confrérie*. The tough attitude of the song thus serves to mute any lingering critique of the abject emptiness of Tsotsi's subjectification/subjection to the law by smuggling back the old thrill of political resistance and the cool attitude of gangsterism—but gangsterism purely as style, of course, not as a real threat to the status quo. The song allows us, as Coetzee might put it, to indulge in the fantasy that we might remain outlaws—that our subjection to the state is not irreversible after all. The sound track then modulates into a gentler call-and-response number, "E Sale Noka," featuring the moving voice of Vusi Mahlasela, with its unmistakably South African timbre. The song resolves, finally, into a dominant chord, with all the attendant feelings of transcendence and (as the choir's singing suggests) national or human community. In this chord the audience may savor the satisfying sense of closure and social resolution to which the developmental plot gestures but leaves quite vacuous in terms of real potentiality for the *Bildungsroman*'s protagonist.

· 4 ·

Without leaving our two *Tsotsis* and their politically resonant conclusions behind, I would now like to reflect in somewhat finer detail on the shape of the postcolonial state today. To do so, I would like to bring into play a range of insights suggested by Jean Comaroff and John L. Comaroff's essays on the law and disorder in South Africa—a body of work that offers an extraordinarily rich account of the impact of neoliberal trends on the world's newest postcolonies. Three tropes—that of youth, victimhood, and crime (plus, inevitably, the police)—seem to me central to their work, and these are also, almost uncannily, the three tropes that most clearly mark the differences between the two *Tsotsis* and, by extension, between the apartheid and postapartheid state. These three tropes are obviously entwined. Nevertheless, each illuminates a slightly different aspect of the contemporary state: new patterns of inclusion and exclusion, new meanings of citizenship, and new dimensions of sovereignty and power, respectively.

First, youth. In their essay "Millennial Capitalism," the Comaroffs underscore the "growing pertinence," or "more accurately,… impertinence" (307), of youth to any understanding of our "brave neo world" (Jean Comaroff, "Beyond Bare Life" 215). A "youth," the Comaroffs note, is not the same thing as a "teenager," a term that tends to apply to pre-adults who are privileged and white. We are speaking here of "adolescents with attitude" (307), usually black and almost always male, who in urban spaces the world over have become threatening, if marginal, presences. This situation has everything to do with the nature of the global economy and the "inability of governments to subject the workings of international capital to their own rules and regulations" (Jean Comaroff, "Beyond Bare Life" 210). As the labor market becomes feminized, and as production migrates toward optimal and often distant sites, the postcolonial (and, specifically, the postapartheid) state has found itself incapable of creating work opportunities for all its citizens and protecting them from destitution. One result of this tendency is a frightening degree of unemployment, particularly of young, unskilled black males. Poverty thus becomes racialized, gendered, and "youthenized," as the Comaroffs' pun would have it, while class anxieties are displaced on to generational ones ("Criminal Obsessions" 804). If, as Franco Moretti has argued in relation to the European *Bildungsroman*, youth was traditionally the master trope of modernity (6), it now seems as if youth or rather *youths* come to stand for the grotesque inversion of the progressive project of modernity. Drawn to global styles like hip-hop but excluded from the world of work and wages, juveniles become, as the Comaroffs put it, a kind of counternation operating in a twilight zone between the local and the global and viewing themselves as "ironic mutant citizens of a new world order" ("Millennial Capitalism" 309).[23]

All this is readily applicable to our focus text. While youth (or, more exactly, developmental potential) is hugely important in Fugard's

---

23. The film version of *Tsotsi* reminds us, in one of its most visually and emotionally arresting sequences, of another, even more disconcerting and ever-waxing group of marginalized persons—AIDS orphans and homeless children.

novel, his Tsotsi is more of an experimental literary device—an emblem of stalled chronicity—than a youth in any sort of historically specific sense. But in Hood's film, this is precisely what the Tsotsi figure becomes. In fact, he is decisively staged as such in the very title sequence. A medium-range track-shot captures him center screen, dressed in a black jacket, walking threateningly toward the camera with this gang, while the first of Zola's throbbing kwaito songs is heard on the sound track. While announcing a locally distinct (though internationally recognizable) urban style, this sequence also introduces an all-too-familiar anxiety—one that might be pleasurable in the context of a movie but is nevertheless tied to very real transnational concerns about the ability of society to reproduce itself, especially given the retreat of the state from so many of its former educational and disciplinary functions. These pervasive anxieties (also expressed in the film's concern with AIDS and infants) are firmly set to rest at the conclusion, when, as we have seen, both the law and the normative nuclear family (in a kind of ideological double whammy) reassert their power over the erstwhile leader of threatening youths.[24] The last shot of the film, significantly, features Tsotsi from behind, alone in a dark street, in the lights of the cop cars. His gang has now dispersed, and his gesture of surrender is readily contrasted with the defiant "up yours" gesture he makes in the film's opening moments. If "youth," in sum, has become all the more threatening since the late 1950s, its incorporation and safe-making needs to be presented all the more melodramatically and decisively today. Hood's film does precisely this and, in so doing, suggests that the new South Africa—the much-welcomed successor to apartheid's police state—shares something of the generally punitive temper of contemporary states.

Next, the victim. To understand this motif, we need to begin by reflecting on the fact that the new democracies that came into being

---

24. Here we may rewrite one of Jameson's more risky observations: he has noted that the third world *Bildungsroman* must necessarily involve a movement of the modernizing individual away from family, the source of tradition and stability (173). But one should bear in mind that the bourgeois nuclear family, especially an affluent one like that in the film version of *Tsotsi*, is not the African norm but rather a kind of postmodern telos for the upwardly mobile: it *is* the new thing, into which the wayward or the aspiring individual (or so the film suggests) must be incorporated.

in the wake of the fall of the Soviet Union all adopted progressive constitutions based on fundamental rights and freedoms. However, as the Comaroffs remind us, it is not clear to what extent these inspiring documents really serve to empower their citizens: "Not one of them actually speaks of an entitlement to the means of survival. They do not guarantee the right to earn or to produce, only to possess, to signify, to consume, to choose" ("Millennial Capitalism" 330). The neoliberal state, in fact, *insists* that we choose, as Coetzee sardonically points out, with the result that "freedom" becomes a rather constrained matter (*Diary* 8).[25] There is much to be said, of course, for the heightened sense of rights that such constitutions have instilled; but the effect has also been to turn citizens into consumers and, where the state seems to fall short in its pared-down mission of delivering services and ensuring law and order, into rather aggrieved ones. This attitude is further fueled by the emergence of what the Comaroffs call a "worldwide politics of suffering" ("Figuring Crime" 225), where disadvantaged groups of various stripes turn increasingly to legal rather than political means for redress. The result is that citizens tend no longer to mobilize as classes (especially given the reduced emphasis on the citizen-producer), but rather as "claimants in class actions" (228). Victims of all sorts are thus more likely to behave like the irate, litigious, ill-served clients of the state than as its political opponents.

One should bear in mind, too, that as the welfare or developmental state morphs into the neoliberal one, all citizens are increasingly

---

25. The passage is worth citing: "Faced with a choice between A and B, given the kind of A and the kind of B who usually make it onto the ballot paper, most people . . . in their hearts inclined to choose neither. But that is only an inclination, and the state does not deal in inclinations. Inclinations are not part of the currency of politics. What the state deals in are choices. The ordinary person would like to say; *Some days I incline to A, some days to B, most days I just feel they should both go away:* or else, *Some of A and some of B, sometimes, and at other times neither A nor B but something quite different.* The state shakes its head. *You have to choose,* says the state: *A or B.* . . . 'Spreading freedom' means creating the conditions for people to choose freely between A and B" (8–9). Compare here Marianne Hirsch's description of the *Bildungsroman*'s plot trajectory as also dealing in the rather constrained choice of A or B: "Its projected resolution is an accommodation to the existing society . . . each protagonist has the choice of accepting or rejecting this projected resolution" (298).

exposed to risk; thus in contexts where violent crime rates are high, they may readily identify and mobilize, across all other social divisions, "on the basis of their vulnerability to violation." The "citizen-victim," in other words, becomes everyman: "'The public'... becomes an aggregate of the imperiled, in which identity is defined in terms of hurt and trauma" ("Figuring Crime" 228). And when this sense of peril manifests itself in a call for more police, we return again to the contradiction I gestured toward at the beginning of this essay: that minimal government, under pressure from a frightened citizenry (redefined as consumers and victims), can readily turn into its authoritarian opposite.

Again, these matters resonate in almost uncanny ways with our focus text. Fugard's novel is certainly interested in the gangster's victims. In fact, their stories are told in some detail in various subplots. Tsotsi's leadership of his gang, moreover, is affirmed by the fact that he *chooses* the victims, and one of the major things he learns in the course of the novel—the thing, in fact, that begins to liberate him from the recursive temporality of trauma—is that he could choose not to have a victim at all. But significant though this interest in the idea of the victim (and choice) may be, it is nowhere near as central to the novel as it is to the film version of *Tsotsi*, which clearly taps into the contemporary culture of victimhood I sketched out above. A crucial scene here is the one where the father of the missing baby berates the police for their lack of progress in tracking down the child and the carjacker. There is, to be sure, some pleasure to be had in seeing black South Africans represented as persons who can make demands on the state—and Hood's *Tsotsi* may be the very first internationally circulated narrative in which we see them in this role, rather than as abject victims or heroic opponents of the police. But the prominence of the victimized family, it seems to me, shifts the affective charge of the story in ways that reduce its critical power. While Fugard's *Tsotsi* deals in what Northrop Frye calls the ironic mode, which excludes any simple emotional identification with characters who are all presented as "inferior to" the audience with regard to their capacity for action and the transformation of their world, the suffering middle-class victims in the film are obvious surrogate figures for both the national and the international audience of the film. We could easily find ourselves in their shoes. True, the director also cues us to feel sorry for the criminal, but there is no question that the citizen-victims are, ultimately, the normative figures; it is their right to have their trauma redeemed that drives the narrative resolution. Nor is it accidental, I would argue, that so much is made in the film of the interior of their luxurious home, which is presented as the site of normative, inspirational consumption. The fact that Tsotsi returns what Hood calls the "gift" of the baby in a shopping bag may therefore be taken as a revealing detail: the outlaw is shown, by the end of the film, as moving not just toward universal person-hood but, however tenuously, toward the status of the citizen-victim or citizen-consumer.

Finally, to the overarching matter of crime and the police. In their essays on the law and (dis)order in South Africa, the Comaroffs cite Mark Seltzer's argument that publics are increasingly constituted today around the scene of the crime ("Criminal Obsessions" 804). It is in the melodrama of cops and crooks, vicious criminals and tough men with badges, they argue, that the social order is most obviously tested. It is here that the liberal state may reveal the naked power that it usually conceals and may do so with the relieved assent of the citizenry. Violent crime, in particular, allows the state to "state," loud and clear, its claim to dominance. These assertions are all the more pertinent, as the Comaroffs demonstrate, in the context of the postcolony, where the forces of disorder are often so potent as to overwhelm the state's capacity for control—thus requiring, both in actual practice and in imaginative forms, a highly theatrical, even melodramatic display of its sovereignty. Crime has of course been rife in postapartheid South Africa, where the ANC government is perceived to have reneged on its promise of a redistribution of wealth in favor of IMF and World Bank–friendly policies. For some—the unskilled, the hungry, the angry—this reversal of macro-economic policy has virtually necessitated a life of lawlessness; for others, the inefficiency of the state's redistributive and welfare functions has made the minimal basics like law and order seem all the more crucial: the very test, in fact, of its legitimacy. The result has been that crime rates, crime statistics, and crime anecdotes have become "a prime currency of public culture, a prime index of order, a prime gauge of effective rule" ("Figuring Crime" 238–39).

The cinematic updating of Fugard's *Tsotsi*, once again, seems to furnish some striking insights into these sociopolitical processes. Fugard's novel, as we have seen, reveals a deep interest in the etiology of crime. Violence, he implies, is both the cause and the result of the nonprogressive temporalities of trauma. But while crime was certainly rife in the 1950s townships in which his novel is set, it was not treated as an occasion for assessing the state of the nation at large. (Indeed, such a way of thinking, as the Comaroffs point out, emerged as a possibility only when South Africa became an undivided polity and a democratic public sphere was brought into being.) Gangster stories or *policiers* from the 1950s, in other words, would not readily translate into national allegory. But in the case of Hood's film, such readings seemed instantly feasible. Even the introduction to the new edition of Fugard's novel, republished in the wake of the film's success, concludes along such lines: "The new South Africa," it declares, "is attempting to overcome persistent crime and unemployment and to offer all its citizens the hope of a better future. Earthbound, lost, blinded by the pain of his oppression but finally capable of transcendence, Tsotsi turns out to be a surprisingly prophetic model for his country's redemption" (xv).

Maybe so. But this optimistic allegorical twist, scarcely sustained by the novel, depends in good measure on the way in which the film version of *Tsotsi* represents the actions of the police. While in Fugard's novel the police are the nefarious, prowling agents of an oppressive state, the film version gives considerable and very sympathetic screen time to a multiracial team of cops, led by a white detective who speaks fluent isiZulu. The first scene in which the cops appear is telling in this regard. It presents their discovery of the stolen car (the scene of the second crime, if you will) and of the disturbing fact that the thief has made off with the owner's baby. In the beautiful, panaromic wide-angle shot that concludes the sequence, we see the team of cops from behind, flanking the stripped vehicle, gazing, in the thin light of dawn, across a strip of open veld toward the vast, hazy township—the place where they must, somehow, find the perpetrator and retrieve the infant. It is hard, especially since the camera makes us share their visual point of view, not to sympathize with the white cop's heartfelt, "*Aag, fok!*" as he assesses the difficulty of the task ahead. "We" become, to recall Mark

Seltzer's insight, members of a public who need the police to succeed. But the heightened importance of the cops in the updated *Tsotsi* is most decisively underscored by their prominence at the film's finale, where they restore order and, as it were, compel the criminal's "free" subjection. The police in the film thus contribute decisively to its overriding ideological burden: that of dramatizing the state as "our illusory common interest" (Marx and Engels 42) and, not at all incidentally, of reassuring overseas audiences of the nation's "democratization, stability, creditworthiness, and the like" ("Figuring Crime" 224).[26]

We are left, in sum, with the curious phenomenon of a film that exposes the failure of the postapartheid state to guarantee a decent living for all its citizens, but that nevertheless comes to be received as what the director calls "an advert for [its] country" (De Bruyn). *Tsotsi* has been met with considerable and perhaps justifiable patriotic pride. "If we do win the Oscar," declared the lead actor, Presley Cheweneyagae in an early 2006 interview, "it's good for all of us in the country" (Marx 5). And so, I suppose, it has been. But to say so involves a certain slippage from the diegetic to the extradiegetic, from the dubiously happy ending for a lead character who learns to accept the compulsory as desirable, to the undoubtedly happy ending the film brought to its actors, its director, and the South African National Film and Video Foundation. But the patriotism that has accompanied such "proudly South African film-making" (writingstudio.za) should not necessarily be seen as a sign of the strength of the postapartheid nation-state. It reveals, rather, the economic exigencies that accompany cultural production in all the new postcolonies, where the state has come to serve as "a business in the business of attracting business," a megamarketing enterprise in which all citizens can claim a share, even as they desire greater global citizenship (Comaroff and Comaroff, "Naturing the Nation" 636). It is precisely because of the tenuousness of the state's ability to ensure the welfare of its citizens in a world where it no longer has

---

26. The Comaroffs' comment on the function of crime statistics is entirely pertinent here: "To argue, both for foreign and domestic consumption, that rates of violent disorder are declining, at worst 'stabilizing,' or that the police are 'winning the war against crime,' is to assert . . . the state" ("Figuring Crime" 224).

full control of economic policy—or of the flow of people, commodities, currencies, and styles across its borders—that it must become a vigorous marketer of national culture to the world at large. South African cultural products—whether the writings of Athol Fugard, the four-part harmonies of the struggle songs, or the gangster rap of the contemporary township (or even, perhaps, the horrors of apartheid itself, viewed in comfortable retrospect)—must be sold internationally. They must become commodities "to be patented, made into intellectual property, merchandised, consumed" (634). And if they sell, they are in a sense success stories, irrespective of their content.

But not irrespective of form. It is clear that the twinned genres of national allegory and the affirmative *Bildungsroman* are by far the most consumable forms through which postcolonial writing can enter the global literary marketplace. Indeed, these narrative forms may be, as Slaughter has argued, the sole reliable key for admission to the contemporary canon (*Human Rights* 304–16). We may detect, in other words, a certain parallel between the fate of the Tsotsi-character and the fate of the contemporary *Tsotsi*-text: in order to be welcomed into what we may call (though I do not love the phrase) the "world republic of letters," our quasi-mythic story must be rewritten in a significantly constrained way. It must surrender its modernist eccentricity, its irony, its dimension of protest and become more standardized, recognizable, upbeat. The outlaw, or the once-unpublished outlaw text, must become—well, more manageably different, just different enough for the consumer to feel satisfied that he or she, all of us, are virtuously on our way to a fuller humanity, even as the director intended:

> When you strip away what seems to be our differences...and get right down to the core of what it means to be human, we are surprisingly similar and hopefully, *Tsotsi* reveals that within its characters....You start off watching a movie about people that are very different from yourself, but by the end of the movie you feel that, but for a different roll of the dice, that could have been your own life.
>
> ("Interview" 47)

The irony here—that the metaphor of gambling, the selfsame figure that long ago struck Walter Benjamin as precisely the negation of continuous personal development and narrative potentiality (175–82), should here be put to such comfortable uses—is something that, in our era of casino capitalism, we may have to savor for quite some time.

University of Pennsylvania

WORKS CITED

Abrams, Philip. "Notes on the Difficulty of Studying the State." 1977. *Journal of Historical Sociology* 1.1 (1988): 58–89.

Althusser, Louis. "Ideology." *Lenin and Philosophy and Other Essays*. Trans. Bill Brewster. New York: Monthly Review P, 1971.

Anderson, Benedict. *Imagined Communities: Reflections on the Origin and Spread of Nationalism*. 2nd rev. ed. London: Verso, 1991.

Barnard, Rita. *Apartheid and Beyond: South African Writers and the Politics of Place*. New York: Oxford UP, 2007.

———. "Oprah's Paton, or, South Africa and the Globalization of Suffering." *English Studies in Africa* 47.1 (2004): 85–108.

———. "*The Smell of Apples, Moby-Dick,* and Apartheid Ideology." *Modern Fiction Studies* 46 (2000): 207–26.

Benjamin, Walter. "On Some Motifs in Baudelaire." *Illuminations*. New York: Schocken, 1986. 157–96.

Casanova, Pascale. *The World Republic of Letters*. Trans. M. B. DeBevoise. Cambridge, MA: Harvard UP, 2004.

"Cinematographer of Oscar-nominated Film about Carjacker Carjacked." 26 Feb. 2006. 28 Dec. 2007 <http://news.monstersandcritics.com/africa/news/printer_1132947.php>.

Coetzee, J. M. *Diary of a Bad Year*. London: Harvill Secker, 2007.

———. *Doubling the Point: Essays and Interviews*. Ed. David Attwell. Cambridge, MA: Harvard UP, 1996.

Comaroff, Jean. "Beyond Bare Life: AIDS, (Bio)Politics, and the Neoliberal Order." *Public Culture* 19.1 (2007): 197–219.

Comaroff, Jean, and John L. Comaroff. "Criminal Justice, Cultural Justice: The Limits of Liberalism and the Pragmatics of Difference in the New South Africa." *American Ethnologist* 31.2 (2004): 188–204.

———. "Criminal Obsessions, after Foucault: Postcoloniality, Policing, and the Metaphysics of Disorder." *Critical Inquiry* 30 (2004): 800–824.

———. "Figuring Crime: Quantifacts and the Production of the Un/Real." *Public Culture* 18.1 (2006): 209–46.

———. "Millennial Capitalism: First Thoughts on a Second Coming." *Public Culture* 12.2 (2000): 291–343.

———. "Naturing the Nation: Aliens, Apocalypse, and the Postcolonial State." *Journal of Southern African Studies* 27.3 (Sept. 2001): 627–51.

Comaroff, John L. "Reflections on the Colonial State, in South Africa and Elsewhere: Factions, Fragments, Facts and Fictions." *Social Identities* 4.3 (1998): 321–61.

De Bruyn, Pippa. "Soft Target." *South African Mail and Guardian* 3 Mar. 2006.

Esty, Jed. "The Colonial *Bildungsroman*: *The Story of an African Farm* and the Ghost of Goethe." *Victorian Studies* 49 (2007): 407–30.

———. "Virginia Woolf's Colony and the Adolescence of Modernist Fiction." *Modernism and Colonialism*. Ed. Richard Begam and Michael Valdez Moses. Durham, NC: Duke UP, 2007. 70–90.

Frye, Northrop. *Anatomy of Criticism: Four Essays*. Princeton, NJ: Princeton UP, 1971.

Fugard, Athol. *Boesman and Lena*. *Blood Knot and Other Plays*. New York: Theater Communications Group, 1991.

———. *Notebooks, 1960–1977*. New York: Knopf, 1984.

———. *Tsotsi*. New York: Grove, 2006.

Gray, Stephen. "Third World Meets First World: The Theme of `Jim Comes to Joburg' in South African English Fiction." *Kunapipi* 7.1 (1985): 61–80.

Hirsch, Marianne. "The Novel of Formation as Genre: Between Great Expectations and Lost Illusions." *Genre* 12.3 (1979): 293–311.

Hood, Gavin. "Interview." Conducted by David Archibald. *Cinéaste* 31.2 (Spring 2006): 44–47.

———, dir. *A Reasonable Man*. African Media Entertainment, 1999.

———, dir. *The Storekeeper*. Miramax, 2005.

———, dir. *Tsotsi*. Miramax, 2005.

Jameson, Fredric. "On Literary and Cultural Import-Substitution in the Third World: The Case of the Testimonio." *The Real Thing: Testimonial Discourse and Latin America*. Ed. Georg M. Gugelberger. Durham, NC: Duke UP, 1996. 172–91.

Kurosawa, Akira, dir. *The Seven Samurai*. Toho Company, 1954.

Lang, Fritz, dir. *Metropolis*. Universum, 1927.

Mamdani, Mahmood. *Citizen and Subject: Contemporary Africa and the Legacy of Late Colonialism*. Princeton, NJ: Princeton UP, 1996.

Marx, Karl, and Friedrich Engels. *The German Ideology. Part One*. London: Lawrence, 1970.

Marx, Lesley. "Redeeming the Gangster: *Boy Called Twist* (2004) and *Tsotsi* (2005)." Unpublished essay.

Mbembe, Achille. "The Banality of Power and the Aesthetics of Vulgarity in the Postcolony." Trans. Janet Roitman. *Public Culture* 4.2 (1992): 1–30.

Miller, Andie. "Journey of a Lost Story." *South African Mail and Guardian* 24 May 2006.

Miller, D. A. *The Novel and the Police*. Berkeley: U of California P, 1988.

Moretti, Franco. *The Way of the World: The Bildungsroman in European Culture*. Trans. Albert J. Sbragia. London: Verso, 1987.

Nuttall, Sarah. "City Forms and Writing the 'Now' in South Africa." *Journal of Southern African Studies* 30 (2004): 731–50.

Rushdie, Salman. "Notes on Writing and the Nation." *Harper's Magazine* Sept. 1997: 22–23.

Simone, Abdoumaliq. "Globalization and the Identity of African Urban Practices." *Blank* ____: *Apartheid, Architecture and Beyond*. Ed. Hilton Judin and Ivan Vladislavič. Cape Town: David Phillip, 1998. 173–87.

Slaughter, Joseph. "*Clef à Roman*: Some Uses of Human Rights and the Bildungsroman." *Politics and Culture* 28 Dec. 2007 <http://aspen.conncoll.edu/politicsandculture/pages.cfm?key+244>.

——. *Human Rights, Inc.: The World Novel, Narrative Form, and International Law*. New York: Fordham UP, 2007.

Thornton, Robert. "What Is 'Civil' about 'Civil Society' in Africa." *Pretexts: Literary and Cultural Studies* 8.1 (1999): 93–112.

White, Hayden. *The Content of Form: Narrative Discourse and Historical Representation*. Baltimore, MD: Johns Hopkins UP, 1990.

Writing Studio. "Proudly South African Filmmaking: Tsotsi." 22 Mar. 2008 <www.writingstudio.co.za/page914.html>.

MATTHEW HART

The Third English Civil War: David Peace's "Occult History" of Thatcherism

Published to wide acclaim in 2004, David Peace's *GB84* is "a fiction…based upon [the] fact" of the 1984–85 miners' strike, when Margaret Thatcher's government defeated a strike action by the National Union of Mineworkers (NUM), long recognized as the militant vanguard of the trades union movement.[1] My goal in this essay is to show how the political vision of *GB84* informs its generic and formal qualities. The first and longer section of what follows therefore deals with the novel's paranoid ambience and its status as a work of historical fiction, reading Peace's self-described "occult" style as an intensifying device

---

1. In 1972, an NUM strike caused power cuts across Britain, leading the government to establish a shortened working week (the infamous "three-day week") in a bid to preserve energy. The pressure thus caused allowed the union to negotiate improved pay and bonuses. A second NUM strike in 1974 led Conservative Prime Minister Edward Heath to call a snap election—which he lost—on the question "Who Governs Britain?" By beginning with a government conspiracy, Peace implies that the 1984–85 strike was not caused by NUM militancy but was rather the result of Thatcher's desire to redress the defeats of 1972 and 1974. This goal became possible in 1984 thanks to her government's landslide reelection the previous year—a victory often credited to Thatcher's leadership during the victorious 1982 war with Argentina. These implications are lent *prima facie* support by then–Shadow Secretary of Energy Nicholas Ridley's 1978 report on privatization and industrial relations in Britain's nationalized industries. The report anticipates union resistance to Conservative policies and advises Thatcher to counter the "political threat" of the unions by provoking a strategic battle in an industry of her own choosing (qtd. in Deller 21). It also advocates "[cutting] off the money supply to the strikers, and [making] the union support them" and training "a large, mobile squad of police" to combat the ability of union pickets to move quickly between targets, or between one region of the country and another (Deller 21). These strategies play a central role in Peace's narrative.

Contemporary Literature XLIX, 4   0010-7484; E-ISSN 1548-9949/08/0004-0573
© 2008 by the Board of Regents of the University of Wisconsin System

through which he foregrounds the existential nature of the struggle between the miners and the state. The final section considers more abstract political questions. It explores *GB84*'s representation of the cruel paradoxes of government in the Orwellian year of 1984—a critical moment in Britain's transition between welfare-corporatist and neoliberal versions of statehood, when Thatcherism's characteristic oscillation between liberal and authoritarian modes was especially visible. What *GB84* does, in its poetic but brutal way, is work at the contradiction in what Stuart Hall dubbed Thatcher's "authoritarian populism"—that is, the way that while Thatcherism represented itself as antistatist "for the purposes of populist mobilization," it nonetheless remained "highly state-centralist" in its orientation toward power ("Authoritarian Populism" 117). *GB84* deals with this history, I suggest, by showing us a world full of political combat but bereft of meaningful parliamentary activity. It therefore presents the miners' strike as a betrayal of the political agonism that, in the language that Chantal Mouffe has appropriated from Carl Schmitt, is the best guarantee that violent conflict does not overwhelm the pluralist values and institutions of democratic states like the United Kingdom.

GB84 begins with a short prelude, "The Argument," the title of which alludes to the introductory glosses to the twelve books of John Milton's *Paradise Lost*.[2] Like Milton, Peace writes in the wake of civil strife and mortal sin; unlike Milton, he doesn't give us a summary of Satan's fall from grace and a premonition of "man's first disobedience" (Milton, line 1). It's hardly needed. The world of *GB84* has long since fallen; we need no abstract to grasp its darkness. We enter it through the malnutritious space of a motorway service-station café, a place of transit and assignation in which a man and woman have come to share secrets. But although this seems like a modern and wholly material world, its difference from Milton's

---

2. Although the association between Milton's title and Peace's is mine, Peace has spoken about his interest in the structuring potential of *Paradise Lost* in a comment that quickly moved to the topic of his "Argument" (Peace, "Interview" 557). While this evidence remains circumstantial, I consider it significant.

"place of utter darkness" (l. 5) is as small as the fluorescent tubes that light the scene. And indeed, those lights are crucial. The first sentence of "The Argument" is one word long, cut off by an em-dash so that everything we are about to read, the passage that follows and all the routine and terror of Britain circa 1984, is concentrated in the incandescence of a single word:

> *Electricity—*
>> Harsh service station light. Friday 13 January, 1984—
>> She puts a cigarette to her lips, a lighter to her cigarette.
>> *A dog starv'd at his Master's Gate—*
>> He waits.
>> She inhales, her eyes closed. She exhales, her eyes open.
>> He picks at the solid red sauce on the plastic ketchup bottle.
>> "Early March," she says. "South Yorkshire."
>> He rolls the solid red sauce into a soft bloody ball.
>> She stubs out the cigarette. She puts an envelope on the table.
>> He squashes the ball between his fingers and thumb—
>> *Predicts the ruin of the State.*
>> She stands up.
>> He shuts his eyes until she's almost gone. The stink still here—
>> *Power.*

Power is the subject of *GB84*: the electrical power that in 1980s Britain was largely generated by burning domestic coal, and the political power that came from controlling coal extraction and therefore the production and distribution of energy. Such are the stakes of this brief encounter beside a highway, when an unnamed woman tells an equally anonymous spook when to expect the onset of Britain's last great industrial conflict.[3] As in the William Blake poem, "Auguries of Innocence," from which he quotes the dismembered couplet about the starving dog and the ruined state, Peace asks us to "see a World in a Grain of Sand." In the events of his novel, then, we should see not just the misfortunes of the unionized coal industry,

---

3. It becomes apparent that the woman is an MI5 agent, Diane Morris, while the man is a semi-freelance operative, Neil Fontaine. MI5 ("Military Intelligence, Section 5"; also known as the Security Service) is charged with counterespionage, counterterrorism, and counterinsurgency activities. Diane is possibly modeled on Stella Rimington, the first female director general of MI5 and in 1984–85 the head of F-2, the counterinsurgency branch.

but a bigger lesson about the victory of conservative neoliberalism over welfare-state capitalism—and about a commensurate breakdown in the nature of politics itself. Just as the strike is a metonym for wider socioeconomic patterns, so does this compressed and paratactic opening scene depict in microcosm the themes and motifs of the fifty-three chapters to come, one for each week of the strike. Thus do we have the bad omen that is Friday the 13th, the endless cigarettes and interminable waiting, the blank envelopes and unmarked bills, the centrality of Yorkshire to the national drama, the vague intimations of sexual grief, and the stink of secret plans that begin in artificial brightness and lead only to the "dark heart" of England (63).

In a recent interview, Peace described *GB84* as a "natural continuation" of his earlier *Red Riding Quartet*, a fictional tetralogy that offers a disturbing, historically rich, and formally disjunctive take on the hard-boiled genre of crime fiction ("Interview" 568). Readers of Peace's writing since *Nineteen Seventy Four* (1999) will surely recognize similarities of style and content between his early and later work. They share, in the first place, their date-heavy titles, which wink at the historical novel's promise to transport readers across time, bringing a rooted past to life in the flux of the present.[4] Often described as "Yorkshire Noir," the *Red Riding Quartet* is based on extensive research about the cultural and social history of northern England in the 1970s and 1980s.[5] With interlocking plots based on events like the "Yorkshire Ripper" attacks, it paints a bleak portrait of a time when cops and crooks, journalists and lawyers, alternately exploited and exposed a violence that seemed to inhere in the very pores of the region—a onetime "citadel of self-help" lately mired in cultural and economic depression (Samuel 163). As a Yorkshireman educated in Manchester, Peace has a native's perspective on the English North—a viewpoint that leads him to describe the miners' strike as "an attempt to destroy the place where I am from and the people who I lived among" ("David Peace on GB84").

---

4. *GB84* is in this sense an obvious successor to the series that ended with *Nineteen Eighty Three*. The title also alludes to David Irving's right-wing paramilitary organization, "Great Britain 1975" (McNamee).

5. "Yorkshire Noir" was coined by Andrew Vine in his 1999 review of *Nineteen Seventy Four*. It has become *de rigueur* in press descriptions of Peace's fiction.

GB84 and the *Red Riding Quartet* therefore share their orientation to the North and development of forms of documentary realism. And yet this description, though accurate in general terms, doesn't begin to describe the often-shocking experience of entering Peace's fictional world. In the first place, his novels are far from straight-forwardly realist. Though irreducible to any one literary mode, they owe much to the crime-fiction genre, in which narrative verisimilitude goes hand-in-hand with stock diction, sensational violence, and the intercession of detective *deus ex machinae*. In *Nineteen Eighty* (2001), for instance, the central plot momentum comes from a dissolute lawyer's attempt to free a young man who was unjustly convicted of a series of child murders. (The true killer, we learned in *Nineteen Seventy Four*, escaped prosecution due to his links to local elites but was nonetheless buried alive by that novel's antihero.) Meanwhile, in Peace's latest, *Tokyo Year Zero* (2007), an implicit allegory between Japan in 1946 and Iraq sixty years later is organized around a detective's investigation into the real-life Kodaira murders. If these plots suggest Peace's affinity with a writer like James Ellroy, that's no coincidence.[6] For even if *GB84* owes as much to the political thriller as to the crime novel, its overlapping narratives of life on the picket line and in the corridors of power are motivated by a sense of the strike as a *social* crime, a historical injustice made possible by secret acts of violence and betrayal.[7] This is in part what Peace means when he describes *GB84* as an attempt to write an "occult history" of the strike ("Interview" 566). In an interview with Mark Lawson, he explains that the adjective in "occult history" signifies the state of being hidden or occulted more than the realm of the supernatural. In this sense, then, "occult" refers to the unknown or obscured elements of British political history—to whispers and echoes like the news that MI5 surveillance of the NUM depended on monitoring techniques pioneered against the Irish Republican Army. But this is

---

6. The front jacket of the 2004 Faber and Faber paperback edition of *GB84* quotes Ian Rankin's judgment that "David Peace is the English James Ellroy."

7. See, for example, Peace's answer to a question about how it felt, writing *Tokyo Year Zero*, to "return" to crime writing: "Well, you see, I think *GB84* and *The Damned Utd* [2006] are crime novels, so I never really felt I had been 'away'" (Peace, "Q & A").

only part of what Peace means by that phrase. For that term has implications beyond the uncovering of things we do not know. With its connotations of haunting and ritual violence, "occult history" suggests that the political history of Britain—and the narrative form required to uncover that history—is subterranean in more than one sense, a matter of bodies that will not stay buried as well as stories that have not been told.

Beyond broad questions of genre lie narrower matters of style. Unusually for an author associated with the no-nonsense syntax of the hard-boiled genre, Peace's writing sometimes reads like prose poetry or modernist montage. That's not to say that he goes in for Jamesian prolixity or Joycean excess. On the rare occasions when the sentences of *GB84* lengthen beyond simple subject-object constructions, they tend to be quoted materials or reported speech, as when a Nottinghamshire miner called Fred Wallace reads out the principles of the antistrike National Working Miners' Committee: "Our legal constitution states that our aims are: a) to ensure that the NUM and its constituent areas are controlled by and for the membership and to protect the democratic processes of the Union; and b) to ensure the legal rights of all members of the Union and their relatives and dependants, and to protect them from or compensate them for any loss arising from the abuse of such rights" (245). Such sentences sound both empty and corrupt. This effect is clearly intended—after all, Wallace is spouting legal boilerplate, having been wheeled out for media consumption by Stephen Sweet, an entrepreneur and antiunion activist modeled on Thatcher confidant David Hart. Yet such speech is dubious as much for its syntax as for the way Wallace's demotic origins obscure his manipulation by more powerful forces. By contrast, the formal bedrock of *GB84* is made of staccato phrases of relentless activity, so that the very grammar of judicial discourse sounds dishonest next to the dark exigencies that narrating the strike demands.

In *GB84*, then, language is not contemplative or circular; it is either declarative and instrumental or broken down into fragments, with the stylistic atmosphere of the whole taking shape between these antinomies. Peace's use of short sentences that echo and undercut one another creates a tense and frightening atmosphere, even when the "action" being described is dully bureaucratic. The following passage takes place in an NUM meeting. The events are seen from the perspective of Terry Winters, a character based on the union chief executive, Roger Windsor:

> The President had done it once. The President would do it again—
> This time he would do it alone. This time he had no choice.
> The ISTC at Rotherham had refused to black the Orgreave coke.
> The President ranted. The President raved—
> The President couldn't tell the difference between union and management—
> Management and government—
> Government and police—
> Police and—
>
> (113)

Although he goes unnamed, "the President" is Arthur Scargill, and the thing he "will do...again" is repeat the NUM's victories of 1972 and 1974. Historians of the strike differ about the extent to which Scargill ought to be seen as the cause of the strike's origins and ultimate failure.[8] In Peace's hands, the NUM president is a paranoid Svengali whose rantings are the symptom of a political monomania, an appetite for victory that is as "insatiable" as that which drives Margaret Thatcher (115). For all that, however, the President is barely in control of events, constantly undone by the formal and informal machinations of government, by the regional and factional interests of the NUM, and by the sheer pace of events. Yet if the President is an ultimately futile character, his scenes never bog down into an equivalent narrative stasis: even his rages produce "occult" knowledge. In the passage above, for instance, his ravings end with "Police and—" but the reading eye, accustomed to zipping past the ends of Peace's fragmentary sentences, continues unabated onto the next line: "Terry looked up from his calculator. Paul Hargreaves was staring at him again" (113). This visual parataxis between reported speech and third-person narrative therefore implies what the President doesn't

---

8. Compare, for instance, Samuel et al. with Adeney and Lloyd. Whereas the latter identify Scargill's leadership as a major cause for the strike and its failure, Raphael Samuel insists that "leaders—especially charismatic leaders...—are not so much causes as effects" (17), adding that Scargill's control over NUM policy was secondary to "local initiative" (20–21).

know and the reader can so far only suspect: that Terry is leaking information to MI5: "The President couldn't tell the difference between…Police and— / Terry."[9]

Yet for all its disjunctive prophecies, *GB84* can't be described as antirealistic. As historical fictions, Peace's novels operate on multiple social and diegetic levels. *Nineteen Eighty Three* (2002), for example, features a range of characters and points of view that stretches from the highest ranks of the constabulary to an abject rent boy. Likewise, the main chapters of *GB84* are made up of four relatively autonomous third-person narratives. Two largely italicized sections tell the stories of David Johnson ("The Mechanic"), a security-service freelance in bad odor with his bosses, and Malcolm Morris, an MI5 eavesdropper trained in Northern Ireland and now active in "domestic" counterinsurgency operations. The two largely roman print voices, meanwhile, concern Terry Winters's job at the top of the NUM and the actions of Neil Fontaine, another veteran of the military-security complex now assisting Stephen Sweet, whom he honors with the racist epithet "The Jew." Against these narratives, which depict the high- and mid-level machinations behind the strike's failure, we have two first-person narratives, arranged in chronological series and organized in two tightly printed columns that take up the left-hand page before the start of each numbered chapter. Fictionalized out of Peace's interviews with miners and research in the published oral histories of the strike, these stories— told first by a striking miner, Martin, then by an NUM shop steward, Peter, and then by Martin again—provide the subaltern experience missing from the political drama of the main chapters.

Peace is clearly determined to handle a wide array of characters and subplots, adding weight to his claim that *GB84* is an attempt to write "the whole 'occult history' of the Miners' Strike—from top to bottom, from left to right" ("Interview" 566). He is not driven, however, by a Lukácsian sense of social and aesthetic totality, where the job of a historical novelist is to depict the material structures and

---

9. Seumas Milne reports on the allegations (the subject of a House of Commons Early Day Motion in 1991) that Roger Windsor was an MI5 plant within the NUM (139–75). Peace's Terry Winters is no James Bond; he is rather a mix of fantasist, incompetent office politician, and willing victim of a security service "honey trap."

interests that connect the atomized experiences of striking miners and their political masters. Though Peace has what might be called an "Old Labor" sense of the strike's roots in the class structure of the British state, his desire to grasp the strike in whole cloth is as much a question of genre (of the way the crime novel works to unravel mystery and assign blame) as it is of a belief in historically redemptive forms of narrative totalization. What's more, his fidelity to the sociocultural "fact" that he finds in contemporary pop culture, oral testimony, and print sources is more than matched by the uncanny elements that lend *GB84* a uniquely haunted character. This is a book, after all, that begins with an intertextual allusion to Satan's fall and ends with suicide and defeat. It is here that we come to the secondary implications of the phrase "occult history."

This tension between realism and the unreal is apparent throughout *GB84*, even when, as in the "Martin" and "Peter" sections, its documentary character is most apparent. These passages, which build upon the precedent of *Nineteen Eighty*'s baroque accounts of the Yorkshire Ripper attacks, are laudable for their attention to the everyday lives of miners and their families. Here, for instance, is the scene in Cath and Martin's bedroom on the day news breaks about the closure of Cortonwood colliery:

> Wake up, says Cath again. Wake up, Martin. I turn over. I look at her. They're closing Cortonwood, she says. You'll be out now. I sit up. I reach for my cigarettes. She moves packet out of my reach. I say, Pass them here. She throws them on bed. Expensive habit that, she says.
>
> (2)

So far, so naturalistic. Notice the clear but unobtrusive use of dialect syntax; the intimations of old arguments, which the strike will only exacerbate: how Cath is already anticipating the economies that signal no more holidays, meaner meals, and bank foreclosure. Martin and Cath's marriage is the earliest victim of the strike—not the first to fall but the first we meet, foreshadowed in these five actions, six utterances, and one look.

One could cite many such examples, each testament to Peace's deft handling of vernacular detail. And yet what I've obscured till now is that Cath's "Wake up" doesn't really begin Martin's narrative, which in fact opens with four very different sentences, italicized so as to suggest some alternate consciousness: *"The dead brood under Britain. We whisper. We echo. The emanation of Giant Albion*—Wake up, says Cath again. Wake up, Martin" (2). The narrative alludes, here, to William Blake's myth of the giant Albion, son of Poseidon and founder of Britain before its takeover by the human descendants of the Trojan Brutus. It is not just Martin who wakes, the longer quotation suggests, but the buried dead of England's earliest conflicts. And these occult allusions do not only appear as nightmarish visions within the miners' oral testimony: as we read later on in the main narrative, "England was a séance, within and without" (166).

Both the first-person realism of the Martin and Peter sections and the third-person crime narrative of the main chapters are undercut by a presence that is "occult" in the sense that it is beyond the range of ordinary knowledge. Peace isn't trying to construct some mythopoeic structure that explains or transcends the events of 1984–85. He rather frames his realism with an obscure under-mythology that, obeying no particular theology or precedent, continually erupts through the crust of his historical fiction. The effects of this strategy are sometimes clear, as when the whispers and echoes that begin Martin's story recur at the end. Here, as the double columns that have structured the miners' stories give way to a single column centered on the novel's last page, Martin's account of the strikers' pageantlike return to work turns into a vision of a "Union of the dead" that rises from the pitted earth of South Yorkshire: "Their muted pipes—That whisper. That echo—Their funeral marches. Their funeral music…The country deaf to their laments" (462). In this moment, the historical fact of the miners' return to work becomes an allegory for the death of militant labor. The italics that have adorned Martin's and Peter's occult visions here give way to a consistent use of roman type, suggesting that there is now no meaningful difference between the actual march of exhausted but valiant strikers and the Benjaminian night of the living dead that is the "long march of labour halted" (462).

At other times, however, Albion's ghosts emerge in murkier ways. For instance, the language of whispers and echoes that links *GB84*'s first and last pages is reiterated on the day that Martin comes home after being beaten by the police on a picket, his skull fractured and his marriage in tatters. "Whisper" and "echo" are here translated into their Old English equivalents: "I close my eyes. Tight—*Under the ground, we brood. We hwisprian. We onscillan. Under the ground, we scream*" (110). The imagery of burial remains consistent between the three passages, but in the last example, myth and allegory break down into something more vague and suggestive. It is difficult to judge whether this arcane imagery is supposed to signify the torments that the miners face as a matter of their everyday labor or, rather, their revolutionary potential— the way, as one commentator puts it, that "a miners' strike, with all its symbolical associations, as a revolt from the lower depths, gen- erates anxieties out of all proportion to its economic and industrial effects" (Samuel et al. 1). Moreover, as the novel continues, a third possibility arises: that the miners' agitations, both physical and political, have released a new—Thatcherite—malevolence that now controls the country, destroys their livelihood, and breaks their bodies.

The "occult history" that is *GB84* doesn't ask us to believe in giants, for these images of a troglodytic Albion can be read as secu- lar allegories, correctives to the strain of utopian English radicalism that stretches from Blake through E. P. Thompson to its current manifestation in the Arcadian ramblings of the pop group Babyshambles.[10] *GB84* is a revisionist history, inspired by conspira- torial accounts of the British security state like Ken Loach's film about the "shoot-to-kill" policy in Ulster, *Hidden Agenda* (1990), and Seumas Milne's investigation of the "secret war" against the NUM, *The Enemy Within* (1994). As a fictional contribution to labor history, *GB84* is critical of union holy cows like the idea that the so-called Battle of Orgreave—the standoff at the Orgreave coking plant that culminated in a mounted police charge of union lines, a key event in *GB84* as in every history of the strike—was anything other than a distraction, significant only as a month-long demonstration of the police's superiority over the mobile groups of "flying pickets" that proved so effective in the 1970s.

---

10. Thompson is well-known as a writer on Blake and his importance to an English radical tradition. The lyrics of Babyshambles may be less well-known but are no less Arcadian, as in "Albion": "So come away, won't you come away / We could go to / Deptford, Catford, Watford, Digberth, Mansfield / Ahh anywhere in Albion // Yellowing classics / And canons at dawn / Coffee wallahs and pith helmets / And an English song."

In his radio interview with Mark Lawson, Peace concedes that for all his stress on the quotidian meaning of "occult," he is happy that the term has darker connotations, since the histories he writes are as "grotesque" as they are simply hidden. *GB84* is in this sense consciously ambivalent in character, since its demystifying qualities match its paranoid atmospherics, where both miners and state operatives are trapped in a web of violence and mystery that they can neither escape nor fully control. The character Neil Fontaine epitomizes this quality. Neil is in one sense a creature of pure calculation. Factotum and nursemaid to a man he despises as "the Jew" but serves as an agent of state power, he is crucial to the material fact of the state's secret antiunion activities. Neil selects the Orgreave plant as a battleground that favors the riot-control tactics pioneered in the 1981 disturbances at Toxteth and Brixton, plans the transportation of Polish "scab coal" from the North Sea coast to power stations, and somehow finds time to manipulate and finally murder a second character, The Mechanic, in the wake of an unrelated (and terribly botched) "sneak and peek" operation against an elderly antinuclear campaigner.[11] And yet for all that Neil is the Machiavellian instrument of sovereign power, he can no more escape the strike's violence than Martin or Peter. Driven by passions both sexual and political, his narrative ends when he kills himself in his patron's suite at Claridge's Hotel. Cast in this moment as a ronin, or masterless samurai, Neil's dying thoughts dramatize the catastrophe that results when occult intimations become dark self-knowledge:

> He thinks and he thinks and he thinks and he thinks—
> *The Earth tilts. The Earth turns. The Earth hungry. The Earth hunts—*
> He thinks and he thinks and he thinks—
> *This is the way the world works. This is the way—*
> He thinks and he thinks—
> *There are the things I know. The things I don't—*
> Neil thinks. Neil knows—
> *For both, there is a price.*
>
> (461)

---

11. At the height of the Orgreave violence, Stephen Sweet shouts: "Thank you, Brixton.... Thank you, Toxteth" (138). The murder of the nuclear protester is based on the conspiracy theories surrounding the March 1984 murder of Campaign for Nuclear Disarmament activist Hilda Murrell.

An instrument of political realism driven to madness and empathy, Neil becomes an unwilling medium for the transmission of occult insights. This confusion of real and unreal is symbolized by the way that Peace's allusion to T. S. Eliot's "The Hollow Men" (1925) combines the language of *Realpolitik* with a sense of apocalyptic knowledge—Eliot's famous incantation, "This is the way the world ends," being rewritten as a futile justification of the deeds Neil has done in the interest of the state: "*This is the way the world works.*" And indeed, Neil has been here before. Driving to Orgreave months before, he is stopped by a vision of defeated rebels from another age: "*Roundheads lead their horses across the road. Bloody. They are beaten. In retreat*" (112). And he is not the only character to view 1984–85 through the eyes of past conflicts. On Day 68 of the strike, Martin awakes from a nightmare: "*We lie among corpses. Thousands of them. We are parched. Drowned in blood. Stained armour. Fallen crowns*" (82). This dream of bloody usurpation creates a submerged link between the actions of the picketing miners and the history of English revolution and counterrevolution that returns in Neil's vision and continues in Peter's narrative. Peter's account of the Orgreave fighting ends when he is struck over the head, prompting a memory in which Yorkshire becomes a map of internecine war:

> He'd felled me. This copper—*Listen to the voice.* Ground was hard—*The voice saying, Follow me.* Sun right warm—*Follow me.* Lovely on my face— My father used to take us as a lad to many of fields from Roses and Civil Wars: Wake-field. Ferry Bridge. Towton. Seacroft Moor. Adwalton Moor. Marston Moor—Picnics in them fields. Flask of tea in car....He was dead now, was my father. Ten years back. I was glad he was, too. Not to see me in this field. Here—Orgreave. South Yorkshire. England. Today— Monday 18 June 1984. Sun on my face. Blood in my hair. Puke down my shirt. Piss on my trousers—I was glad he was dead. I closed my eyes. *Forgotten voices. A lost language. A code. Echoes*—Like funeral music. Drumming was. They beat them shields like they beat us. Like we were air. Like we weren't here.
>
> (136)

The theme is finally solidified on the very next page, when Neil and Stephen Sweet watch the police charge from a vantage point high above the field:

"Have you ever, ever, seen anything like this before, Neil?"

Neil Fontaine shakes his head. He never, never, has seen anything like this before:

The Third English Civil War.

Neil Fontaine closes his eyes. He never, never, wants to see anything like this again.

(137–38)

By presenting the Miners' Strike as "The Third English Civil War," staging it in a landscape haunted by the ghosts of old battlefields, Peace signals the historical depth of the conflict between Yorkshire miners and the Westminster government.[12] More than this, however, he foregrounds its extraordinary virulence. As one miner puts it, comparing the costs of policing the strike to the wages he would earn back at work: "Fucking hell, [Thatcher] must really hate us. Really fucking hate us" (158). There is a fundamental gap in *GB84* between the way the miners see their work and the way they are viewed by their opponents. Describing the press reaction to strikers' complaints of police brutality, Peter laments how the "whole of state jumped to [their] defence," contrasting this with the way that a miner, "who had served this country, man and boy for thirty year" can't even picket without risking arrest or worse (150). Peter's defense of mining as a form of national service has some basis in reality, since legislation like the National Service Act of 1948 used to exempt miners from military conscription due to their importance to the state. But as we see it from the other side of the divide, in the speeches and slogans dreamed up by Sweet and his allies, the miners are not public servants but socialist fifth columnists, an "enemy within" that must be ground into the dust in the name of national security (170).

Peace's allusions to English civil wars remind us that the implacable loathing between the government and the NUM has its roots in

---

12. "Third English Civil War" alludes to Jeremy Deller's 2001 performance piece, *The English Civil War Part II*, in which the Turner Prize–winning artist staged a dramatic reenactment of the Battle of Orgreave. Peace cites Deller's book about his reenactment as a source for *GB84* (465) but adds a northern twist by suggesting that the conflicts of the 1640s shouldn't take numerical priority. As Peter implies, the *first* civil war was the War of the Roses, when the houses of York and Lancaster fought for the crown.

the historical struggle between South and North, metropolis and province, capital and labor. But these historical oppositions are a commonplace of strike narratives and could anyway be accomplished without breaking with realist verisimilitude. The occult language of civil war works, then, as a kind of *intensifying* device that foregrounds the exceptional nature of the 1984–85 strike. This bitterness is something that Milne points out, referring to a speech that also features in *GB84*:

> The virulence of the denunciations of Scargill and the miners...went far beyond the established boundaries of modern-day mainstream British politics. It reached a peak in the summer of 1984, when the Prime Minister compared the struggle with the miners to the war against the Argentine junta over the Falklands/Malvinas islands two years earlier. "We had to fight an enemy without in the Falklands," she declared at a gathering of Conservative backbench MPs. Now the war had to be taken to "the enemy within, which is much more difficult to fight and more dangerous to liberty."
>
> (19)

As Ian Aitken reported at the time, by comparing the NUM to "terrorist gangs" and "terrorist states," Thatcher describes an industrial dispute as if it were a war over "the very principle of parliamentary democracy and the rule of law itself." Peace's occult style is his primary means of bringing in the existentially high stakes of that martial element. Still more importantly, the apocalyptic intensities of his haunted history suggest how the strike metastasized from a political agonism based in a disagreement about industrial policy into a realm of hatred—an *antagonism* so fundamental that the parties to it are incapable of settling their differences through rational means (Mouffe 20). The liberal ideal of a political community that regulates itself through competitive self-interest or free discussion has here devolved into anomie and self-slaughter. This is not to say that *GB84* is nostalgic for pre-Thatcherite political life. Peace holds no illusions about the sixties and seventies, when what Hall describes as the collectivist and interventionist trend of Keynesian political economics "edged towards an alternative form of decision-making to that of Parliament [alone]—the process of *corporatist* bargaining between state, capital (the CBI) and labour (the TUC)"

("State" 13).[13] Indeed, as Peace shows in *Nineteen Seventy Four* and *Nineteen Seventy Seven*, the corporatist period not only featured some of Britain's worst industrial conflicts; its compromise of class interests and political expediency also serves as a social metaphor for pettier collusions between criminals and lawgivers. But whereas Peace is happy to describe his earlier novels as a kind of "I Hate 1974" corrective to pop-cultural nostalgia for the era of flares and glam rock, that hatred is located nowhere so much as in the heart of the New Right ("Interview" 555). The conclusion of *Nineteen Eighty Three*, for example, cuts between a suicide, Thatcher's second election victory speech, and a repeated phrase, "The Hate" (404). It is in this sense that the occult intensities of *GB84* dramatize how a political struggle that was once conceived (if not actually experienced) as a war of position between competing stakeholders in a single community became indistinguishable from what Carl Schmitt would have called a fight to the death between political enemies.

———

In this final section, I want to invoke Schmitt so as to read *GB84* as a novel about political failure—and not only the failure of the left but also the failure of politics as such. I begin with a question that no one has so far asked about *GB84*: Why does a novel so drenched in the operations of power, set in a country with high regard for parliamentary ritual and maneuver, have so little to say about the institutions and personalities of representative democracy? In a fight between "the Prime Minister" and "the President," where is "the Welsh Windbag"?

That last soubriquet refers to Neil Kinnock, leader of the Labor Party from 1983 to 1992. For a dispute often understood as a battle between right and left, Peace's version of the miners' strike has almost

———

13. Hall's acronyms refer to the Confederation of British Industry and the Trades Union Congress, the major national umbrella groups for capital and labor. By "corporatism" he refers to experiments like the National Economic Development Council, where the government would broker economic policy with representatives of the TUC, CBI, nationalized industries, and the Bank of England. Founded by Harold Macmillan in 1962, the NEDC was marginalized by Margaret Thatcher—who described it as an "abomination"—and finally abolished by John Major in 1992 (Thatcher, *Downing Street* 7).

no time for the U.K.'s official parliamentary opposition. Kinnock has but a small role in the book, when the NUM president appears at the 1984 Labor Party Conference to denounce the government's "top-hatted Fascism" (265). This narrative follows a real incident in which Arthur Scargill spoke in support of a pro-strike motion that denounced "police violence" without also condemning the violent acts of some pickets.[14] The passing of the motion was seen at the time as a defeat for Kinnock, committed as he was to expunging the militant left from the Labor Party, and Peace appears to endorse this interpretation of events: "[T]he President loved to see their leader suffer. The Welsh Windbag. His face as red as his hair. The man who had described the President as the labour movement's equivalent of a First World War general. The President loved to see him suffer" (265).[15]

And that's it. Despite its constitutional links to the NUM, the party of organized labor henceforth disappears from the narrative. But lest one dismiss this as just another symptom of the left's eclipse, it is important to point out that the parliamentarians of the Conservative Party are just as irrelevant. The center of antistrike activity in *GB84* is Stephen Sweet, who decries the miners as an "extra-parliamentary opposition" but is himself a master of extra-parliamentary scheming (65). He works tirelessly, and sometimes against the declared policy of the government he supports, to entangle the NUM in a "Gulliver strategy" of multiple civil and criminal lawsuits, much as Jonathan Swift's hero was rendered helpless by the many slender ligatures that tied his giant frame to the earth.[16] Sweet convinces the government not to use the strikebreaking powers enshrined in the Employment Acts of 1980 and 1982, thereby making room for himself to frame the strike less as a clash between state and union than between English Davids and a Stalinist Goliath. In a phone call with an unidentified official, he berates the faint hearts in government: "No, no, no. . . . The nation perceives this dispute to be about the assault and intimidation of ordinary men who simply want to go to work. . . Assault and intimidation are a matter

---

14. For this angle on the news of the day, see "Labour Party Conference: Scargill Ovation in Acrimonious Debate" and "Laborites Assail Police."

15. For the perception that Scargill defeated Kinnock, see "Kinnock Loses Key Votes at Party Congress" and "Leading Article: Emotion Just Sweeps Them All Away."

16. For the historical roots of this plot detail, see Milne 266–67.

of criminal law not industrial legislation. The individual [legal] actions by members against their own Union underline this perception" (146). He curses a cabinet minister who dares to negotiate with the union (365) and stalks the corridors of the National Coal Board, on the lookout for "Suits out to settle" with those he has vowed to destroy (368). The relative silence of MPs and ministers derives, in part, from Peace's sense of how the government downplayed the political dimensions of the strike (whether by using unelected proxies like Sweet or by asserting that extraordinary events were really business as usual) while ratcheting up its ideological stakes.[17] It also has roots in the way labor leaders like Kinnock distanced themselves from the NUM, even as they tried to identify themselves with the economic hardship of the union's rank and file.[18]

And yet just as the strike's pedigree in historical enmities between capital and labor can't fully explain the occult element of *GB84*'s style, neither can we historicize away the curious political absence at the heart of the novel. What is missing from these historical accounts is the way this absence figures as a negative symbol of a deeper sociopolitical fracture, where the nation devolves into something like civil war. Halfway into the strike, Neil Fontaine wakes from another occult nightmare, shaken by an image of "[a] scar across the country" (175). A page later, in yet another echo between Neil's narrative and the experiences of the men he plots against, Peter is driving to a picket in Nottinghamshire when a hit song comes on the radio, "Two Tribes," by Frankie Goes to Hollywood: "Must have heard that bloody song ten times a day now for weeks. Ought to make it bloody National Anthem, said Sean" (176). Against this atmosphere of deep-rooted and mysteriously persistent conflict, the compromises of parliamentary negotiation are futile. As the song says: "When two tribes go to war, / One is all that you can score."

---

17. For instance, the attorney general of England and Wales, Sir Michael Havers, is quoted early on in *GB84*: "*If* [the strike] *does involve a lot of extra police work, then so be it. It is not involving the government in the dispute*" (19). Against this, Tony Bunyan concludes that "there is little doubt that overall policing policies and strategies were determined by [the 'MISC 101' Civil Contingencies Unit committee] under the Prime Minister" (300). Havers was a member of this committee.

18. See, for example, "Leading Article: If Tuesday Were the Only Day" and "Laborite Chief Assails Mine Strike Violence."

For Schmitt, the German jurist whose compromise with Nazism long made him *verboten* in Western intellectual circles, the division of the world into "two tribes" is far from anomalous; it is, rather, constitutive of politics as such. His 1932 book, *The Concept of the Political*, begins by disentangling the abstract notion of "the political" from the idea or institutions of a state like Great Britain. As a form of government, Schmitt says, the state already presupposes the political (19). It is therefore necessary, he claims, to define the political in such a way that it retains its autonomy from modes of government or elements of social life, turning instead to the "concrete and existential" antithesis between friends and enemies as the "distinction to which political actions and motives can be reduced" (27, 26). This distinction, Schmitt says, is not a matter of judgment or favor. The enemy need not be thought ugly, or heretical, or culturally other. Nor is the friend/enemy antithesis reducible to economic ideas of competition or ethical notions of adversarial debate. Rather, "the enemy exists only when... one fighting collectivity of people confronts a similar collectivity. The enemy is solely the public enemy, because everything that has a relationship to such a collectivity of men, particularly to a whole nation, becomes public by virtue of such a relationship" (28). It was on the basis of this adversarial we/they relation that Schmitt denounced what he saw as the vapidity of liberal political theory, which in its conception of political power as existing in the several constituencies of state, church, and civil society possesses "no liberal politics, only a liberal critique of politics" (Schmitt, *Concept* 70).[19] In its dissolution of the corporatist compromise of the 1970s and its instinctive hostility toward the politics of consensus, Thatcherism has an affinity with Schmitt's theorization of political power as indivisible and antagonistic.[20]

Schmitt's friend/enemy distinction best describes the multipolar world of international relations. As he writes in dismissing the idea

---

19. Also quoted in Mouffe 12. Gopal Balakrishnan explains how for Schmitt the liberal pluralist account of political power "was one step away from a condition of civil war in which there would be no judge to determine 'mine and thine'" (124).

20. See, for example, Thatcher's description of 1970s corporatism as the "illusion . . . that state intervention would promote social harmony and solidarity" rather than "snarling envy and motiveless hostility" (*Downing Street* 8).

that there could be politics in a world state: "The political world is a pluriverse, not a universe" (53). But Schmitt's antithesis, which he developed at a time of intense internal conflict within Weimar Germany, can also pertain to events such as those narrated in *GB84*. Schmitt writes of how the state (the major political instrument of modernity, if not the horizon of politics as such) possesses the terrible power "to demand from its own members the readiness to die and...kill" (46). Indeed, it is this life and death dimension that gives the political its truly existential character.[21] And whereas this power can be directed outside, at a foreign nation, it can also be directed within the state, against a domestic enemy (*hostis*) that—like the miners Margaret Thatcher described as the "enemy within"— must be fought "outside the constitution and the law" in an exceptional situation (*Ausnahmezustand*) that, in its very betrayal of ethical or juridical norms, paradoxically defines the nature of political sovereignty (47). Like a god who reveals his dominion over the natural world by suspending its laws in the performance of miracles, Schmitt's sovereign is "he who decides upon the exception" to the constitutional order (*Political Theology* 5). Defined in this way, politics is not a normative arena of rights or duties; still less is it a competition between rational actors for an agreed-upon prize. It is an antagonistic struggle predicated on the "ever-present possibility of conflict" and the "real possibility of physical killing" (Schmitt, *Concept* 32–33).

This frightening prospect returns us to the "Third English Civil War." Speaking to the Conservative Party conference in October 1984, the morning after the Provisional IRA bombed the hotel in which she was staying, Margaret Thatcher described the miners' strike as the work of an "organized revolutionary minority...whose real aim is the breakdown of law and order and the destruction of democratic parliamentary government." This speech, quoted at length in *GB84*, is explicit in identifying the NUM as an enemy in

---

21. Balakrishnan quotes two lines of verse written by Schmitt that suggest how the friend/enemy distinction is existential in two senses. In the first place, it entails a struggle for existence (the sense that I depend on in this essay). Second, it implies how political conflict makes human existence truly consequential: "Woe to him who has no friend, for his enemy will sit in judgment upon him. / Woe to him who has no enemy, for I myself shall be his enemy on Judgement Day" (Balakrishnan 132).

Schmitt's sense, opposed to "the law of the land [and] the heritage of the people" (Thatcher, "Speech"). And although Thatcher makes no mention of the extralegal methods deployed by the state in response to this threat, Peace leaves no doubt about the consequences of her language, with Stephen Sweet's tears of joy at hearing her speech swiftly compared to water "[s]treaming down mountains" and "running in rivers" and these images giving way to yet another occult vision: *"Rivers of blood. Mountains of skulls"* (281).

I do not mean to imply that Thatcherism—which many commentators claim hardly merits the status of an "ism"—is wholly or even consciously modeled after Schmitt's concept of the political.[22] Nor am I suggesting that Peace has read Schmitt or would agree with him that the antithesis between friends and enemies is an "inherent reality" of all political life (*Concept* 28). My claim is that the way the strike was fought rendered it existential in the Schmittian sense— and that the occult tendencies of *GB84* are Peace's way of registering the violent chasm between a conception of politics as civic struggle and a commitment to politics as civil war. The tension between Thatcherism's dual orientations toward liberalism and authoritarianism—"free market, strong state," as Hall puts it— reaches a critical point in the occult history of the miners' strike, where the defense of English freedoms requires the beating and bugging of British citizens, and the defeat of the state's enemies involves the marginalization of its representative institutions. What results from this is an *antagonism* that Chantal Mouffe, trying to think "with Schmitt against Schmitt," would describe as the betrayal of pluralistic *agonism*, where victory over one's political enemies is indistinguishable from the defeat of democracy as such (14).[23] In a recent critique of "third way" political theory, Mouffe invokes Schmitt in order to retain his sense of the political as an adversarial field in which oppositions like the one between capital

---

22. See, for example, Eric Evans: "[Thatcherism] offers no new insights and, although profoundly ideological on one level, it is better seen as a series of non-negotiable precepts than as a consistent body of thought" (2).

23. Mouffe depends upon the semantic distinction between *agonism* as a bounded competition or prize for a contest and *antagonism* as a potentially boundless logic of mutual resistance or active opposition.

and labor remain meaningful. Like Peace, however, she balks at the notion that an existential antagonism—a battle in which "the two sides are enemies who do not share any common ground"—can avoid the sort of scapegoating and abuses of power that render a state like Britain a democracy in name alone (20). And it is this situation, more than the failure of the strike to save jobs, which *GB84* comes to mourn. For whereas Hall can end his 1985 essay on authoritarian populism with the hope that we might eventually understand Thatcherism, "the better to defeat and destroy it" (124), Peace writes twenty years later, amid the worldwide rout of any meaningful counterforce to the neoliberal economic principles that underpinned Thatcherism's violent assault on the unionized left.

It is this historical loss that finally explains the occult antagonisms of *GB84*. I have already mentioned how the novel ends with a ghostly vision of "the long march of labour halted." Standing above the "matchstick men" of labor's death march is an unnamed female figure—surely Thatcher herself—who calls out, in a terrible composite of Cath's morning greeting, George Orwell's patriotic essays, and Pol Pot–style end-of-history rhetoric: "Awake! Awake! This is England, Your England—and the Year is Zero" (462). *GB84* is in this sense a story of victory and defeat—Thatcher's victory, the miners' defeat— but it is also a novel about a shared failure to resist a Schmittian definition of the political, when an economic grievance over the future of Britain's traditional industries could no longer be worked out within a political structure or process that might safeguard the coexistence of market rationalities and unionized labor. To borrow from Michel Foucault, power is everywhere in *GB84*, but because it is everywhere, it is nowhere—nowhere, that is, but in an occulted and unequal zone where the state took aim and destroyed an "enemy within."[24] More than a narrative about the end of militant labor, *GB84* is a savage polemic about political violence—about the costs of a conflict that, defined on both sides as a battle for a way of life, is waged in the occult zone of the under-state, where Albion lives and the jackboot thrives and every night is a night of long knives.

University of Illinois, Urbana-Champaign

---

24. Cf. Foucault: "Power is everywhere, not because it embraces everything, but because it comes from everywhere" (93).

WORKS CITED

Adeney, Martin, and John Lloyd. *The Miners' Strike 1984–85: Loss without Limit.* London: Routledge, 1986.

Aitken, Ian. "Thatcher Raises Terrorist Spectre to Attack Miners / British Premier Equates Trade Unionists with IRA and Libyan Terrorism." *Guardian* 27 Nov. 1984. *Lexis-Nexis Academic.* 4 Mar. 2008 <http://www.lexisnexis.com/>.

Babyshambles. "Albion." By Peter Doherty. *Down in Albion.* Rough Trade, 2005.

Balakrishnan, Gopal. *The Enemy: An Intellectual Portrait of Carl Schmitt.* London: Verso, 2000.

Blake, William. *Blake's Poetry and Designs.* Ed. Mary Lynn Johnson and John E. Grant. New York: Norton, 1979.

Bunyan, Tony. "From Saltley to Orgreave via Brixton." *The State v. The People: Lessons from the Coal Dispute.* Ed. Phil Scraton and Phil Thomas. Spec. issue of *Journal of Law and Society* 12 (1985): 293–303.

Deller, Jeremy. *The English Civil War, Part II: Personal Accounts of the 1984–85 Miners' Strike.* London: Artangel, 2001.

Eliot, T. S. *Collected Poems, 1909–1962.* London: Faber, 1963.

Evans, Eric. *Thatcher and Thatcherism.* New York: Routledge, 1997.

Foucault, Michel. *History of Sexuality.* Trans. Robert Hurley. Vol. 1. New York: Vintage, 1990.

Frankie Goes to Hollywood. "Two Tribes." By Peter Gill, Holly Johnson, and Mark O'Toole. *Welcome to the Pleasuredome.* ZTT Records, 1984.

Hall, Stuart. "Authoritarian Populism: A Reply to Jessop et al." *New Left Review* I/151 (1985): 115–24.

———. "The State in Question." *The Idea of the Modern State.* Ed. Gregor McLennan et al. Milton Keynes: Open UP, 1990. 1–28.

"Kinnock Loses Key Votes at Party Congress." *Financial Times* 2 Oct. 1984: 1. *Lexis-Nexis Academic.* 4 Mar. 2008 <http://www.lexisnexis.com/>.

"Laborites Assail Police." *Washington Post* 2 Oct. 1984: A12. *Lexis-Nexis Academic.* 4 Mar. 2008 <http://www.lexisnexis.com/>.

"Laborite Chief Assails Mine Strike Violence." *New York Times* 3 Oct. 1984: A7. *Lexis-Nexis Academic.* 4 Mar. 2008 <http://www.lexisnexis.com/>.

"Labour Party Conference: Scargill Ovation in Acrimonious Debate / Backing for the Coalminers' Strike." *Guardian* 2 Oct. 1984. *Lexis-Nexis Academic.* 4 Mar. 2008 <http://www.lexisnexis.com/>.

"Leading Article: Emotion Just Sweeps Them All Away." *Guardian* 2 Oct. 1984. *Lexis-Nexis Academic.* 4 Mar. 2008 <http://www.lexisnexis.com/>.

"Leading Article: If Tuesday Were the Only Day / Keynote Speech by Labour Leader Kinnock at Blackpool Conference." *Guardian* 3 Oct. 1984. *Lexis-Nexis Academic.* 4 Mar. 2008 <http://www.lexisnexis.com/>.

Loach, Ken, dir. *Hidden Agenda.* Chapel Films, 1990.

McNamee, Eoin. "Hand-held Narrative." *Guardian Unlimited Books* 30 Apr. 2004. <http://books.guardian.co.uk/news/articles/01206954,00.html>. 4 Oct. 2007.

Milne, Seumas. *The Enemy Within: MI5, Maxwell, and the Scargill Affair*. London: Verso, 1994.

Milton, John. *Paradise Lost*. Ed. Scott Elledge. New York: Norton, 1975.

Mouffe, Chantal. *On the Political*. London: Routledge, 2005.

Peace, David. *The Damned Utd*. London: Faber, 2006.

———. "David Peace on *GB84*." n.d. *Faber.co.uk*. <http://www.faber.co.uk/article_detail.html?aid=23503>. 19 Sept. 2007.

———. *GB84*. London: Faber, 2004.

———. "An Interview with David Peace." Conducted by Matthew Hart. *Immigrant Fictions: Contemporary Literature in an Age of Globalization*. Ed. Rebecca L. Walkowitz. Spec. issue of *Contemporary Literature* 47 (2006): 546–69.

———. Interview. Conducted by Mark Lawson. *Front Row*. BBC Radio 4. 3 Apr. 2004.

———. *Nineteen Eighty*. London: Serpent's Tail, 2001.

———. *Nineteen Eighty Three*. London: Serpent's Tail, 2002.

———. *Nineteen Seventy Four*. London: Serpent's Tail, 1999.

———. "Q & A with David Peace." *Yorkshire Post* 3 Aug. 2007. <http://www.yorkshirepost.co.uk/books/Gripping-vision-of-crime-and.3084853.jp>. 19 Sept. 2007.

———. *Tokyo Year Zero*. New York: Scribner's, 2007.

Samuel, Raphael. *Island Stories: Unravelling Britain. Theatres of Memory*. Vol. 2. Ed. Allison Light. London: Verso, 1998.

Samuel, Raphael, Barbara Bloomfield, and Guy Boanas, eds. *The Enemy Within: Pit Villages and the Miners' Strike of 1984–5*. London: Routledge, 1986.

Schmitt, Carl. *The Concept of the Political*. 1932. Trans. George Schwab. Chicago: U of Chicago P, 1996.

———. *Political Theology: Four Chapters on the Concept of Sovereignty*. Trans. George Schwab. Chicago: U of Chicago P, 2005.

Thatcher, Margaret. *The Downing Street Years*. London: HarperCollins, 1993.

———. "Speech to Conservative Party Conference (October 12, 1984)." *Margaret Thatcher Foundation*. <http://www.margaretthatcher.org/speeches/default.asp> 4 Mar. 2007.

Thompson, E. P. *Witness against the Beast: William Blake and the Moral Law*. New York: New P, 1993.

Vine, Andrew. "New Star Shines in a Winter's Tale." Rev. of *Nineteen Seventy Four*, by David Peace. *Yorkshire Post* 6 Oct. 1999: 14.

JOHN MARX
Failed-State Fiction

Fiction has a stake in the state's future, which it demonstrates by treating civil war as a setting for literary experimentation. Recent novelistic experiments largely complement political scientific research in defining the "failed state" as a more or less normative condition in much of the world. Writing in both disciplines subordinates the notion of the state as setting for national development to that of the state as context that shapes and is shaped by experts in their administration of populations. As a result, the ideal of citizenship cedes center stage, as scholarship and literary prose strive to present competent management as an aspiration every bit as compelling as the goal of national liberation it displaces. Fiction diverges from its interdisciplinary collaborator, however, on the matter of who qualifies as a manager. For example, novels including Chimamanda Ngozi Adichie's *Half of a Yellow Sun* (2006) identify a problem for political science, as well as for conventional wisdom, when they consider child soldiers and refugees as participants in state organization rather than mere symptoms of state failure.

If national literature presupposed a world composed of nations, literary elaboration of the state has a more than local scope as well. When a fiction such as *Half of a Yellow Sun* portrays life during wartime as both intensely violent and remarkably ordinary, it suggests that what goes on in the most unstable of states is never so extreme that it cannot be normed. Here as elsewhere, the most conventional novelistic content of household intrigue and personal growth thrives amid coups and mass killings that would otherwise define a "state of exception." In Adichie's account of the Nigerian crisis that culminated in the Biafran War, couples fall in and out of

Contemporary Literature XLIX, 4   0010-7484; E-ISSN 1548-9949/08/0004-0597

love, families mourn, and children grow up in communities displaced and devastated by conflict. People starve and die in the refugee camp where the novel's final chapters are set, but they also write poetry, have sex, and engage in intellectual debate about, for instance, "racism... as a basis of conquest" (Adichie 402).

Influential work in the social sciences shares the conviction that pragmatic questions of governmentality predominate precisely where one might anticipate crises of legitimacy and bare life. Where social science privileges quantitative data, however, literature counters with the quality of local color. Adichie's *Half of a Yellow Sun* supplements think-tank statistics with a narrative of the Biafran War written from the standpoint of its survivors. In so doing, the novel operates as if it might contribute meaningfully to the body of knowledge concerned with how states work. Social scientists who acknowledge literary efforts tend to think of fiction as giving crisis a human face. "[D]evelopment studies generally conceives of the Third World as a problematic of progress that can be arrayed well in statistical terms," notes scholar of international relations Christine Sylvester, whereas "Everyday lives feature in...novels" (66).[1] Literature reveals anomalies that do not register on statistical curves, "inconsistent objects," Sylvester calls them, "that beckon our attention" (70). With stories that "stick to the gut and the brain," postcolonial fiction makes it difficult for social scientists to turn away from "biopolitical horrors [that] stand side-by-side, incongruously, with clear markers of development" (75, 70). If fiction forces "the coolly distant development expert to the inside of a maelstrom" (75), political science entices fiction to perceive the state less as art's habitual antagonist—the sovereign power that censors and bans, imprisons and exiles—than as an object that art might help to reform. Political science imagines a collaborative model in which fiction brings anomalies to the attention of researchers, who then

---

1. Stephen Chan similarly characterizes fiction as "a medium that does not claim it is *knowledge*, as much as it claims to represent an *unknowable* interior of disproportion, dislocation and terror, that is simply *felt*" (372). Literary scholars often affirm such disciplinary distinction. Peter Hitchcock argues that the "wild imaginings" of Nuruddin Farah offer temporary escape from "brute materiality," reminding us that "the lives in play need more than statistical adjustments and infrastructure plans" (745).

tweak their statistical analyses and policy recommendations to account for this new data.

But fiction does not simply flesh out social-scientific practice. Instead, it shapes a counterdiscourse. While fiction does offer a humanizing counterpoint to the cold facts of statistical calculation, it also portrays life in the failed state as an education—the sort of education, in fact, that might make one more expert than the experts. Just so, Adichie delegates the authority to compose the definitive book on Biafra to a home-schooled refugee. *Half of a Yellow Sun* goes even further when it stipulates that serving time in the army helps prepare one to do the work of writing. The singular importance of this gesture lies in its effort to democratize expertise. The heroes of Adichie's novel are not political scientists making charts in the London School of Economics or pulling strings at the World Bank. They are the sorts of people whom empire builders treated as native informants. As much as fiction privileges expertise, therefore, it also reimagines the hierarchy of global administration. It imagines a redistribution of the authority to describe atrocities and to show how such events relate to the state's more normative aspect. In this effort, Adichie's novel is not without precedent, and considering its precedents allows us to see literary tradition anew. The issue of how the literary present revises its past must wait, however, until I have specified the meaning of the "failed state" in twenty-first century political and academic commentary.

Failure Is Normal

There are marked differences between the normative model of state failure and the competing legalistic definition of political crisis. The distinction is perhaps most readily apparent in discussions about intervention. Commentators who consider state failure in normative terms tend to speak less of humanitarian emergencies or legal exceptions. Instead they proceed as if state and civil society were alive if not well in war zones and refugee camps, and they encourage intervention that fortifies both the semblance and substance of political stability. "It is frequently assumed that the collapse of state structures, whether through defeat by an external power or as a result of internal chaos, leads to a vacuum of political power," write the editors of the volume *Making States Work* (Chesterman et al., "Introduction" 1). "This is rarely the case," they argue, for "[e]ven where non-state actors exist as parasites on local populations, political life goes on." "Even in a failed state," echo scholars at the London School of Economics Crisis States Research Centre, "some elements of the state, such as local state organisations, might continue to exist" (Crisis States Workshop). In addition to discovering order in disarray, normative study locates pockets of failure in otherwise stable states. Oft-cited instances include the U.S. Gulf Coast after Hurricane Katrina and the *banlieues* of Paris in 2005; one might also adduce Kashmir and, in the recent past, Northern Ireland.[2] The normative approach treats such differing examples not as exceptions but as data to be assimilated to a statistical model. To see how, we can consider what may well be the most evocative example of this style of thinking, the "Failed States Index" published annually by *Foreign Policy* magazine and the Fund for Peace.

Foreign Policy began disseminating the notion of state failure in 1992, when in its pages Gerald Helman and Steven Ratner argued, "a disturbing new phenomenon is emerging: the failed nation-state, utterly incapable of sustaining itself as a member of the international community" (3). By the late 1990s, the journal had ceased trumpeting the novelty of such crises and started presenting them as usual enough to deserve an annual update. The "Failed States Index" tabulates data on 177 countries culled from open-source articles and reports using a proprietary methodology called CAST (Conflict Assessment System Tool). That data yields country-specific case studies, a world map, and the Failed States scores. The score chart is color-coded: on the Fund for Peace Web site, a critically unstable red shades into a broad swath of borderline orange, stable yellow, and most stable green.[3] Red in 2008 featured Somalia, Zimbabwe, Burma, and Pakistan. Green in 2008 identified the most stable polities as Sweden, Finland, and Norway. In years past, much is the same: Scandinavia is consistently the most stable region in the world;

---

2. Katrina and the Paris riots brought down the rankings of the U.S. and France, respectively, in the 2006 Failed States Index (52).

3. The color-coding on the truncated rankings available via *Foreign Policy* are slightly different and represent only the sixty least stable countries ("Failed States" [2008] 67).

Sudan and Iraq are among the least stable states. Lest readers mistake such predictability as a statistical constant, the editors of *Foreign Policy* are careful to note significant changes year to year.[4] In the 2007 report, they observe that "the first multiparty elections in more than 40 years" allowed Congo to drop out of the top-five most-failed category ("Failed States" [2007] 59). In 2008, they identify "the implosion of the U.S. subprime market" as primary among the "year's shocks" while also remarking of Israel that ongoing "inability to fully integrate its Arab minority" and "the increased factionalization of its political leaders" resulted in the country's "first appearance in the top 60" of most unstable states ([2008] 66, 68).

The Failed States Index is a comparative environment all its own. Strange (if alliterative) bedfellows Liberia and Lebanon sit side by side in the imaginary space of the 2007 rankings. One imagines the two states crossing paths as Liberia moves toward the orange of greater stability while Lebanon hurtles into the most unstable red ("Failed States" [2007] 59). There is no singular recipe for failure or success. Liberia "continued to make gains" in 2008 "due to a renewed anticorruption effort and the resettlement of nearly 100,000 refugees," while "Bangladesh took this year's hardest fall" after a "devastating cyclone…left 1.5 million people homeless" and "the imposition of emergency rule…dragged on" ([2008] 68). As the analysts behind the index sum up, "Failing states are a diverse lot" ([2007] 56). With this assertion, they not only sidestep political-scientific jostling to stabilize the definition of state failure but also avoid becoming mired in the discipline's more general and fundamental disagreement about what a "state" is, about whether it is

---

4. We may situate the risk of mistaking consistency for constancy in what James Ferguson describes as a vogue for geopolitical comparison that abjures the teleology of development. The logic of modernization "transform[ed] a *spatialized* global hierarchy into a *temporalized* (putative) historical sequence," which meant countries finding themselves behind the times had the chance of catching up (178). "Once modernity ceases to be understood as a *telos*," however, "the question of rank is de-developmentalized, and the stark status differentiations of the global social system sit raw and naked, no longer softened by the promises of the 'not yet'" (186). In theory, a normative scheme that treats all states as comparably fragile never treats inter-state differentiation as permanent. In practice, the regular division between stable and unstable states runs the risk of making stability seem a privilege for the few.

best defined in Lockean, Weberian, or more broadly juridical terms.[5] Instead of legalistic definition, the Failed States Index encourages normative comparison among demonstrably different combinations of civil war and natural disaster, bureaucratic corruption and economic malaise.[6]

The philosophical shorthand of Michel Foucault versus Giorgio Agamben goes a long way in capturing the difference between efforts to norm state failure and the contrasting legalistic definition of crisis.[7] Foucault theorizes a state devoted to "normalization," the "government of men" guided by the collection of statistical information about the health and welfare of subject populations (*Abnormal* 49).[8] In contrast, Agamben's state is defined by its reliance on legal exception, "fictitious lacuna in the order for the

---

5. Sebastian von Einsiedel rehearses these definitional debates (14–15). He attributes the most-cited definition of state failure to William Zartman, "for whom collapse means 'that the basic functions of the state are no longer performed'" (15).

6. The researchers divide their "indicators" into various subcategories: the social category includes mounting demographic pressures, massive movement of refugees, a legacy of group grievance, and chronic and sustained human flight; the economic category includes uneven economic development along group lines and sharp and/or severe economic decline; the political category includes criminalization and/or delegitimization of the state, progressive deterioration of public services, suspension or arbitrary application of the rule of law, a security apparatus operating as a "state within a state," the rise of factionalized elites, and the intervention of other states or external political actors. The Fund for Peace researchers define as core institutions "a competent domestic police force and corrections system; an efficient and functioning civil service or professional bureaucracy; an independent judicial system that works under the rule of law; a professional and disciplined military accountable to a legitimate civilian government; a strong executive/ legislative leadership capable of national governance." And then there are STINGS, an acronym for "Surprises (e.g., currency collapse); Triggers (e.g., assassinations, coups d'état); Idiosyncrasies (e.g., non-contiguous territory, a deference to authority); National Temperaments (e.g., cultural or religious perspectives); Spoilers (e.g., disgruntled followers, excluded parties)." See the explanation of CAST methodology for a complete description of these terms (Fund for Peace, *Methodology*).

7. Distinguishing the work of these two thinkers is rapidly becoming a cottage industry. See, for instance, Bull, Fassin, and Medovoi.

8. François Ewald defines the key term thusly: "Normalization, then, is less a question of making products conform to a standard model than it is of reaching an understanding with regard to the choice of a model. The *Encyclopaedia Britannica* stipulates in its article on standardization that 'a standard is that which has been selected as a model to which objects or actions may be compared. In every case a standard provides a criterion for judgment.' Normalization is thus the production of norms, standards for measurement and comparison, and rules of judgment" (148).

purpose of safeguarding the existence of the norm and its applicability to the normal situation" (*State* 31). For Foucault, the "suspension of, or temporary departure from, laws and legality" is less an exception than one in a range of periodic eruptions: coups d'état, acts of sedition, or civil war, all appear "normal, natural phenomenon, immanent as it were to the life of the *res publica*…like tempests, they arise periodically when they are least expected, in the greatest calm, in periods of stability" (*Security* 267).[9] "[R]aison d'État," as Foucault discovers it in the likes of Francis Bacon and B. P. von Chemnitz, "must command, not by 'sticking to the laws,'" but by controlling "the laws themselves, which must adapt to the present state of the republic" (*Security* 261). Where Agamben imagines sovereignty that survives by creating exceptions to laws it professes to uphold, Foucault better describes the administration envisioned by the Failed States Index when he depicts a highly adaptable art of government that conceives of "no prior, external purpose," "no problem of origin, of foundation, or of legitimacy" (*Security* 259). "[N]othing in this definition refers to anything other than the state itself," Foucault allows; "we are always already in a world of government, *raison d'État*, and the state" (*Security* 257–59).

From the perspective of what Foucault calls "a government which nothing escapes," it is possible to imagine that every social condition might be catalogued, every population segment recognized and understood, every geopolitical location identified (*Birth* 296). The research program of contemporary political science expresses ambition on this scale. In his working paper outlining the current

---

9. This distinction, Mika Ojakangas observes, boils down to different ways of defining exceptions. Foucault understands exceptions as "extensions of the norm," as opportunities to bring new objects of study within a disciplinary purview (16). To this way of thinking, "*all* forms of life…are exceptions," Ojakangas explains; "exceptions are not…taken out (*ex-capere*), but taken in (*in-capere*)" (16). Where Agamben's law masks the hand of a sovereign judge who decides what counts as an exception, Foucault's norm operates in the open through disciplines that encourage the proliferation of manageable differences. "Such a power has to qualify, measure, appraise, and hierarchize," Foucault contends; "it does not have to draw the line that separates the enemies of the sovereign from his obedient subjects; it effects distributions from the norm" (*History* 144). "[T]he norm still refers to a standard measure that allows us to distinguish what is in conformity with the rule from what is not," Ewald elaborates, "but this distinction is no longer directly linked to the notion of rectitude" (140).

phase of study for the Crisis States Research Centre, James Putzel offers two "over-arching questions": "A) Why and how, under the conditions of late development, are some fragile states able to respond effectively to contestation while others collapse and/or experience large-scale violence? B) What are the factors that contribute to and impede state reconstruction in post-war periods?" (3). The answers would amount to nothing less than a total historical mapping of geopolitical variation.

In studies published by the Crisis States Research Centre and elsewhere, governance takes myriad forms, from the all-enveloping "societies of control" described by Gilles Deleuze (4), to the attenuated states described by Anna Simons and David Tucker in *Third World Quarterly*:

> If we consider Lebanon in the 1980s, Yugoslavia in the 1990s, Afghanistan both before the rise of the Taliban and immediately thereafter, and Somalia still....To anyone on the outside[,] life [in such places] may have appeared chaotic, but the fact that local residents in Beirut, Mogadishu, Sarajevo, and Kabul knew exactly where they could safely venture, whose militia would protect them, and who would gun them down points to latent order within the chaos.
>
> (391)[10]

In these examples, governance is patchy. It is in flux. Its agents are subject to change. It may prove fully intelligible only to insiders with experience and outsiders expert in their observation. If what Simons and Tucker notice qualifies as state administration, however perverse, then the problem facing scholars and policymakers is not only discerning how states fail but also learning how to differentiate among states in crisis. "All states consistently fail some portions of their population," Simons and Tucker argue, which means that understanding the variety of failure must entail an overhaul of the distinction between functioning and dysfunctional (400). This is not a merely academic distinction for Simons and Tucker, whose interest in "the kinds of failure that matter most" stems from concern about the relationship between instability and terrorism (400). Even

---

10. See also Pierre Englebert, who addresses "why Congo persists" even though it seems as if it "should have collapsed some time ago" (119).

if, they argue, all states fail to some extent, not every state fails in a manner that leads to what gets called terrorist violence. Thus U.S. Secretary of State Condoleezza Rice was wrong to maintain that "weak and failing states...serve as global pathways that facilitate... the movement of criminals and terrorists" (Simons and Tucker 387). Some do and some do not, and if commentators wish to discover which do, they must learn to differentiate among failure's permutations, including its appearance in states the U.S. has enlisted as allies in the "war on terror," like Pakistan or Israel.[11]

The old rules no longer apply: states must no longer be thought of as defined by their ability to monopolize violence within their borders. A far more partial enactment of the aspiration to control may indicate administration that is statelike. Or, perhaps, state lite. Not only war-torn cities but also refugee camps can be seen as evincing this kind of aspirational administration. Where Agamben describes "the refugee" as "nothing less than a limit concept" and "the camp" as "the pure space of exception," normative scholarship detects sundry familiar agents and activities of state formation.[12] Jacob Mundy argues in the *Journal of Modern African Studies* that even the stark Western Saharan camps in southwest Algeria represent an "experiment in pre-figurative national pedagogy and socio-political organisation. The camps' institutions derive from a nationalist project and mirror them in all their aspects" (284–85). For Jacob Stevens, that evolution of camp into proto-state creates new administrative challenges, as "camps become a parallel economy that draws money and skills away from the locality" that hosts them, generating a hybrid form with its own distinctive social dynamics (66).

---

11. On Pakistan as a failed state, see Zaidi (10–11). On Israel, see the 2008 "Failed States Index" (68) and the bracing polemical account by Retort (108–9, 26).

12. As many have noted, Agamben is following Hannah Arendt, who described "an ever-growing new people comprised of stateless persons, the most symptomatic group in contemporary politics" (277). "The refugee must be considered for what he is," Agamben argues, "nothing less than a limit concept that radically calls into question the fundamental categories of the nation-state, from the birth-nation to the man-citizen link, and that thereby makes it possible to clear the way for a long-overdue renewal of categories in the service of a politics in which bare life is no longer separated and excepted, either in the state order or in the figure of human rights" (Agamben, *Homo* 134). For an attempt to reckon with this appropriation of Arendt, see Butler and Spivak (36).

A more diverse sense of the state suggests a different notion of state power than that associated with the rule of law. Agamben considers "the Rwandan child...the most telling contemporary cipher of the bare life that humanitarian organizations, in perfect symmetry with state power, need."[13] But this is what state power needs only if state power is thought of as the capacity to say who lives and who dies.[14] For Foucault, such was the right of the medieval sovereign. But governmentality, he famously argues, replaces the "ancient right to *take* life or *let* live" with the "power to *foster* life," to regulate, manage, and discipline it (*History* 138).[15] This is a power that, unlike sovereign rule, presumes multiple agents and a good deal of competition.[16]

---

13. This passage reads in full: "It takes only a glance at the recent publicity campaigns to gather funds for refugees from Rwanda to realize that here human life is exclusively considered (and there are certainly good reasons for this) as sacred life—which is to say, as life that can be killed but not sacrificed—and that only as such is it made into the object of aid and protection. The 'imploring eyes' of the Rwandan child, whose photograph is shown to obtain money but who 'is now becoming more and more difficult to find alive,' may well be the most telling contemporary cipher of the bare life that humanitarian organizations, in perfect symmetry with state power, need" (Agamben, *Homo* 133).

14. How, Foucault queries, if we understand power as disciplinary, "can the power of death, the function of death, be exercised?" (*Society* 254). The answer, he argues, lies in racism, which enables murder to take on a Darwinian cast and for death to appear the very means of guaranteeing a healthy life: "the death of the other, the death of the bad race, of the inferior race (or the degenerate, or the abnormal) is something that will make life in general healthier: healthier and purer" (*Society* 255). Mahmood Mamdani describes the Rwandan genocide in just such terms when he emphasizes "the perversely popular aspect of the genocide," egged on by state institutions that encouraged "ordinary Bahutu" to see themselves as "native" and to kill a target identified as "alien" ("African States" 503). A BBC source alleges comparable complicity on the part of Kenya's government in the Rift Valley massacres following the 2008 election: "Three members of the gang met at State House...and after the elections and the violence the militias were called again and they were given a duty to defend the Kikuyu in Rift Valley and we know they were there in numbers" (*State*).

15. Leerom Medovoi observes, "Neither [Michael] Hardt and [Antonio] Negri nor Agamben seriously entertains Foucault's underlying proposition about liberal modernity: within the general economy of power, sovereignty (despite its continued visibility) has steadily retreated, giving way to less dramatic but far more effective disciplinary and regulatory regimes of power that can administer life from the individual level of the body all the way up to the statistical amalgam of the population" (56).

16. On this topic, see Slavoj Žižek, who argues that Agamben "precludes the very possibility of the emergence of political subjectivity" (341–42), and Judith Butler, who contends: "[I]f the language by which we describe destitution presumes, time and again, that

Mahmood Mamdani's commentary on Darfur makes the practical implications of foreclosing politics abundantly clear. He describes the UN and NGO view of "the people of Darfur" as employing terms that Agamben would have us see as defining contemporary governance, but that Mamdani sees as far more narrowly instrumental. They are "as wards in an international rescue operation with no end in sight" (Mamdani, "Blue-Hatting" 20).[17] By characterizing local populations as "minority victims of ongoing barbarities," Mamdani contends, aid organizations justify their presence ("Politics" 8). The need to reproduce a dynamic of victim and savior keeps the NGOs from recognizing, much less supporting, indications of social order in Darfur. Bringing together "political figures and representatives of civil society for an open discussion" is discouraged, Mamdani explains, for to do so "risks conveying a feeling that normality is returning to Darfur, when it is actually the depth of the crisis that should be emphasized" ("Blue-Hatting" 20).[18]

If Mamdani's NGOs strive to disempower those they help by talking like Agamben, Mamdani himself strives to recontextualize Darfur's violence as part of an "internal political process" ("Blue-Hatting" 20). What might look exceptional—the particularly brutal activities of the Janjawiid, for instance—reappears as a challenging but recognizable problem of state administration. "They are nomadic forces on horseback," Mamdani quotes General Henry Anyidoho of Ghana and the African Union as saying; the Janjawiid "are spread across Sahelian Africa: Niger, Sudan, Chad, the Central African Republic. The problem is that the AK–47 has replaced the bow and arrow. The Janjawiid should be disarmed before the rebels

---

the key terms are sovereignty and bare life, we deprive ourselves of the lexicon we need to understand the other networks of power to which it belongs, or how power is recast in that place or even saturated in that place. It seems to me that we've actually subscribed to a heuristic that only lets us make the same description time and again, which ends up taking on the perspective of sovereignty and reiterating its terms" (42).

17. Didier Fassin argues that this "process essentializes the victims: against the thickness of biographies and the complexity of history, it draws a figure to which humanitarian aid is directed" (512).

18. "The 'humanitarian' effort is itself based on the conviction that both the crisis and its solution are military, not political," Mamdani concludes, and so long as the world remains so convinced, there will be "little appetite for an internal political process designed to strengthen democratic citizenship" ("Blue-Hatting" 20).

turn in their arms" ("Blue-Hatting" 20). The point of normalizing violence in Darfur is not to affirm it, but to think of intervention as facilitating conciliation among parties designated as players in a political process. In this way, Mamdani envisions shifting the international mission from one of keeping people alive (which requires that they be always on the brink of extermination) to one of fostering the governance of intelligible political, cultural, or other sorts of social differences. This would require us to contemplate the possibility that the real news about life in Sudan is not its abject lawlessness but rather its continuity with dynamics facing states everywhere. Not every administration has Janjawiid to deal with, the normative approach allows us to acknowledge, but every population contains wild cards of some sort or another, potentially destructive agents that in challenging state stability also provide the occasion for state power to extend its reach.

This politics of conciliation conceives of population as not simply ordered by but also produced by the state. We will mistake Mamdani's proposal if we understand the dynamic of state and population in the traditional terms liberalism supplies, in which the state generates unity out of a civil society composed of seemingly preexisting groups and interests. Instead, government strives to reproduce, adapt, and revise social order comprising group dynamics it defines as relevant. Mamdani summarizes one familiar version of this process when he notes that administrations "in colonial and post-colonial Uganda, as in other parts of Africa colonized by Western powers in the twentieth century, defined every individual as belonging to a race or an ethnic group" ("African States" 494).[19] Ethnicity and culture are not the only divisions states produce, of course, nor does their production necessarily lead to violent

---

19. Mamdani elaborates: "From Sudan to Ethiopia, Uganda to Mozambique and Angola, and Ivory Coast to Liberia, most political violence in post-colonial Africa seems to be organised along ethnic lines. Why is that? Some have suggested that it has to do with the importance of ethnicity in African culture. I argue instead that it has to do with the politicisation of culture in the African colonies. When colonial reform replaced 'direct' with 'indirect' rule through compliant local authorities the effect was to make cultural difference the basis for administrative, legal and political organisation, thereby politicising ethnic difference and making ethnic identity the basis for political discrimination" ("Letters" 4).

conflict.[20] Instead, it is through such divisions, of whatever sort, that the state gives shape to politics, that "civil peace," as Foucault calls it, continues war by other means (*Society* 16). Foucault argues, "Civil society is…a concept of governmental technology" through which states designate both their limits—the domains they consider private as opposed to public—and "field of reference," the population and economy that the state promises to nurture and develop (*Birth* 295–96).

If we read Mamdani's argument in light of Foucault's, it is possible to say that the Janjawiid are not a given part of civil society, but that government technologies might extend civil society to include them. Precisely because it is codified in legislation and law, the state's public is as mutable as changing governmental policy and rule-making allows. Its groups and relations, hierarchies and castes are as modifiable as state administration can make them, and as particular as the rights and privileges, grievances and petitions the state is able to recognize. The successful state would know how to incorporate the Janjawiid and their ilk.[21] If it cannot do this, for whatever reason, then the state fails a little bit. State failure, in this way of thinking, is the inverse of state flexibility. The most stable state is the one most capable of adapting its demographic criteria, designating new and changing populations, and increasing the detail of its census.[22] From its philosophical inception in the

---

20. "Nor should policy makers or academics infer that ethnic diversity is the root cause of civil conflict," argue James Fearon and David Laitin. Rather they should attend to the ways that states in crisis produce and redefine group dynamics. "We find little evidence that civil war is predicted by large cultural divisions," they argue. "But it seems quite clear that intense grievances *are produced by* civil war" (88).

21. Thus this policy recommendation: "What I counsel in lieu of a military intervention is a political process with two objectives in mind: a reform of the state that will build on the peace settlements in the south and east by extending power-sharing to insurgent elites in the west; and a resource-building initiative (the conflict in Darfur is driven in part by a lack of resources that the international community is best equipped to address but has yet to show serious interest in). The example to emulate is not NATO's intervention in the former Yugoslavia, but the political settlement in the south of Sudan, which the Bush administration can count as its solitary foreign policy success" (Mamdani, "Letters" 4).

22. "[F]or those who govern," Foucault contends, "it is not only a matter of taking into account and taking charge of the activity of groups and orders…. [T]here is no limit to the objectives of government when it is a question of managing a public power that has to regulate the behavior of subjects" (*Birth* 7).

eighteenth century, the state manifests increasing flexibility in conceiving the divisions that run through its public, and it does so in the name of extending dominion. Nothing could be farther from the Hegelian ideal of statecraft, in which a civil society learns to set aside its differences and found a democracy.[23]

Accordingly, it should come as no surprise that parenting, rather than debate, provides the framework for prevailing discussions of how to reform statecraft. In their 1992 outline "Saving Failed States," Gerald Helman and Steven Ratner maintain, "The conceptual basis for the effort should lie in the idea of conservatorship" (12). Domestic discipline provides the model for international order: "In domestic systems when the polity confronts persons who are utterly incapable of functioning on their own," Helman and Ratner explain, "the law often provides some regime whereby the community itself manages the affairs of the victim. Forms of guardianship or trusteeship are a common response to broken families....It is time that the United Nations consider such a response to the plight of failed states" (12). As it turns out, the editors of the "Failed States Index" find that a "common thread links" the "most improved players" on the 2008 chart: "All three host U.N. peacekeeping operations" ([2008] 68). "[T]here are many problems with the trusteeship model," cautions Oxford international relations professor Richard Caplan, and "these include its neocolonial overtones" (242).[24] Simon Chesterman, the executive director of the Institute for International Law and Justice at New York University, is among those to defend trusteeship, contending that "local ownership...must be the end of

---

23. Hegel's formulation is in paragraph 182 of *The Philosophy of Right*: "If the state is represented as a unity of different persons, as a unity which is only a partnership, then what is really meant is only civil society.... [T]he whole sphere of civil Society is the territory of mediation where there is free play for every idiosyncrasy, every talent, every accident of birth and fortune, and where waves of every passion gush forth, regulated only by reason glinting through them" (266–67). In Michael Hardt's gloss, "civil society takes the natural human systems of needs and particular self-interests, puts them in relation with each other through the capitalist social institutions of production and exchange and, thus, on the basis of the mediation and subsumption of the particular, poses a terrain on which the State can realize the universal interest of society in 'the actuality of the ethical Idea'" (25).

24. "[I]t is possible to identify remedies that can soften the rough edges of international control," Caplan allows, but the tendency of international actors to "give insufficient weight to capacity building" and to "accountability" is "difficult to overcome" (242).

a transitional administration, but it is not the means" (344).[25] Literature contributes to this discussion, questioning whether the normative study of state crisis must yield a stringently hierarchical approach to policy implementation, wherein global experts solve problems caused by local agents by mentoring them.

Failure in Fiction

Although contemporary fiction reproduces certain aspects of political scientific treatment of state failure, it does not reproduce that discipline's international division of labor. Instead, it retools an identifiably novelistic approach to representing subjectivity as the means for introducing new sorts of local, and often unaccredited, expert participants in the project of administration. Adichie's *Half of a Yellow Sun* presents the Biafran War as an instance of state failure twice over—first, a Nigerian failure so severe that it led to civil war and a breakaway republic and, second, the Biafran state's own collapse under attack from Nigeria and its international allies. This presentation appropriates the terms of political science in the service of a counterdiscourse: in *Half of a Yellow Sun*, the question of who is best qualified to analyze and to manage the failed state is up for grabs.

In addition to revising political scientific hierarchy, *Half of a Yellow Sun* supplements the most habitual literary approach to portraying political subjectivity. The novel performs a makeover on the home, which appears less as a private venue for the generation of public individuals than, alternatively, as the setting for a kind of ad hoc professional training. By simultaneously politicizing and professionalizing the household, furthermore, *Half of a Yellow Sun* performs a kind of gesture familiar to readers of postcolonial novels. If reaction to Fredric Jameson's argument about the "necessarily… political dimension" of postcolonial literature taught us nothing else, it taught us to appreciate the enormous variety of ways contemporary fictions reconfigure the public/private distinction we have been taught to

---

25. It only makes sense that outsiders are the best guides to stabilization, Chesterman claims. "Since the malevolence or collapse" of local political dynamics "is precisely the reason that power is arrogated to an international presence," he reasons, "the light footprint is unsustainable as a model for general application" (344).

think of as traditionally bourgeois.[26] In the instance of *Half of a Yellow Sun*, the domain once called "private life" is the place for politics, as demonstrated by the story of Odenigbo and Olanna, husband and wife as well as educators in the fields of mathematics and sociology, respectively. The air raid interrupting their wedding reception exemplifies a motif: throughout the novel, the couple's romantic turmoil directly parallels Nigeria's defining postcolonial crisis, as well as being punctuated by it (202–3).[27] In and of itself, this is not a radical innovation. *Half of a Yellow Sun* has a lowbrow cousin who can be found in the "historicals" section of the romance-novel shelf. But such a combination is still significant in suggesting, first, that problems which over two centuries of novel writing have taught readers to understand as normal still organize lives during political strife and, second, that the form of domestic romance is perfectly capable of stretching to accommodate the setting of civil war. That said, these refugees are not helpless victims or ciphers of bare life. Neither does their home provide a setting for the formation of reading persons whose self-discipline equips them to be national citizens.[28]

---

26. Jameson's thesis drew fire for stipulating geopolitical uniformity and a strictly allegorical mode: "Third-world texts, even those which are seemingly private…necessarily project a political dimension in the form of national allegory" (69).

27. The couple court one another by arguing about dictatorship and African nationalism, while Olanna fears that marriage "would flatten" their relationship "to a prosaic partnership" (52). Later, as Nigerian politics become increasingly fractious, their domestic life changes too when Odenigbo sleeps with a "village girl" his mother wants him to marry, fathering a child whom Olanna agrees to adopt (227, 251). Later still, with the war entering its last, punishing phase, Odenigbo sinks into depression, spends his days drinking at the "Tanzania Bar," and rebuffs Olanna's advances at night with a blank, "I'm tired, *nkem*" (332). When news comes that one of their best friends has been killed, they finally fall into each other's arms, have loud, therapeutic sex, and sink into a "sad and unsettling peace" (392).

28. There is a fuller argument to be made about how the novel presents Olanna's sympathy, which crosses lines of ethnicity and class and has her comforting and taking comfort in the familiarity of "barely educated" neighbors with whom she "had nothing in common" (265). She extends her sympathetic reach by opening a school to "make sure that when the war is over" the region's children "will all fit back easily into regular school" (291). Although there is an undeniably patriotic component to this—"We will teach them pride in our great nation," Olanna declares—the emphasis is on establishing scholastic continuity between the times of war and peace (291). For a more thorough narrative consideration of what it means to nationalize women's labor to "help sustain the soldiers," the most notable references are Flora Nwapa's *Never Again* (13) and the title story of Chinua Achebe's collection *Girls at War* (101–20).

Odenigbo and Olanna are such persons, but *Half of a Yellow Sun* establishes no such relation between private and public.

Instead, the novel transforms the function of the household by centering Olanna and Odenigbo's domestic life on their intellectual salon, a group whose membership includes key figures in the secession—among them Okeoma, the novel's incarnation of the poet and war hero Christopher Okigbo—as well as a cast that combines demographic diversity with academic authority. Participants include Professor Ezeka, whom Adichie reports she "modeled on the Biafran leader Chukwuemeka Odumegwu Ojukwu"; Dr. Patel, "the Indian man who drank Golden Guinea beer mixed with Coke"; Miss Adebayo, loud, Yoruban, and flirtatious, nothing like what one expects "a university woman to be"; and Richard Churchill, an Englishman researching Igbo-Ukwu art who also publishes eyewitness journalism from inside Biafra (Adichie, "Memory"; *Half of a Yellow Sun* 18–19, 36). The salon does not encompass a civil society so much as provide a university setting for demographic categories privileged by Nigerian politics in the 1960s. It focuses attention, in other words, on the very group distinctions highlighted by the plotting of politicians and army officers in the years immediately following independence, distinctions that were only reinforced when the young state of Nigeria was rocked by massacres, secession, and the Biafran War.[29]

The salon does not present dispute among its participants as solely or even primarily a discussion about self-interest among citizens. By doubly marking discussants as expert and ethnic, it distances them from the citizenry they might otherwise represent. They argue as

---

29. Chinua Achebe observed regretfully in 1983 that in postcolonial Nigeria, a "self-conscious wish to banish *tribe* has proved largely futile because a word will stay around as long as there is work for it to do. In Nigeria, in spite of our protestations, there *is* plenty of work for *tribe*" (*Trouble* 6). Herbert Ekwe-Ekwe notes the persistence of colonial regionalization in Nigerian politics (35). Pade Badru argues that the January 1966 coup "brought ethnicity to the fore of Nigerian politics" (75). And Frederick Forsyth's popular account of the Biafran War argues that the label "Igbo coup" provided rhetorical cover for ethnic cleansing executed by political and military functionaries in the North in response to what was, in fact, an "all-party coup in January" (56). See Zeleza on the variety of postcolonial African state responses to the colonial treatment of ethnicity (421). See Bayart for a wide-angle approach to the "assumption that a so-called 'cultural identity' necessarily corresponds to a 'political identity'" (ix).

scholars, even when they argue about what it means to be Nigerian or, later, Biafran. When his fellows accuse Odenigbo of being a "hopeless tribalist," they are not cajoling him into setting differences aside in the name of national unity so much as they are making a conceptual point about the historical derivation of such notions as "pan-Igbo" identity (20–21). "Professor Ezeka snorted and shook his head," the narrator recounts, before beginning a pocket lecture: "The pan-Igbo idea itself came only in the face of white domination. You must see that tribe as it is today is as colonial a product as nation and race" (20). Scholarly independence, rather than critical publicity, explains why these specialists do not consistently or narrowly represent the interests of their respective ethnic groups.

When it domesticates coffeehouse congregation, in sum, Odenigbo and Olanna's salon does more than simply reverse Jürgen Habermas's formula of private people coming together as a public to debate the common concern. Adichie's emphasis on the scholarly aspect of political dialogue confirms what Habermas himself avers, namely, that the era of "bourgeois representation" is over (Habermas 37). Instead of salvaging the public sphere, *Half of a Yellow Sun* offers a model for reproducing the feel of the seminar or colloquium when the universities are all closed down. And indeed, though the war forces them to relocate more than once, and to less welcoming abodes each time, Odenigbo and Olanna continue to preserve a space for political argument among experts. They welcome new interlocutors and encourage old ones to stop by as they are able.[30] When Okeoma visits from the front, Olanna recaptures the salon's civility by inviting him to read one of his poems and asking, "Please remove your grenade while we eat" (324).

The Author-Function of State

Half of a Yellow Sun confirms the social scientific hypothesis that life during civil war is not entirely abnormal—which is to say, life

---

30. Ezeka occasionally visits from his office at the Biafran directorate (286, 340). New regulars include the army contractor "Special Julius" and Professor Ekwenugo, the designer of battlefield explosives.

during civil war is not life as it should be, but something enough like the ideal to appear a significant deviation from it, rather than an exception to it. Even though the novel accepts that hypothesis, it does not cede authority to describe such normality to think tanks and resource centers run out of Geneva, London, or Washington. Instead, it describes the salon managed by its two Nigerian educators as the perfect setting for a young man to become an indigenous expert on failed states. *Half of a Yellow Sun* marshals the usual diachronic logic of *Bildung* for this effort, but in its revised domestic setting, what might otherwise appear as personal experiences of growing up seem more like aspects of professional training.[31]

Ugwu is the houseboy whom Odenigbo and Olanna raise as a son and invigilate like a promising graduate student. After a time of intense preparation, he demonstrates his membership in the class of people who "know Book" by writing a volume of his own (129). His labor is a secret until the novel's final lines, however. Only then does it become clear that Ugwu, the boy readers have watched develop over the course of some four hundred pages, is the author of the book within a book whose composition appears in sections at the end of several chapters of *Half of a Yellow Sun*, in a different typeface from the main narrative, under the heading, "The Book: The World Was Silent When We Died." Ugwu is the answer, in other words, to a good old-fashioned question of "What matter who's speaking?" (Foucault, *Language* 138).

This author-function is complicated by the various disciplines and styles of writing employed in "The Book."[32] One chapter speaks in the manner of colonial history when it chronicles the disastrous implementation of indirect rule among the "non-docile and worryingly ambitious" Igbo (115).[33] Another approaches civil war from

31. The novel thus offers a departure from what Joseph Slaughter calls the "mutually enabling fictions" of human-rights law and *Bildungsroman*: "each projects an image of the human personality that ratifies the other's vision of the ideal relations between individual and society" (1407).

32. "The Book" sounds themes that recur habitually in case studies of state failure. For an illustrative example, see Frederick Golooba-Mutebi's "Collapse, War, and Reconstruction in Uganda," published in January 2008 by the Crisis States Research Centre.

33. The scholarly literature on this episode is, needless to say, substantial. See, for instance, Afigbo, Isichei, and Ekechi.

the standpoint of international politics in considering what it meant that "Biafra was 'under Britain's sphere of interest'" (258).[34] A third foregrounds the economics of state failure, what commentators call the resource curse, and the foibles of neocolonial planners "too interested in aping the British" (205).[35] Even greater stylistic range appears in an initial section that recalls the memoir of witnessing—it describes a woman fleeing massacre in northern Nigeria, holding a calabash with a "child's head inside: scruffy braids falling across the dark-brown face, eyes completely white, eerily open, a mouth in a small surprised O" (82). A late section, finally, takes the form of poetic apostrophe:

> Did you see photos in sixty-eight
> Of children with their hair becoming rust:
> Sickly patches nestled on those small heads,
> Then falling off, like rotten leaves on dust?
>
> (375)

The puzzle of who might be capable of doing the failed state in such different voices is hardly restricted to the novel's plot. It also shapes expectations about the author whose name is on *Half of a Yellow Sun*'s cover. A bibliography and "Author's Note" only encourage such conjecture by referencing materials from an array of disciplines and citing survivors and relations whose interviews facilitated the novel's composition (434–36). In assigning the fictional author-function to the unlikely Ugwu, *Half of a Yellow Sun* satisfies a craving for unity invoked by that range of sources in Adichie's "Note."

More significant still than the author-function readers attach to Ugwu or Adichie is the authority *Half of a Yellow Sun* claims for the

---

34. John Stremlau's work remains a key reference point for the international-politics approach to Biafra.

35. On the resource curse, a 2003 World Bank study observes that "the presence of abundant primary commodities, especially in low-income countries, exacerbates the risks of conflict" (Bannon and Collier ix). In a survey of state failure for Harvard's Center for International Development, Robert Bates labels this paradoxical curse one of the primary themes of scholarship on political disorder (20). In *Half of a Yellow Sun*, Olanna's sister Kainene is among the characters to give voice to this argument: "It's the oil" that ensures Nigeria will wage war against the breakaway Biafran state: "They can't let us go easily with all that oil" (180).

novel as a genre. Fiction appears herein as an assemblage of humanities and social scientific forms that combine to provide a fuller picture of political crisis. Odenigbo and Olanna's professorial salon, like Ugwu's precocious authorial talents, reference the novel's heteroglossia. Ugwu's *Bildung* puts the experience of warfare on the novel's interdisciplinary curriculum. More than a participant-observer, he is an expert whose authority derives from an intimate relation to his object of study, a relation that social science must disavow to preserve objectivity and analytic distance. Ugwu's education is not only thoroughly sentimentalized but also rooted in a mentoring model that looks downright populist when compared to the university program for generating accredited experts. His mentorship begins in the novel's first chapter and in the *locus classicus* of postcolonial fiction—a library filled with tomes acquired in the course of a colonial education.[36] This archive appears as the very definition of the quiet, well-lit place: "Sunlight streamed in through the windows, and from time to time a gentle breeze lifted the curtains" (5). As is typical in such settings, the holdings on display range widely, encompassing everything from *Non-Parametric Methods* to *An African Survey*, from *The Great Chain of Being* to *The Norman Impact upon England* (6). As if to demonstrate the extent to which the library dominates the house in which Ugwu works and grows up, Adichie lingers over books that spill out into bedrooms and hallways, piled high on "shelves and tables...on the sink and cabinets," and "stacked from floor to ceiling in the study" (6). The eclectic holdings of this home-cum-library encourage omnivorous reading habits: Ugwu avidly studies everything from *The Mayor of Casterbridge* to the *Socialist Review*, from books Odenigbo

---

36. There are any number of precedents for this setting, and they would include primal scenes of reading from works of English-language fiction dating back to the eighteenth century, but perhaps the most relevant is the library in Tayeb Salih's *Season of Migration to the North*, with its "four walls from floor to ceiling...filled, shelf upon shelf, with books and more books," from Gibbon to Woolf, "Not a single Arabic book" but instead "A graveyard. A mausoleum" of colonial materials (136–38). From these volumes, Salih's leading man Mustafa Sa'eed acquires an insider's knowledge of English writing, which he transforms into an insurgent weapon. "So deliberate are Salih's mimetic reversals," Edward Said observes, "even Kurtz's skull-topped fence is repeated and distorted in the inventory of European books stacked in [Mustafa] Said's secret library" (211).

recommends to magazines scrounged as the household flees east to escape the Nigerian army.[37]

Odenigbo shows Ugwu how the library can be used to "decolonize our education" by explaining how to read against the grain (75). "How can we resist exploitation," he catechizes his pupil, "if we don't have the tools to understand exploitation?" (11). Ugwu internalizes what he is told: although he may not understand Odenigbo's argument that "America was to blame for other countries not recognizing Biafra," Ugwu reproduces "Master's words... with authority, as though they were his" (295). He persists in this mode when composing his book: the last chapters of the novel find Ugwu listening attentively "to the conversations in the evenings, writing in his mind what he would later transfer to paper" (399). Ugwu's dedication for "The Book" affirms the mentoring model by recycling one of Odenigbo's favored phrases: "For Master, my good man" (433).

Like any student, Ugwu comes into his own by submitting to a power relationship. To the habitual dynamic of mentor and pupil, however, *Half of a Yellow Sun* adds a sentimental supplement, Ugwu's motivating sense of guilt for his actions as a conscript in the Biafran army. When he is first pressed into action, being a teenage soldier perversely echoes life in the academic home. Ugwu's battalion has its headquarters in a former primary school where, in one of the classrooms, he finds a copy of the *Narrative of the Life of Frederick Douglass*.[38] The platoon treats him as the class nerd: his teenage comrades

37. As Nigeria lurches into civil war, Ugwu balances his attention to newspapers and political writing with avid consumption of fiction. After the "Igbo Coup," he supplements newspaper reading with *The Mayor of Casterbridge* (126). After the second coup and reprisal killings, he reads *The Pickwick Papers* in an attempt to make the change "hurtling toward him...slow down" (175). He hoards all manner of reading material rescued "from the study dustbin," from the "incomprehensible" *Mathematical Annals* to the only slightly more intelligible *Socialist Review* (210). After the war has been lost, he salvages what he can from Odenigbo's library, its books "heaped together before being set on fire," and laments the books burned in Nsukka's main square (418–22).

38. He handles this volume just like those from Odenigbo's library. He reads with care, sometimes out loud, and commits key sentences to memory, such as, "Even if it cost me my life, I was determined to read. Keep the black man away from the books, keep us ignorant, and we would always be his slaves" (360). That Douglass's volume is itself a story of education provides a sharp contrast: where readers find in the *Narrative* an account of the

mock his reading habits and tear out pages from Douglass's *Narrative* to use as rolling paper. Orders to kill and maim interrupt this middle-school dynamic soon enough, however, and the novel enlists Ugwu in wartime atrocity when he and his comrades cram into a saloon, drink steadily, and gang rape the "bar girl." Ugwu is goaded into participating: "[A]ren't you a man?" his comrades taunt. Much to his dismay, he achieves "a self-loathing release" (365). This display of force confirms that Ugwu is not in charge of his own development: "He was not living his life; life was living him" (364).

Rather than undermining his authority, the memory of the rape helps make Ugwu into a writer.[39] After escaping the battlefield, he writes in order to repress: "the more he wrote the less he dreamed" (398). Precisely because reminders of what he has done are ever present—he even learns that his sister has been raped and beaten to death by soldiers (421)—this process of sublimation proves reproducible. The internalized voices of his mentors are cops in Ugwu's head: he knows only too well what Odenigbo, Olanna, and her sister Kainene "would say, what [they] would do to him, feel about him, if [they] ever knew about the girl in the bar" (399). What they cannot know, he must remember—an act of atrocity that produces guilt that yields writing. The very title of his book confirms the productivity of this formula: "*The World Was Silent When We Died*. It haunted him, filled him with shame. It made him think about that girl in the bar," which makes him continue working (396).

If the remembrance of rape reinforces the dynamic of mentoring, and with it the authority such discipline bestows upon Ugwu, there

---

triumph of mind over body, liberal subjectivity over corporeal definition and suffering, *Half of a Yellow Sun* features an expert whose authority derives at least in part from violence in which his body seems to act on its own accord. I thank Tom Allen for suggesting this reading.

39. Adichie acknowledges the precedent of Chukwuemeka Ike's 1976 Biafran novel *Sunset at Dawn*, but where that earlier novel narrates the transformation of its Dr. Amilo Kanu from medical researcher into field commander and thus labors to explain how professionals under duress might evolve into battlefield heroes, *Half of a Yellow Sun* reverses that story when it turns Ugwu's time spent as a soldier into part of his training to become a political scientist (Ike 71–72, 210–17). More broadly, one might also suggest, *Sunset at Dawn* treats administration as an impoverished form of service when compared to soldiering.

is no character in *Half of a Yellow Sun* capable of describing how this process works or what it means. For that we must rely on the novel's narrator, a figure who represents the pedagogy of mentoring and the violence of war, and who explains that the two converge to generate Ugwu's unaccredited expertise. Such an author-function has been widely disseminated in recent years. It is associated with names as various as those of Aminatta Forna and Dave Eggers. Forna's name is on the byline of journalistic commentary about international justice and on the cover of both a memoir of political turmoil in Sierra Leone and the 2006 novel "of how it was to live as a woman in our country's past" called *Ancestor Stones*. The acknowledgments at the close of Forna's novel present the novelist as interviewer and researcher as well as writer of a book that, like Adichie's, does more than represent the disempowered. Both authors, and both novels, are in the business of representing the victims of state crisis as the authors of their own stories (318).[40] *What Is the What* (2006) is too: its preface describes Eggers responding to Sudanese Lost Boy Valentino Achak Deng's appeal for "an author to help me write my biography."[41] Though such examples indicate the current ubiquity of an author-function defined by its eagerness to give voice to unaccredited experts akin to Ugwu, in truth, fiction has been generating something like this authority for a while. A necessarily truncated genealogy will have to suffice to suggest something of the twentieth-century precedence for a recent novel such as *Half of a Yellow Sun*.

Experts in Atrocity

Where social science displaces emotional investment on to fiction in order to claim scholarly distance, *Half of a Yellow Sun* uses Ugwu's

---

40. Forna's memoir of her father in Sierra Leone in the 1970s is *The Devil That Danced on the Water* (2002).

41. *What Is the What* proclaims itself both autobiography and novel, and indeed the book ratifies the sorts of author-function activated by both genres, as the preface suggests when it explains how Deng and Eggers came to work together. "[I]n spite of the public-speaking opportunities available, I wanted to reach out to a wider audience by telling the story of my life in book form," Deng says in the preface. "Because I was not a writer, I asked Mary [Williams, of the Lost Boys Foundation] to put me in touch with an author" (Eggers xiii).

guilt to sentimentalize education. This recipe for generating expertise is echoed by what amounts to the novel's guiding philosophy, put into words by Olanna's grandfather, who "used to say, about difficulties he had gone through, 'It did not kill me, it made me knowledgeable'" (347). By disavowing such a sentimental supplement, political science makes it appear as though knowledge and credentials are the same thing. *Half of a Yellow Sun* is not the only novel to pull those concepts apart and to propagate the idea of an uncredentialed expert of the war zone.

Yvonne Vera's 2002 fiction *The Stone Virgins* identifies a kind of knowing-by-suffering that it compares to the more conventional archival mode of "replicating histories" (184).[42] Memoir-style child-soldier novels ranging from Ken Saro-Wiwa's 1985 *Sozaboy* to Chris Abani's 2007 *Song for Night* represent killers as subjects of self-knowledge and graduates of unnervingly specialized forms of education.[43] Timothy Mo's 1991 *The Redundancy of Courage* establishes the basis for including knowledge earned on the battlefield in multivariate analyses of crisis. This novel narrates the invasion of East Timor as, first, a war about American influence; second, a demonstration of revolutionary nationalism; and third, a conflict whose causality is of less importance than its effective revision of local

---

42. Veena Das's study of "knowing by suffering" concentrates on Indian Partition violence (75–78).

43. *Sozaboy*'s Mene takes part in a catechistic exercise that Saro-Wiwa renders as a kind of linguistic discipline: "Just I will repeat what Bullet or the soza captain have said. And I will say it carefully with my mouth and with style so that if you hear me talking by that time, you will even think that I am oyibo man" (93). Abani's child-soldier My Luck is a minesweeper whose training involves complete self-mastery: "first our eyes were made keen so we could notice any change in the terrain no matter how subtle.... Having trained our eyes, they began to train our legs, feet, and toes" (32–33). Finally, "a week before graduation," My Luck and his colleagues are "led into surgery," where their vocal cords are severed so that if one of them gets blown up by a mine they neither alert the enemy to their presence nor "scare each other with...death screams" (35). Mute but articulate, My Luck masters a sophisticated sign language and narrates his own tale: "I am not a genius," he notes; "I am just better versed at the interior monologue" than most (21). There are social scientists who work this vein as well, although they are not in the majority. See David Keen's argument that "War appeared to be a system" (2), Michael Ignatieff's investigation of strategic thinking in a "war economy" (302), Kate Meagher's consideration of the "Bakassi Boys" and "property rights" in Nigeria's Abia state (96), as well as Krijn Peters and Paul Richards's interviews with Sierra Leone "youth combatants" (183).

social organization. This last sort of change seems best analyzed from the ground-level perspective of the novel's participant-observer, Adolph Ng.[44] James Kelman's 2001 *Translated Accounts* provides a veritable catalog of the characters, settings, and scenarios that populate literary as well as political-scientific treatment of state crisis. "Securitys" compare themselves to football players and "logicians, we killers" (319); foreign VIPS, lawyers, and journalists encourage the locals to "respect humanity" (284); witnesses regret that memory of those killed and tortured "slips from my mind" (315). Familiar scenes of killing and rape, tenderness and domestic routine fill out fifty-four fragmented chapters, all set in an unnamed "occupied territory or land where a form of martial law appears in operation" (ix). Kelman's novel does not vest absolute authority with its putative translator and collator of eyewitness statements. Instead, *Translated Accounts* represents fractious engagement among various narrative agents, many of whom refer to one another quasi-professionally as "colleagues" rather than as citizens or neighbors, and who knowingly "irritate international experts" (87), acknowledge that "we take part in our own subjection" (306), and observe, "'Official politics' is 'you must listen politics'" (170). "I could be anywhere," says one character, underscoring that state failure is no more a uniquely third-world phenomenon than failed-state fiction is a third-world genre (307).

To the extent that these fictions help readers recognize discrepant forms of expertise around the world, they collaborate with *Half of a Yellow Sun* in shaping an alternative to the most habitual means of

---

44. Marginally successful hotelier Adolph Ng turns a "Chinese" affinity for "the make-shift, the third-hand, the modified, the refurbished" into the basis of mastery over the jungle booby trap, the guerrilla bomb, the cobbled-together mine, the "Adolf Ng special" (169, 311). With this skill, Adolph not only earns a place among the rebels but also effectively goes native: he acquires "tribal eyes" (275). On his way into exile, Ng pauses to have coffee in New York with a UN emissary who provides a differently expert understanding of the invasion of Danu, Mo's thinly veiled fictionalization of East Timor. "It's funny sitting here," Adolph tells him, "so remote from Danu." "Remote?" the emissary counters. "This isn't remote.... This is where it's determined; this is where it began; this is where it will end" (404). Adolph learns that there is a deep-water channel running right past Danu that the U.S. requires for its submarines, and that this is what led Danu's next-door neighbor to invade it, apparently on American orders.

attributing specialized knowledge to those with university degrees. This is a paradoxical democratization of expert hierarchy, no doubt, which draws attention to the insights of unaccredited characters but still maintains that their knowledge has value because it is specialized. Expertise against expertise, we might call it, a counterdiscourse that widens the circle but never extends to include the social totality. Instead, fiction specifies a range of types—the child soldier, the witness to atrocity—whose specialized knowledge grants them authority to supplement and even contest the accounts of credentialed professionals.

The creation of noncredentialed experts was pioneered by earlier writers. Saadat Hasan Manto's Indian partition stories from the late 1940s and early 1950s forecast an intimacy with atrocity taken more or less for granted in later fiction.[45] They thereby helped establish a connection between personal life and expert understanding of crises in subsequent novels. His tales establish bloody parallels between the loss of domestic household order and the failure of incipient state organization.[46] Though small in scope—some of Manto's partition stories are as brief as a page—they accumulate to give the sense of massive governmental failure. That there is no official presence in many of these stories does not mean that chaos rules. Instead, social structure emerges through the repetition of

---

45. Though in truth Manto wrote on a variety of themes, critics often turn to him for his portrayal of partition's violence, a topic that remains more an episode in than the centerpiece of much prominent midcentury fiction. Niaz Zaman observes that the subgenre "literature of partition" lacks the biggest names of South Asian writing in English from the period. Bhabani Bhattacharya suggests that the likes of Raja Rao, R. K. Nayaran, and Mulk Raj Anand were "too dazed by recent history to make it their material," and as a result, they hardly deviated from their usual theme of transition from colonialism to independence (qtd. in Zaman 19–21). Alex Padamsee notes that nationalist narration treats partition as an interruption and communalism as the "dark 'Other'…'beyond the pale' of representation" (1).

46. In "Colder Than Ice," a woman accuses her lover of cheating. His confession is an uncanny revision of the ordinary extramarital affair. The husband explains that he spent the night rioting, and that he killed every member of another family but one, an attractive young woman whom he dragged off to rape in private. After some time, however, he realized that she too was dead and that he had been carrying around a corpse (29). Aamir Mufti places the "female victim of 'communal' sexual violence" in the context of Manto's fiction as a whole (203).

similar incidents, habitual personae, and chronic tropes.[47] "Bitter Harvest" induces a pattern from the story of a father who comes home to find "the blood-soaked body of his wife" and "the nearly naked body" of his daughter (143). Enraged, he runs into the street, killing three men with his axe before breaking into a house and pouncing "like a wild beast" on a girl hiding inside (145). Where his daughter's killer was, he now is. The story ends with his victim's own father running into the house, recognizing what is going on (and recognizing his daughter's assailant as well), and rushing back outside, ready to perpetuate a daisy chain of slaughter.[48]

By making the regularity of atrocity visible, Manto makes atrocity difficult to bracket as outside the norm. He teaches a pragmatic lesson, one that runs contrary to the habit Gyanendra Pandey discerns among "journalists and other investigators" fond of identifying "exceptional circumstances...behind such acts of collective violence" (30).[49] Manto's fiction suggests that if partition's massacres are no exception, there ought to be continuity between the sorts of administrative practices required to curtail what tends to get called "communal" violence and those more generally responsible for reproducing a stable India. His writing inscribes the possibility, even a tendency, of state failure at the very inception of independent Indian administration.

In its narrative of postcolonial Yugoslavia, Rebecca West's 1941 *Black Lamb and Grey Falcon: A Journey through Yugoslavia* provides a

---

47. "The Dutiful Daughter" underscores this regularity by identifying a shadow management apparatus emerging to fill the administrative vacuum. A mother searches for a daughter abducted by remarkably efficient traffickers: "Sometimes it seemed to me that the entire operation was being conducted like import-export trade" (98).

48. Veena Das and Ashis Nandy gloss Manto's use of female characters in a manner suggestive of Vera's much later plot in *The Stone Virgins*: "Women . . . are the media through which men concretise the pact of violence but, because they are not simply things to be looted and plundered but also subjects, they retain the memory of this loot, rape and plunder. The definition of the victim emerges in new relief since the victim is now defined as the object of, as well as the witness to, violence" (193).

49. Even "riots on the scale and with the frequency that we have seen since the 1980s" have not shaken faith in "the cherished national traditions of nonviolence and peaceful coexistence," Pandey contends (33). "The message of much of the writing on riots in the country since 1947 is the same as that found in the nationalist histories of the pre-Independence period," in contrast to which Pandey would offer a sense of collective violence in India as a "social fact" (32).

significant early precedent for such challenges of self-governance: "The chief problems of Yugoslavia were its poverty and the antagonisms felt by sections of the populations which had different cultures" (603). "Such politics we know very well in Ireland. They grow on a basis of past injustice," West argues. "A proud people acquire a habit of resistance to foreign oppression, and by the time they have driven out their oppressors they have forgotten that agreement is a pleasure and that a society which has attained tranquility will be able to pursue many delightful ends" (82). Formerly colonized populations "continue to wrangle" out of habit, she alleges, "finding abundant material in the odds and ends of injustices that are left over from the period of tyranny and need to be tidied up in one way or another."

West does not offer a recipe for such administrative tidying up, but she does present her readers with a narrative theory for making a link that would become habitual in later fiction between the care of the self and the order of the postcolonial state. To sort out the "bad book" of Yugoslav history, West proposes the "analogy [of] the sexual affairs of individuals" (55). Bosnia's colonization by Turkey finds analogy in "a kind of human being, terrifying above all others, who resists by yielding" (301).[50] West works this analogy by parsing her guide's marriage. He is Constantine, a.k.a. Stanislav Vinaver, aide to the Serbian leader Stojadinovic.[51] He fought in World War I ("very gallantly"), is Jewish as well as the son of a Russian émigré, and, thus, embodies Yugoslavian multiculture as well as helping to administer it. This paragon is unfortunately married to Gerda, "a stout middle-aged woman, typically German," whose prolific abuse of her husband is authorized by the "conqueror's point of view"

50. West offers a plurality of other, similarly suggestive types, including the effete intellectuals who "though poor almost to the point of beggary . . . are sustained in happy gentility by their possession of Western clothes and urban status" (1078). These decadents speak a "flowery German" and tend to fall into a "complaining and exultant whine." Without "strength or skill or land," all brain and no talent, West imagines they "would not have lasted out a single winter under a Nazi regime."

51. The reviewer Stoyan Pribichevich outed Constantine, whose real name West does not provide. Pribichevich notes: "'Constantine' was a 'writer and a poet,' as Miss West calls him. But he was first of all Stoyadinovich's official; second, a talker; third, a writer; and fourth, a thinker" (qtd. in Colquitt 89n8).

(457–58, 800). Gerda is "allergic to Jews," dismisses Serbs as "stupid," gypsies as "dirty and stupid," Slavs as "ungrateful," the poor as "horrible people," and Yugoslavia itself as "only a mish-mash of different peoples who are all quite primitive and low" (466, 464, 507, 660, 662). "But it's precisely because there are so many different peoples that Yugoslavia is so interesting," West interrupts her, "and it is fascinating to see whether they can be organized into an orderly state." "How can you make an orderly state out of so many peoples?" Gerda persists. "They should all be driven out" (662). If the best that can be said of Constantine is that he resists his wife's aggression by yielding to it to preserve some degree of domestic amity, West is clear that such resistance does not constitute management. When Constantine "bared his throat to Gerda's knife," West writes, "he had offered his loving heart to the service of hate, in order that he might be defeated and innocent" (916). If only, West laments, Constantine could care about himself enough to take care of his state as they both suffer German abuse. Or, to put this in the related terms offered by Adichie in *Half of a Yellow Sun*, if only Constantine and his wife could do a better job of modeling civil discussion about the administrative challenges facing Yugoslavia, even as those challenges increase under pressure of German invasion and dissident unrest.

West confirms that such arguments about how to manage a state in crisis need to be hashed out not only in postcolonies but also in bastions of stability such as England. The Yugoslavian army's battlefield prowess provides her with an exemplary demonstration that she holds up as a model to the British trying to keep things together during the Blitz. Finishing her book in a shell-shocked London, West takes inspiration from Yugoslavia's effort.[52] "[W]hen I have thought of invasion," she writes, "or when a bomb has dropped near by, I have prayed, 'Let me behave like a Serb'" (1126). With her prayer, West threatens to demote Britain from its status as the epitome of modern nationhood and to treat it as a potentially

---

52. There was no chance that Yugoslavia could win this fight, West willingly acknowledges; that it was willing to undertake it regardless is what matters. "The Yugoslav Army never capitulated, although it was destroyed," she contends. "In this war, as in the one before it, they have made out of their defeats great victories" (1147–49).

failed state like any other.[53] It would be too much to argue that this prayer alone inaugurates the normative scheme I have identified in later fiction and political science. Yet it is perfectly reasonable to conclude that West signals a different mode of comparison than the older center-periphery scheme that made European nations the inside to their colonial outsides.

Although this brief genealogy from Adichie to West casts a focused thematic net, it might motivate a revised account of the relationship between state and novel more broadly conceived. It is conventional to think of fiction as putting flesh on the bones of the bourgeois citizen-subject. It is, further, conventional to understand this dynamic as coming undone in the twentieth century. Canonical postcolonial tomes such as Ngũgĩ wa Thiong'o's 1977 *Petals of Blood* and V. S. Naipaul's 1979 *A Bend in the River* confirm the end of what Samir Amin calls the era of anti-imperial "Bandung regimes" and "their bourgeois national project" (129).[54] By portraying what is often described as the "failure" of the postcolonial intellectual to salvage the nation, such novels also provide motivation to grant that figure a revised job description.[55] *Half of a Yellow Sun* takes up that

---

53. This is but one aspect of West's reconsideration of England's geopolitical position. An "exasperated critic" of British imperialism, West identifies its primary sin as transforming colonial populations into "helpless people" and staffing offices with administrators who "regard [their subjects] as children" (1089, 91).

54. These are among the most recognizable fictions from that moment Said describes when "disenchantment" with third-world nationalism "overtook many people during the 1970s and 1980s" (265). *Petals of Blood* famously concludes with Ngũgĩ's scholar-activist Karega contemplating the possibility of working-class revolution, uncertain that he has any place in it—"Tomorrow . . . tomorrow . . ." he muses (345). *Petals of Blood* is set in a city undergoing what might be called industrialization without modernization. Simon Gikandi takes up this neocolonial dynamic at length (135–48). The conclusion of Naipaul's novel marks the end of the line via Ferdinand, a well-schooled "évolué" and political officer who sees only bare life in his country's administrative collapse. "We're all going to hell," he tells the novel's protagonist, Salim. "Nothing has any meaning. . . . The bush runs itself. . . . It's a nightmare" (272). For Sara Suleri, Naipaul's is the neocolonial novel *par excellence*: it displays an "uncanny ability to map the complicity between postcolonial history and its imperial past" (156).

55. That story of failure emerges out of Frantz Fanon's description of the "unpreparedness of the educated classes" in "The Pitfalls of National Consciousness" (148–49). Pheng Cheah reads Ngũgĩ as positioning the postcolonial intellectual as a proxy for the nation as a whole. Ngũgĩ's nationalism is not a "nativism," he argues, "but a process of *Bildung* in which the nation can digest foreign elements and make them part of its organic

challenge. Instead of characters whose principal function is guiding a national citizenry, Adichie's novel considers whether its protagonists demonstrate the expertise to grasp why states fail and thus, perhaps, how to manage them. A genealogical glance toward partition writing and *Black Lamb and Grey Falcon* begs questions about whether we fully understand the social function being imagined for the highly educated heroes and heroines in even earlier novels. Failed-state fiction invites speculation about whether the novel might long have been more interested in producing managers than citizens.[56]

With such speculation in mind, we might better appreciate what is at stake in failed-state fiction's delegation of expert authority. When novels take up the political scientific campaign to normalize state crisis, they also ask all sorts of questions about what expert agency looks like in this context. Literature provides alternatives to the London School of Economics researcher and the UN policy wonk with characters like Rebecca West's Constantine, Timothy Mo's Adolph Ng, and Chimamanda Ngozi Adichie's Ugwu. These heroes are unaccredited analysts, unwilling participants in civil wars, and flawed government flacks. Fiction strives to make their expertise intelligible as specialized knowledge every bit as consequential as that of development economists and political theorists. In so doing, failed-state fiction might be said to promote a dramatic revision of the division of labor that abides in policy circles. These novels do not alter the political scientific formula in which experts speak on behalf of populations rather than speaking as the people.

---

body" (365). The "ambivalent sociological figure of the postcolonial intellectual . . . is simultaneously the exemplary agent" of this process "and also the most likely channel for neocolonial cultural influences." Kwame Anthony Appiah sums up "the predicament of the postcolonial intellectual [as] simply that as intellectuals—a category instituted in black Africa by colonialism—we are, indeed, always at the risk of becoming otherness machines, with the manufacture of alterity as our principal role" (356).

56. Along these lines, Nancy Armstrong and Leonard Tennenhouse argue that both American and British novel traditions in the eighteenth and nineteenth centuries "registered a growing tension between 'the people' and 'the population'" (16). They identify a mid-nineteenth-century form of the genre that served as "the means of bringing the problem of population from the background squarely into the foreground of the novel where it blocked and dispersed the liberal fantasy of building a nation one individual at a time" (13).

But when fiction broaches the question of who qualifies as an expert in the first place, it identifies a problem political science has yet to fully think through. In this way, fiction claims a special understanding of state politics.

University of California, Davis

WORKS CITED

Abani, Christopher. *Song for Night*. New York: Akashic, 2007.

Achebe, Chinua. *Girls at War and Other Stories*. New York: Fawcett, 1973.

———. *The Trouble with Nigeria*. 1983. Portsmouth, NH: Heinemann, 1984.

Adichie, Chimamanda Ngozi. *Half of a Yellow Sun*. New York: Knopf, 2006.

———. "Memory, Witness, and War: Chimamanda Ngozi Adichie Talks with Bookforum." Interview. Conducted by Kera Bolonik. *Bookforum* Dec.-Jan. 2008.

Afigbo, A. E. *The Warrant Chiefs: Indirect Rule in Southeastern Nigeria 1891–1929*. New York: Humanities, 1972.

Agamben, Giorgio. *Homo Sacer: Sovereign Power and Bare Life*. Trans. Daniel Heller-Roazen. Stanford, CA: Stanford UP, 1998.

———. *State of Exception*. Trans. Kevin Attell. Chicago: U of Chicago P, 2005.

Amin, Samir. *Re-Reading the Postwar Period: An Intellectual Itinerary*. Trans. Michael Wolfers. New York: Monthly Review, 1994.

Appiah, Kwame Anthony. "Is the Post- in Postmodernism the Post- in Postcolonial?" *Critical Inquiry* 17 (1991): 336–57.

Arendt, Hannah. *The Origins of Totalitarianism*. 1951. New York: Meridian, 1958.

Armstrong, Nancy, and Leonard Tennenhouse. "The Problem of Population and the Form of the American Novel." *American Literary History* 20 (2008): 667–85.

Badru, Pade. *Imperialism and Ethnic Politics in Nigeria, 1960–1996*. Trenton, NJ: Africa World, 1998.

Bannon, Ian, and Paul Collier, eds. *Natural Resources and Violent Conflict: Options and Actions*. Washington, DC: World Bank, 2003.

Bates, Robert. "Political Insecurity and State Failure in Contemporary Africa." CID Working Papers 115. Cambridge, MA: Center for International Development at Harvard U, 2005.

Bayart, Jean-François. *The Illusion of Cultural Identity*. London: Hurst, 2005.

Bull, Malcolm. "Vectors of the Biopolitical." *New Left Review* 45 (2007): 7–25.

Butler, Judith, and Gayatri Chakravorty Spivak. *Who Sings the Nation-State?* New York: Seagull, 2007.

Caplan, Richard. "From Collapsing States to Neo-Trusteeship: The Limits to Solving the Problem of 'Precarious Statehood' in the Twenty-First Century." *Third World Quarterly* 28 (2007): 231–44.

Chan, Stephen. "The Memory of Violence: Trauma in the Writings of Alexander Kanengoni and Yvonne Vera and the Idea of Unreconciled Citizenship in Zimbabwe." *Third World Quarterly* 26 (2005): 369–82.

Cheah, Pheng. *Spectral Nationality: Passages of Freedom from Kant to Postcolonial Literatures of Liberation*. New York: Columbia UP, 2003.

Chesterman, Simon. "Transitional Administration, State-Building, and the United Nations." Chesterman et al. 339–58.

Chesterman, Simon, Michael Ignatieff, and Ramesh Thakur. "Introduction: Making States Work." Chesterman et al. 1–10.

———, eds. *Making States Work: State Failure and the Crisis of Governance*. New York: United Nations, 2005.

Colquitt, Clare. "A Call to Arms: Rebecca West's Assault on the Limits of 'Gerda's Empire' in '*Black Lamb and Grey Falcon*.'" *South Atlantic Review* 51.2 (1986): 77–91.

Crisis States Workshop, The. "Crisis, Fragile and Failed States: Definitions Used by the CSRC." *Crisis States Development Research Centre Definitions*. London: London School of Economics, 2006.

Das, Veena. *Life and Words: Violence and the Descent into the Ordinary*. Berkeley: U of California P, 2007.

Das, Veena, and Ashis Nandy. "Violence, Victimhood, and the Language of Silence." *The Word and the World: Fantasy, Symbol, and Record*. Ed. Veena Das. New Delhi: Sage, 1986. 177–95.

Deleuze, Gilles. "Postscript on the Societies of Control." *October* 59 (1992): 3–7.

Eggers, Dave. *What Is the What: The Autobiography of Valentino Achak Deng*. New York: Vintage, 2007.

Einsiedel, Sebastian von. "Policy Responses to State Failure." Chesterman et al. 13–35.

Ekechi, Felix K. *Tradition and Transformation in Eastern Nigeria: A Sociopolitical History of Owerri and Its Hinterlands, 1902–1947*. Kent, OH: Kent State UP, 1989.

Ekwe-Ekwe, Herbert. *Biafra Revisited*. Reading, Eng.: Africa Renaissance, 2007.

Englebert, Pierre. "Why Congo Persists: Sovereignty, Globalization, and the Violent Reproduction of a Weak State." *Globalization, Violent Conflict, and Self-Determination*. Ed. Valpy Fitzgerald, Frances Stewart, and Rajesh Venugopal. London: Palgrave, 2006. 119–46.

Ewald, François. "Norms, Discipline, and the Law." *Representations* 30 (1990): 138–61.

"The Failed States Index." *Foreign Policy* 154 (2006): 50–54.

"The Failed States Index 2007." *Foreign Policy* 161 (2007): 54–63.

"The Failed States Index 2008." *Foreign Policy* 167 (2008): 64–68.

Fanon, Frantz. *The Wretched of the Earth*. Trans. Constance Farrington. New York: Grove, 1963.

Fassin, Didier. "Humanitarianism as a Politics of Life." *Public Culture* 19 (2007): 499–520.

Fearon, James D., and David D. Laitin. "Ethnicity, Insurgency, and Civil War." *American Political Science Review* 97.1 (2003): 75–90.

Ferguson, James. *Global Shadows: Africa in the Neoliberal World Order*. Durham, NC: Duke UP, 2006.

Forna, Aminatta. *Ancestor Stones*. New York: Grove, 2006.

———. *The Devil That Danced on the Water*. London: Harper, 2002.

Forsyth, Frederick. *The Biafra Story*. Baltimore, MD: Penguin, 1969.

Foucault, Michel. *Abnormal: Lectures at the Collège de France, 1974–1975*. 1999. Ed. Valerio Marchetti and Antonella Salomoni.Trans. Graham Burchell. New York: Picador, 2003.

———. *The Birth of Biopolitics: Lectures at the Collège de France, 1978–79*. Ed. Michel Senellart. Trans. Graham Burchell. New York: Palgrave, 2008.

———. *The History of Sexuality*. Trans. Robert Hurley. Vol. 1. New York: Vintage, 1988.

———. *Language, Counter-Memory, Practice*. Ed. Donald F. Bouchard. Trans. Donald F. Bouchard and Sherry Simon. Ithaca, NY: Cornell UP, 1977.

———. *Security, Territory, Population: Lectures at the Collège de France, 1977–78*. Ed. Michel Senellart. Trans. Graham Burchell. New York: Palgrave, 2007.

———. *Society Must Be Defended: Lectures at the Collège de France, 1975–76*. Ed. Mauro Bertani and Alessandro Fontana. 1997. Trans. David Macey. New York: Picador, 2003.

Fund for Peace, The. "Failed States Index Scores 2008." 2008. *Fund for Peace*. <http://www.fundforpeace.org/web/index.php?option=com_content&task=view&id=292&Itemid=452>.

———. "Methodology Behind CAST (Conflict Assessment System Tool)." 2006. *Fund for Peace*. <http://www.fundforpeace.org/web/index.php?option=com_content&task=view&id=107&Itemid=145>.

Gikandi, Simon. *Ngugi wa Thiong'o*. New York: Cambridge UP, 2000.

Golooba-Mutebi, Frederick. "Collapse, War, and Reconstruction in Uganda: An Analytical Narrative on State-Making." *Crisis States Working Papers Series No. 2*. London: London School of Economics, 2008. 1–26.

Habermas, Jürgen. *The Structural Transformation of the Public Sphere: An Inquiry into a Category of Bourgeois Society*. 1962. Trans. Thomas Burger and Frederick Lawrence. Cambridge, MA: MIT P, 1991.

Hardt, Michael. "The Withering of Civil Society." *Deleuze and Guattari: New Mappings in Politics, Philosophy, and Culture*. Ed. Eleanor Kaufman and Kevin Jon Heller. Minneapolis: U of Minnesota P, 1998. 23–39.

Hegel, G. W. F. *Philosophy of Right*. Trans. T. M. Knox. Oxford: Oxford UP, 1967.

Helman, Gerald B., and Steven P. Ratner. "Saving Failed States." *Foreign Policy* 89 (1992): 3–20.

Hitchcock, Peter. "Postcolonial Failure and the Politics of Nation." *South Atlantic Quarterly* 106 (2007): 727–52.

Ignatieff, Michael. "State Failure and Nation-Building." *Humanitarian Intervention: Ethical, Legal, and Political Dilemmas*. Ed. J. L. Holzgrefe and Robert O. Keohane. Cambridge: Cambridge UP, 2003. 299–321.

Ike, Chukwuemeka. *Sunset at Dawn*. London: Collins, 1976.

Isichei, Elizabeth. *A History of the Igbo People*. New York: St. Martin's, 1976.

Jameson, Fredric. "Third-World Literature in the Era of Multinational Capitalism." *Social Text* 15 (1986): 65–88.

Keen, David. "'Since I Am a Dog, Beware My Fangs': Beyond a 'Rational Violence' Framework in the Sierra Leonen War." *Crisis States Working Papers*. London: London School of Economics and Political Science, 2002. 1–22.

Kelman, James. *Translated Accounts*. New York: Doubleday, 2001.

Mamdani, Mahmood. "African States, Citizenship, and War: A Case-Study." *International Affairs* 78 (2002): 493–506.

———. "Blue-Hatting Darfur." *London Review of Books* 29.17 (2007): 18–20.

———. "Letters." *London Review of Books* 29.8 (2007): 4.

———. "The Politics of Naming: Genocide, Civil War, Insurgency." *London Review of Books* 29.5 (2007): 5–8.

Manto, Saadat Hasan. *Mottled Dawn*. Trans. Khalid Hasan. New Delhi: Penguin, 1997.

Meagher, Kate. "Hijacking Civil Society: The Inside Story of the Bakassi Boys Vigilante Group of South-Eastern Nigeria." *Journal of Modern African Studies* 45 (2007): 89–115.

Medovoi, Leerom. "Global Society Must Be Defended: Biopolitics without Boundaries." *Social Text* 25.2 (2007): 53–79.

Mo, Timothy. *The Redundancy of Courage*. London: Vintage, 1991.

Mufti, Aamir. *Enlightenment in the Colony*. Princeton, NJ: Princeton UP, 2007.

Mundy, Jacob A. "Performing the Nation, Pre-Figuring the State: The Western Saharan Refugees, Thirty Years Later." *Journal of Modern African Studies* 45 (2007): 275–97.

Naipaul, V. S. *A Bend in the River*. 1979. New York: Vintage, 1989.

Ngũgĩ, wa Thiong'o. *Petals of Blood*. London: Heinemann, 1977.

Nwapa, Flora. *Never Again*. 1975. Trenton, NJ: Africa World, 1992.

Ojakangas, Mika. "Impossible Dialogue on Bio-Power: Agamben and Foucault." *Foucault Studies* 2 (2005): 5–28.

Padamsee, Alex. "Uncertain Partitions: 'Undecidability' and the Urdu Short Story." *Wasafiri* 23.1 (2008): 1–5.

Pandey, Gyanendra. *Routine Violence: Nations, Fragments, Histories*. Stanford, CA: Stanford UP, 2006.

Peters, Krijn, and Paul Richards. "'Why We Fight': Voices of Youth Combatants in Sierre Leone." *Africa* 68 (1998): 183–210.

Putzel, James. "War, State Collapse, and Reconstruction: Phase 2 of the Crisis States Programme." *Crisis States Working Papers Series No. 2*. London: London School of Economics, 2005. 1–30.

Retort. *Afflicted Powers: Capital and Spectacle in a New Age of War*. New York: Verso, 2005.

Said, Edward. *Culture and Imperialism*. New York: Knopf, 1993.

Salih, Tayeb. *Season of Migration to the North*. Trans. Denys Johnson-Davis. Portsmouth, NH: Heinemann, 1969.

Saro-Wiwa, Ken. *Sozaboy*. 1985. New York: Longman, 1994.

Simons, Anna, and David Tucker. "The Misleading Problem of Failed States: A 'Socio-Geography' of Terrorism in the Post 9/11 Era." *Third World Quarterly* 28 (2007): 387–401.

Slaughter, Joseph R. "Enabling Fictions and Novel Subjects: The *Bildungsroman* and International Human Rights Law." *PMLA* 121 (2006): 1405–23.

State "Sanctioned" Kenyan Clashes. BBC 5 Mar. 2008. <http://news.bbc.co.uk/2/hi/africa/7279149.stm>.

Stevens, Jacob. "Prisons of the Stateless: The Derelictions of UNHCR." *New Left Review* 42 (2006): 53–67.

Stremlau, John J. *The International Politics of the Nigerian Civil War*. Princeton, NJ: Princeton UP, 1977.

Suleri, Sara. *The Rhetoric of English India*. Chicago: U of Chicago P, 1992.

Sylvester, Christine. "Bare Life as a Development/Postcolonial Problematic." *Geographical Journal* 172.1 (2006): 66–77.

Vera, Yvonne. *The Stone Virgins*. New York: Farrar, 2002.

West, Rebecca. *Black Lamb and Grey Falcon: A Journey through Yugoslavia*. New York: Viking, 1941.

Zaidi, S. Akbar. "A Failed State or Failure of Pakistan's Elite?" *Economic and Political Weekly* 12 July 2008: 10–11.

Zaman, Niaz. *A Divided Legacy: The Partition in Selected Novels of India, Pakistan, and Bangladesh*. New Delhi: Oxford UP, 2001.

Zartman, William. *Collapsed States*. Boulder, CO: Lynne Rienner, 1995.

Zeleza, Paul Tiyambe. *Manufacturing African Studies and Crises*. Dakar, Senegal: Codesria, 1997.

Žižek, Slavoj. *The Parallax View*. Cambridge, MA: MIT P, 2006.

ERIC KEENAGHAN

Life, War, and Love: The Queer Anarchism of Robert Duncan's Poetic Action during the Vietnam War

R obert Duncan would achieve national prominence as a featured poet in Donald Allen's anthology *The New American Poetry* (1960), which helped to establish him as one of the innovators of open-form poetics. But the politics underlying his poetics have largely been forgotten. Almost thirty years ago, Sherman Paul asked if it was possible to read Duncan as "writ[ing] the definitive politics of his time" (257). Such a reappraisal, Paul knew, would necessitate adjusting the common left-wing precepts about the relationship between poetry and politics. "There is another way of assessing his politics and coming to an understanding of what it means to be a political poet," Paul mused (262). What the critic leaves us, though, are merely clues about what that other understanding might be: Duncan's "defiance of domineering authority" (241); an early alignment with political anarchism (261); a "commitment to the Heraclitean principle of creative strife" (172); his inviting such strife into his life by "say[ing] 'yes' to eros" (227) so as to ward off an "oncoming, always ever-present death" (273). One factor mentioned by Paul—anarchism—has received little critical attention, but it could help synthesize the various elements of Duncan's poetics to account for his "definitive politics."[1] At its core, anarchism is a political philosophy opposing the

---

1. Allan Antliff (113–32) narrates Duncan's early association with James Cooney's anarchist circle in Woodstock, New York, and the aesthetic politics of the Libertarian Circle he founded with Philip Lamantia in 1946. Stephen Collis (*Phyllis Webb* 100–109)

Contemporary Literature XLIX, 4   0010-7484; E-ISSN 1548-9949/08/0004-0634
© 2008 by the Board of Regents of the University of Wisconsin System

sovereign state so as to promote greater freedom for all individuals. In Duncan's anarchistic philosophy, poetry is not a revolutionary's tool; rather, it is a creative means of striving toward an alternative vision of life, one rivaling the state's idea of what life ought to be.

Despite popular misconceptions, anarchism is founded upon creative, rather than destructive, modes of opposing the state. The nineteenth-century Russian anarchist Peter Kropotkin, one of Duncan's influences, described this creative emancipation as a rediscovery of what he termed "mutual aid," an evolutionary principle whereby living beings "find in association the best arms for the struggle for life" (242). The modern state, with its emphasis on profit and capitalist accumulation, encourages an unrelenting individualism that overshadows life's dependence on association. Creativity might help expose a forgotten groundwork for human collectivity wherein individuals act freely yet, because they cooperatively work together, do not interfere with others' liberties. Emma Goldman, a prominent American anarchist, sympathetically condoned acts of violence if the perpetrators found oppressive socioeconomic conditions "unbearable" because of their "sensitive natures" (92). Ultimately, however, she believed that the spirit of anarchy rested in cooperation as "a creative force," and that every element of experience is "a living force in the affairs of our life, constantly creating new conditions" (56, 63). Duncan's work from the 1960s and 1970s recirculates such anarchistic ideas about vitalist and creative resistance. In a 1969 installment of his serially published *H.D. Book*, he asserts, "As the power and presumption of authority by the State has increased in every nation, we are ill with it, for it surrounds us and, where it does not openly conscript, seeks by advertising, by education, by dogma or by terror, to seduce, enthrall, mould, command or coerce our inner will or conscience or inspiration to its own uses" (2.4: 47).[2] Duncan sees the state as more than a policy-making body that

---

reads Duncan's derivative poetics as part of his anarchistic commitment to publics and commonality; elsewhere he uses Duncan's challenge of linguistic property to ground a theory of "anarcho-scholasticism" (*Through Words*, esp. 9–26, 55–58). Robert J. Bertholf examines Duncan's split with Denise Levertov in light of the general principles informing the former's anarchism.

2. Duncan wrote *The H.D. Book* from 1961 until his death in 1988. The project was originally commissioned for H.D.'s birthday by Norman Holmes Pearson, her literary executor;

polices or conscripts its citizens. The state also attacks freedom through other means, including commercial markets, educational settings, and religious institutions. Much like Louis Althusser's notion of ideological state apparatuses—systems such as schools or the family that help form the capitalist state's ideological subjects— Duncan's ideas about social institutions cast them as responsible for consolidating a social illness. Unlike Althusser, though, Duncan believed that means other than revolution could provide an appropriate remedy: life could be reimagined.

Because art epitomizes the free individual's ability to reimagine the world, Duncan, like the English anarchist poet-philosopher Herbert Read before him, regarded it as the chief means of producing social health.[3] In 1969, Duncan described the poet as "striving to keep alive the reality of his art as revelation and inspiration of Truth or Beauty" while being "at odds with the dominant motives of profit and industry embodied in the society; for Communist and Capitalist alike the work of art is taken to be a commodity of social exchange" (*H.D.* 2.4: 47). Artists' struggle, then, lies in the fight to keep their work alive, thereby testifying to the realities obscured by ideologies operating in the state's interests. Poets should not fancy themselves revolutionaries or make self-interested ideological pronouncements; instead, they must recognize that "meaning is not given to the world about us but derived from the world about us, that our human language is a ground in which we participate in the cosmic language. Living is reading the message or poem that creation is about" (*H.D.* 2.4: 28). In the act of writing, poets venture outside state-prescribed meanings of ("about") life by extrapolating from the life around ("about") them a new sense with which they might "participate." This life-work redefines individualism by overriding a state-endorsed modern cult of personality and rediscovering an anarchistic utopia of association. "Our own dreams,

---

however, the "book" evolved into an extended study of interwar modernism and the relationship between war and poetry. *The H.D. Book* is divided into two parts ("Beginnings" and "Nights and Days"), and Duncan's revision for each constituent chapter is a palimpsest. In 1966 he began to serially publish the rewritten chapters in little magazines such as *Coyote's Journal*, *Caterpillar*, and *Credences*. A complete edited version is being prepared. My citations are to the chapters' first appearances. I note the part, chapter, and then page number.

3. See especially Read's "Poetry and Anarchism" (1938).

like our own lives, are fleeting and insubstantial," Duncan notes elsewhere in the *H.D. Book*, "unless they are delivered over from the personal into the commons of man's dream" (2.3: 146). This poetically discovered association is a "community of feeling" and "a new gain in consciousness" (147).

Today we can recognize how anarchism offers Duncan a language to think about modes of resistance in what Michel Foucault first described in his 1976 seminar as a "biopolitical" regime (*Society* 262–67). For Duncan, poetry introduces more vulnerable subjects who, through their passions, give themselves over to rereading the world. I describe this as a queer subject, whose queerness is not primarily owed to homosexuality. Indeed, Duncan distanced himself from gay minority. As he famously claimed in "The Homosexual in Society" (1944, 1959), one must "disown *all* the special groups (nations, churches, sexes, races) that would claim allegiance," so as to pursue instead "a devotion to human freedom, toward the liberation of human love, human conflicts, human aspirations" (47). The queerness of Duncan's anarchistic project, then, is derived from his impassioned desire to live more freely, to the fullest of his individual potential, while helping realize a commonality that runs counter to an overly prized atomism. Poetically producing such a queer vision of life was a struggle for Duncan, and some of his project's finer contradictions—such as the tension emerging between the free, desire-driven individual and the community—remain unresolved. As we shall see, he even attacked friends' work in the name of promoting a struggle that would favor his own individual and artistic growth. Despite these limits, though, his example can help us rearticulate current conceptions of biopolitics by foregrounding how poetry and desire play significant roles in resisting the state.

From an "Up Rising" to a Metapolitics

In his 1977–78 course Security, Territory, Population, Michel Foucault provocatively suggested, "maybe the state is only a composite reality and a mythicized abstraction whose importance is much less than we think. Maybe" (*Security* 109). For many, this prospect of a state we cannot identify, whether as a tangible oppressor or as a tangible benefactor, is disconcerting. Yet it is a hallmark of late anarchistic and libertarian thought. It is legible in Duncan's disavowal of the state's reality as the only reality; it also can be read in Guy Debord's theorization of the spectacle of late capitalist society. Debord was the most prominent figure from the Situationist International, a group of libertarian French social thinkers and artists who promoted free play and accident as a route to discovering the transformational politics of everyday life. Capitalism, he argues, "asserts that all human life, which is to say all social life, is mere appearance" and thus produces "a visible negation of life" (14). Such anticapitalist ideas influenced many who participated in the Paris May 1968 populist riots, a series of events that Julian Bourg notes as causing the "ethical turn" in Foucault's thought.[4] Indeed, Daniel Guérin reads Situationism's anarchistic influence in the oft-heard "magic word" in the Paris streets during the events of 1968: "self-management" (158). But even if the state is a mere appearance, its power rests in how the state manages the population by promoting consumption and sponsoring social spectacle; Foucault would explore that modality of power further. "What is important for our modernity, that is to say, for our present, is not then the state's takeover (*étatisation*) of society," Foucault argues, "so much as what I would call the 'governmentalization' of the state" (*Security* 109). Governmentality amounts to a biopolitical management of the population, which he summarily defined two years earlier as "State control of the biological" and the postmonarchical sovereign state's "right to make live and to let die" (*Society* 240, 241). The contemporary state's unreality owes to the fact that it is now more an administrative function than an executive body originating law. A biopolitical regime mandates that its people will live, but only under conditions that exclude or harm some.

With his concept of biopolitics, Foucault shifts the locus of "reality" so as to reopen questions about power and resistance. This chief concern is especially evident in the first volume of *The History of Sexuality* (1976). The final chapter, "Right of Death and Power over Life," incorporates conclusions from the Society Must Be Defended

---

4. Foucault treats "life" differently than the Situationists do, and new light could be thrown on Foucault's late concern with freedom and ethics by further exploring his implicit or explicit engagement of Situationism.

course lectures, which Foucault was also authoring at the time. The essay examines social and political power through the lens of the technologies of sex and sexuality. Again, reality is a central issue:

> We must not place sex on the side of reality, and sexuality on that of confused ideas and illusions; sexuality is a very real historical formation; it is what gave rise to the notion of sex, as a speculative element necessary to its operation....It is the agency of sex that we must break away from, if we aim—through a tactical reversal of the various mechanisms of sexuality—to counter the grips of power and the claims of bodies, pleasures, and knowledges, in their multiplicity and their possibilities of resistance.
>
> (*History* 157)

Unlike gay liberation and Front homosexuel d'action révolution-airre in the United States and France, respectively, Foucault did not believe that sex is a means of political resistance, an undoing of repressive traditions, ideologies, or legal proscriptions. Power is diffuse, and inequities are as much a product of its governmental distribution as they are of moralistic codification. One's energies would be misplaced, then, if one concentrated solely on revolting against a state apparatus. Instead, politics—including a sexual politics—should be directed against those processes to which the state has become a mere functionary in the name of managing life.

Foucault associated biopolitics with a *laissez-faire* paradigm that sustains capitalist economic forms and resultant distributive inequities. A (hetero)normative status quo is maintained through an administrative "game" that sets out to maintain the currently accepted order of things by "not interfering, allowing free movement, letting things follow their course" (*Security* 48). If the rules of the game are followed, the majority of the population should prosper, albeit at the expense of a dispensable few. What is more, the welfare and fortune such a biopolitical strategy secures allows for only a rather limited—even illusory—mobility and freedom. Populations can be administered because the majority of individuals deploy strategies for narrating their selves that let them cling to, and continuously defend, secure forms of identity and privacy. The resulting freedom is very limited, however, since it is tied to and circumscribed by the *state*, insofar as it relies on a stable or *static* identity that can be *statistically* measured. As Foucault reminds us, etymologically, *statistics* means "science of the state" (*Security* 101).

Statistical systems and logics reduce freedom, what is by nature unpredictable, to a set of probabilities that can be tracked and predicted. The freedom associated with liberalist individualism, then, is a highly conditioned agency that is recognizable and predictable because individuals function through an identificatory moniker (or intersection of monikers) chosen from available identities and market niches that let them and their respective group be administered and statistically assessed. Foucault dubbed this entire apparatus "liberalism."

For my purposes, though, it is necessary to extricate Foucault's concept of liberalism from his reductively economic, *laissez-faire* definition.[5] Instead, I translate into his biopolitical frame John Dewey's understanding of liberalism—an understanding that may very well have influenced Duncan, who regarded Dewey as sharing William James's distinction of offering a "new testament" about truth, freedom, and consciousness (*H.D.* 1.1: 23).[6] In the pragmatist's framework, liberalism is a historically variable articulation of the democratic ideal of strong individualism. Since the eighteenth century, it has been a matter of natural right to regard individuals as the bearers of certain key qualities: an inviolable integrity, absolutist and atomistic agency, and, most of all, contained privacy. During the Progressive era, capitalistic forces of big business and imperialist enterprises appropriated and deradicalized the earlier liberal thought of John Locke, John Stuart Mill, and Jeremy Bentham. Dewey wished to restore the lost spirit of philosophical liberalism, regarding it as a "radical" strategy for "re-forming, in its literal sense, the institutional scheme of things" (*Liberalism* 66). To do so, though, meant he had to redefine individuality in such a way that the concept is unrecognizable. Individuals are never wholly individuated, never atomistic. They are always partly social. In his late essay "The Crisis in Human History" (1946), Dewey goes so far as to

---

5. For Foucault's extended thinking about biopolitics as linked to and growing out of *laissez-faire* economic regulation of the state, see *Naissance de la biopolitique*.

6. Elsewhere Duncan describes Dewey as an inheritor of William James's pluralistic sense of life, a "sense that What Is is multifarious" (*H.D.* 2.5: 42). Duncan was attracted to the compatibility of anarchism and pragmatism, evident in James's own characterization of the pragmatist as "a happy-go-lucky anarchistic sort of creature" (21, 124).

say that the word *individual* is not a noun but an adjective describing only half of humanity's experience (211). He argues that humans' social nature is a function of language and communication, which condition us and connect us to one another. Because it embodies the individual's irrevocable ties to community, language can serve as the means for increasing freedom by introducing individuals to new associations.

Only life is capable of being individually experienced and collectively shared, even if only through language's mediations. Since this is the case, living differently is a strategy of political opposition to state-mandated ways of life. These conclusions frame Duncan's idea of the sort of political resistance that poetry might offer. Such an understanding of politics, though, is bound to cause a crisis for the liberal- or progressive-minded, whose humanitarianism often equates politics with a preservation of human dignity and thus implicitly idealizes the supposedly untouchable sanctity of private personhood.[7] Duncan struggled to extricate himself from such liberalist language and logics, which not only informed the political hegemony of the day but also the terms of New Left opposition in the 1960s. Poetry, he believed, was an especially useful discursive praxis for reimagining freedom and commonality, outside the biopolitical state's liberalist life model. We can date the start of his earnest struggle to produce such a new idea of political action from 1965. At that time, controversy surrounded the appearance of a particularly inflammatory poem of his in *The Nation*, for which Duncan's friend Denise Levertov was poetry editor.

The Nation had a long-standing reputation as a liberal venue, but the poetry it usually featured could be read as resisting any political reading. In the September 1965 centennial issue, Alexander Laing commends Levertov for her "editorial arrangements." As he narrates it, her efforts recall the magazine's heyday in the 1920s, when poetry editor Mark Van Doren popularized Edna St. Vincent Millay, Edwin Arlington Robinson, and Edgar Lee Masters's poetry but published only the prose of Ezra Pound, a decision that in Laing's

---

7. On the privatizing nature of humanitarian ideals, see Alain Badiou's *Ethics* and, in relation to a biopolitical analysis, Slavoj Žižek's "From Politics to Biopolitics . . . and Back."

terms seemed to leave poetry unaffected by politics yet allowed a poet *some* political voice. By organically weaving her selections into the issues, Levertov, like her predecessors, demonstrates that poetry is "something more than a convenient spatter of type to fill out a column after the prose is all used up." Laing wonders, though: "Politics? Still present, but unobtrusive, as in some of [Wendell] Berry's poems. They already sing, a little, in the depths of the brain." As long as politics remains a sonorous mental hum rather than an interruptive theme, Levertov's selections successfully promote a "kind of newness" while avoiding the more "transient" strands of aggressive politics he associates with the Beats' work (218). Even as *The Nation*'s journalism was explicitly aligned with an emergent New Left in the mid-1960s, its poetic publication recalled earlier editors' lukewarm critiques of the cold war. Historian Robert R. Tomes notes that the magazine's predominant editorial position between 1953 and 1964, though critical, failed to contest "the basic principles of liberal ideals," namely staunch anticommunism and advocacy of strong individualism (103). Notwithstanding the irony that Levertov herself would become a well-known antiwar poet-activist, Laing's impressions about her editorial efforts' continuation of that past moment ring true. Not only did she publish liberal lyricists such as Berry, but the work she included by more experimental writers, such as Robin Blaser, skirted thematic radicalism.

The exception to Laing's narrative was published only one installment before *The Nation*'s centennial issue. Toward the back of the September 13, 1965 issue, right before the crossword, split between the penultimate facing pages (146–47), Duncan's controversial "Up Rising" first appeared in print.[8] Duncan and Levertov had been friends, correspondents, and avid supporters of one another's work since 1953. It is no surprise that she requested a poem from Duncan; and given their common involvement in antiwar activism, it's not surprising that she liked his submission. Unlike many of Levertov's other selections and most of Duncan's own work, "Up Rising" is an unrestrained and venomous condemnation of the Johnson administration for taking military action against North Vietnam. Reading

---

8. I cite "Up Rising" from *Bending the Bow* (81–83). It also appeared with minor changes in the unpaginated chapbook *Of the War*. I preserve Duncan's idiosyncratic spelling.

the letters Levertov sent to Duncan just before and after the poem's appearance, we can see that it was a coup for her and then-literary editor Grandin Conover to get "Up Rising" into *The Nation*'s pages. On September 1, she urged Duncan not to worry about not reviewing proofs; the haste was due to the "conspiracy" she and Conover were conducting "to make damn sure the poem doesn't get killed by someone" (Duncan and Levertov, *Letters* 507). Since this would be Conover's last issue, such a "kill[ing]" was sure to happen if it were not published immediately. On October 30, Levertov wrote to Duncan that the publisher, George Kirstein, "almost flipped his lid over Conover's conspiring with me to print it but [Carey] McWilliams [the editor-in-chief] stood up for it and Kirstein backed down" (515). If her colleague hadn't been leaving already, she intimates, it's likely that he would have been fired.

Why was "Up Rising" so volatile? In part, its subject matter. The poem opens with an unequivocal indictment of the head of the U.S. state for substituting military intervention for international diplomacy. That decision is likened to a form of totalitarianism:

> Now Johnson would go up to join the great simulacra of men,
> > Hitler and Stalin, to work his fame
> > with planes roaring out from Guam over Asia,
> all America become a sea of toiling men
> > > stirrd at his will, which would be a bloated thing,
> > > drawing from the underbelly of the nation
> > > such blood and dreams as swell the idiot psyche
> > > out of its courses into an elemental thing
> > > until his name stinks with burning meat and heapt honors

Duncan's repeated emphasis on the individual "name" and "will" of President Johnson underscores his blatant criminalization of the administration's wartime actions by associating the president with the likes of Hitler and Stalin. Indeed, this "bloated" and monstrous volition has the power not only to manipulate the nation's population but to displace it: the people lose their individuated bodies as they are amassed into "a sea of toiling men." The oceanic metaphor sets the nation and this mob adrift, lacking claim to a national ground upon which they may plant their feet. Rather, laboring under another's will, the crowd is focused on the "underbelly," what lies beneath or on the flip side of the ground supporting them.

As if they were drilling for oil, they extract from the land its "blood and dreams." This physical and ideational operation results in a rancid atmosphere, wherein one state figure's "honors" are noxiously inflected by the smell of the "burning meat" the people have laid upon his altar.

The incendiary scene spreads globally in the second stanza, as "men wake to see that they are used like things / spent in a great potlatch, this Texas barbecue / of Asia, Africa, and all the Americas." Although Duncan wrote "Up Rising" with no foreknowledge of the other contents of this particular issue of *The Nation*, his lyric extends the concerns in Charles W. Tait's featured article "Whatever Happened to the State Department?" which similarly condemns the policy of settling ideological disputes with military force (138). The three geopolitical sites that Duncan notes are specified by Tait as evidence of U.S. policy's recent failures: the sponsoring of Belgian paratroopers dropped in Stanleyville, Republic of Congo; the bombing of North Vietnam; and the invasion of the Dominican Republic (137). Duncan connects the infernal reification of U.S. labor to the conflagrations of imperialist wars abroad. Those Americans who are fortunate enough to "wake" from this nightmare can establish enough distance between themselves and it so as to claim responsibility for contributing, through their labor, to "the burning of homes and the torture of mothers and fathers and children, / their hair a-flame, screaming in agony." Taking responsibility allows sympathy to develop. There is no room for victimization or innocence here: aggressor and attacked are bound together at the destruction of the most intimate of sites, their home spaces.

Duncan's gruesome wartime fantasia explicitly invokes William Blake's and D. H. Lawrence's visionary writing ("As Blake saw America in figures of fire and blood raging," "the ravening eagle of America / as Lawrence saw him"), and he would later cite these passages as evidence that "Up Rising" is a visionary rather than propagandistic piece. Yet when read in light of *The Nation*'s own political journalism, it is difficult to argue that the poem sublimates politics into myth at all, let alone into a pleasant intellectual sonorousness that Laing would appreciate. Rather, it's easy to see how Duncan's named attack on Johnson and Barry Goldwater as "this black bile of old evils arisen anew," "corrupt[ing] the very body of the nation" would worry a Laing or a Kirstein. At this turning point in *The Nation*'s relationship to radical politics, its journalism was only beginning to broach strong criticisms of state policies. Ironically enough, Duncan had not tread such politicized poetic terrain before. Much to his consternation, many readers did not see "Up Rising" as visionary. His anarchism seemed to have resulted in a hyperbolically individualist revolutionary poem, violently and destructively inveighing against the state. Donald Hutter, his editor at Scribner's, wanted to cut "Up Rising" and other polemical pieces from the collection *Bending the Bow* (1968), leading Duncan to tell Levertov, "This one ["Up Rising"] has all along been a stumbling block" (*Letters* 573). "Up Rising" and "Soldiers" had been collected in the provocatively titled chapbook *Of the War* (1966), with an inflammatory cover photograph of a half-undressed body being dragged behind a tank. Referring to prominent poetry figures in the Bay Area, Duncan described how these poems, along with "The Multiversity," "were completely rejected by Blaser and the Spicerean circles as examples of bad verse and the public corruption of my verse" (*Letters* 573). After Duncan attacked her antiwar poetry in 1971 as mirroring the state's "totalitarian" logic (*Letters* 673), Levertov pointed to "Up Rising" as proof that when he rationalized his poetic engagement with the war as an apolitical metaphysics, he engaged in mere "doubletalk and evasion" (*Letters* 679).

The controversy surrounding "Up Rising" resulted, for Duncan, in a year-long writing block, which would lift only in July 1966. Duncan's production was stalled because he was "[w]aiting for the content of 'Up Rising' to undergo its sea change or alchemical phase towards rendering up its purely poetic identity" (Duncan, *Letters* 528). In other words, he was waiting for that poem's content to become, of its own accord, something more than an occasional political piece. But that "alchemy" did not happen on its own. Duncan arduously worked toward articulating a poetics that could intervene in prevailing imaginaries about the life of the nation and its citizens, a route commensurate with an analysis of the state's biopolitical power. What was most at issue was how poetry might establish new understandings of communality. Despite its inflammatory rhetoric beholden to a liberalist cult of personality, "Up Rising" is staked in the very definition of communality. Hence the narrator's rant against state figureheads charts the possibility of individuals awakening so as to disidentify with a formless population laboring under the will of a totalitarian administrator. It is unclear from this poem how such an individual consciousness rises up, but the result is clear—identification with a communality represented by the occupants of those foreign homes destroyed, as Duncan writes, "in terror and hatred of all communal things, of communion, of communism."

One year after "Up Rising" appeared in *The Nation*, a letter from Duncan to Levertov described their shared literary work as part of "the eternal communal experience." Fostering such communality meant poets had to step outside an easy equation of lyric with personal expression; instead, they had to cultivate lyric as an impersonal force and a collective effort at what his letter invokes as "participation." "We labor to make the War *real*," he writes to Levertov, "to make it really happen so that it will speak to us. As we labor to realize life. If we did not so labor we would not, I suppose, experience fear or wrath, our reactions as its reality grows" (Duncan, *Letters* 540). Rather than as a transparent expression of his own antiwar politics, Duncan encourages us to read the outrage or wrath of "Up Rising" as a product of its writing, a community's reaction to the reality of a war in the process of becoming real only as it trickles down from the level of the state to the level of the people. Making the war real through communal poetic endeavors is to partake in the exercise of producing new forms of life, outside the state-endorsed American way of life that idealizes individual personhood.

From Duncan's perspective, then, poetic radicalism cannot inhere in the modes of personal politics and direct action beloved by the then-emergent New Left. As he would warn Levertov when she immersed herself in the antiwar movement, "the monstrosity of this nation's War is taking over your life" (*Letters* 563). The state impinged upon the individual, forcing her to voice her resistance with the same language that the state itself promoted—that of personality and personhood, privacy and privation, property and propriety. Robert Kaufman cogently asserts that Duncan develops an aesthetic politics revolving around "a commitment to the nothing that is in fact the yet-to-be-determined," an engagement with political and ethical possibilities as they present themselves through poetic form and language (118). Art's ability to present such future possibilities is the extent of the action of which it is capable; nonetheless, such lyric action is politicized because of its close association with "the register of experience, of *life*" (102). Duncan attempts to move away from a liberal personal politics toward what Alain Badiou terms a "metapolitics," a meditation on the possibilities of truths that break with prevailing political paradigms. "Doing politics cannot be distinguished from thinking politics," as Badiou puts it (*Metapolitics* 46). Such thinking or, in Duncan's case, such writing constitutes "a subjectification of subjectification," an analysis of our identity as citizens once we're committed to realizing a different political imaginary and way of life (48).

It is dubious, though, whether "Up Rising" itself privileges life over the person. Duncan's attack on the state in that poem seems to demonstrate an egoistic "inflation," as Nathaniel Mackey characterizes it (75).[9] The impetus of Duncan's later work, then, would be to highlight the creative aspect of anarchistic revolution; instead of egoistically pronouncing an uprising against the state, poetry would need to turn consciousness about life wholly away from a biopolitical paradigm. Duncan would change the antagonist of the individual's struggle. No longer would he attack the state and society; instead, he would engage his own self. Anarchistic struggles against biopolitical regimes are internalized, and, for Duncan, that contributes to the particular potency of poetry as an instrument of political action. By opening ourselves to language's sentimental force, we foster an intimacy that lets the truth of the situation, what Badiou terms the "real," disrupt our acceptance of an American way of life and cult of personality prescribed and administered by the state.

The Queer Anarchism of a Life at War

Perhaps as a result of the contradictory weight that anarchism places on both individual freedom and the life of the collectivity,

---

9. Mackey recontextualizes "Up Rising" as a confessional, rather than protest, poem (119–24). Duncan's egoistic rage, he argues, evinces the poet's attachment to imperialist economies and so provides a kind of accountability missing from much antiwar poetry (119–24).

Duncan would never quite escape the inflationary and egoistic quality of his strong individualism. His ardent belief in the individual's independence would cause him to eventually break not only with Levertov but also with Robin Blaser, a friend and fellow member of his poetic coterie during the San Francisco Renaissance of the 1950s. Ostensibly, the dispute with Blaser (as with Levertov) was entirely poetic. The issue here was not the writer's using poetry to advance a particular political perspective, however. Rather, Duncan disapproved of Blaser's careless diction in his translations of Gérard de Nerval. The personal and poetic conflict that transpired evinces Duncan's evolving strategy to anarchistically maintain his own freedom to evolve as an artist, to strive for a new vision of life; he must struggle with himself, but first that necessitates struggling with those closest to him.

In a letter dated April 23, 1966, shortly after "Up Rising" appeared in *The Nation*, Duncan wrote to Blaser: "In order to imagine your poetics...I set my translation of *Les Chimères* at war with your version. Raising ideas out of the heat of battle" ("Returning" 60). His militaristic figures are no coincidence. For much of the letter, Duncan details how his sense of "war" does not merely oppose Blaser's poetic decisions. Opposition was actually the political problem Duncan sought to redress: "At this very time in history when a maddened administration, an ego-maniacal president, and a State Department of conspirators and traitors to international order are laying waste [to] Viet-Nam and plotting in Africa, South America and Asia against governments, in the name of the opposition of capitalism and communism, taking over the terms Marx gave to history as a thesis and antithesis, I should rightly be wary of the war of opposites and should seek the synthesis or syntony [*sic*] of ideas rather than the antithesis" ("Returning" 61). The U.S. adoption of containment strategies following the Marshall Plan era was not just a shift in state ideology or foreign policy; it also inaugurated an epoch overrun by a binaristic "with us or against us" mentality. The cultural majority suspected disagreement or variation from the norm as foreclosing a promised unanimity. To facilely oppose the current order of things, then, was to remove oneself from the national community.

Even if simple opposition were inadequate for critiquing the state, strife, Duncan intuited, still was necessary for poetry to act.

Consequently, he rejected summary dismissals of war as bad, of all conflict as undesirable. Rather than locating opposition between groups and parties as the state and mainstream American culture did, though, Duncan's approach turned his self into the object of strife. It is what kept the individual from buying into an easy equation of democratic individualism with the coherent, knowable individual who gravitates toward like-minded individuals to form a homogeneous American way of life. In his late essay "The Self in Postmodern Poetry" (1979), Duncan wrote that he lived by the tenet "mistrust thy self," a perversion of Emerson's "Self-Reliance." "All of experience seems my trust fund to me; I must cultivate the mistrust that alone can give contrast and the needed inner tension for vital interest" (226). Another way of putting this would be, *One must war not with others but with one's own self*. Life bears intellectual and material benefits only if one "cultivate[s]" a "tension" with one's own experience.

When describing this tension, Duncan deploys a term that I read as crucial to his poetic: *contrast*. "War" or conflict of any kind—whether with nations, other persons, or one's own self—is the process whereby the "intellect seeks to transform *conflicting* elements into *contrasting* elements" ("Returning" 61; emphasis added). Reading this differentiation through Alfred North Whitehead's *Process and Reality* (1929), Duncan stipulates that a desirably contrastive transformation "could never be set into action if elements were conceived as things in themselves complete. So, I see my creative imagination raising a war in things in order to come into the world of opposites and contraries. . . . For, until we see the elements in their dynamic strife, as contraries, we cannot begin to transform contraries into contrasts" (61). Such dynamism, once restored to oppositional elements, would let Duncan rediscover what he calls the "aliveness" of things, in their pluralistic and incomplete natures. "Here, as in physics," he continues, "the difference between the inorganic and the organic, the *bios*, is that between a crystallized form and a form of unresolved inner struggle" (61). Perpetual, internal struggle is the only way we know we're alive. For poetry to help us live, writers must continually combat their precepts and reinterpret their experiences to avoid static—and statist—complacency.

Two years after publicly waging war with Blaser, Duncan further refined his ideas about conflict. No longer would he charge the poet with engaging an abstract *bios*; instead, one must specifically attack one's own way of life, as it is mediated and defined by a wartime state. Duncan developed these ideas most fully in his keynote address for Central Washington State College's Seventh Annual Symposium on American Values, which would be published the next year as the lengthy essay "Man's Fulfillment in Order and Strife" (1969). He described this lecture to Levertov as an opportunity to think about an alternative resistance to the state, apart from a revolutionary "change of the government" (*Letters* 609). What he imagined instead was a kind of "Robin Hood or guerilla existence," a strategic mode of living whose aim "is not how to win but how to keep alive." Essentially, that survivalist mentality relies upon a preservation of "the individual volition, the unsacrificed inner volition" (*Letters* 609). The more Duncan struggled to articulate how poetry acts politically, the more he reappraised commonsense notions of liberal individualism. Consequently, the political will he imagines in his 1968 speech is unlike the oppositional and combative personal politics espoused by various branches of the New Left.

"Man's Fulfillment" immediately likens poetic conflicts to political war. Those conflicts are consolidated into particular positions, poetic camps, and alliances that deafen the participants to the very possibilities poetry bears: "Each of us must be at strife with our own conviction on behalf of the multiplicity of convictions at work in poetry in order to give ourselves over to the art, to come to the idea of what the world of worlds or the order of orders might be" (111–12). This turmoil, to which one consciously and willingly subjects one's self, is a means of "carry[ing] into the public field the inner battles of the individual poet's soul" (112). Contention, war, strife—they transform privacy into publicity; they break the wall whereby the liberal American subject safeguards her own self. Duncan also insists that the writer has a duty to make sure that this war continues: "The very life of our art is our keeping at work contending forces and convictions," no matter if they do prove to be "painful disorders." It is a "creative strife," this "breaking up the orders I belong to in order to come into alien orders." This aesthetic obligation is utterly ethical, a testament to the poet's social responsibility.

Duncan writes of his admiration of Robert Browning's dramatic lyric: "Against the private property of self, he created a community of selves, taking existence in other times and place, other lives, other persons" (113). This community facilitates the writer's development of "*conscience*," which "lies in the depth and wholeness of his involvement in the work where it is" (114). Such "involvement"—in both the senses of "participation" (another recurrent word) and of "folding" (as in the author's invagination into the text)—precipitates what Duncan terms "a crisis in language and world," not a consolidation of one's opinion about either (114). Such disruptions permit the poet to move away, albeit painfully, from an undisciplined, flattened language practice promoting ideological ends that cut him off from life, other persons, and other nations. Duncan fears that "we are in such a perversion of government that no man who means good can be a good citizen. If our manner of speech has come, as it has, to be so much a cover that for the sake of freedom men are drafted against their will; for the sake of peace, armed men and tanks fight in our streets; and for the sake of the good life, the resources of our land are ruthlessly wasted, and waterways and air polluted, then we need a new manner of speaking" (119). Poetry and the crises it provokes promote not only "a new manner of speaking" but also a new experience of *government*. That is to say, if poetry's contrasts expose life's pluralism and experience's possibilities, then they also open new fields of conduct which minimize the discrepancy between longing for a human good and being a good citizen.

The crisis at the heart of Duncan's Vietnam-era poetic is summed up in the following sentence: "All national allegiances—my own order as an American—seemed to be really betrayals of the larger order of Man" (115). If we are not open to the multiple possibilities language awakens us to, if we choose the nation-state and its way of speaking over the other possibilities presented by poetry and its inwardly and outwardly conflicted authors, we lack the resources to productively contrast Americans' liberalist understanding of personhood as private, bourgeois, and propertied, as well as proper and proprietary. We opt to become like President Johnson, who, in "reading a script rationalizing his monstrous actions, written by a public relations agent, is dehumanized by a mediating language" (138). If we read poetry, rather than a propagandistic script, we have a better chance of encountering "an other speech"; our new linguistic contacts reintroduce us to our selves. Alienated and altered, we find ourselves "belonging to the process of the Cosmos," not to the "progress" lauded by modernity and Western nations (123, 114).

By appropriating the disagreeable statist policy of war as his primary metaphor, Duncan ends up offering a contrastive concept challenging the militaristic paradigm shared by the Vietnam-era U.S. state and its countercultural resisters. But if the antiwar poetry he disdained was also interested in exposing the war's dehumanizing nature in the name of life, then we can attribute the distinctiveness of his resistant vitalist poetic to one element. Antiwar poets closely associated their bodies with their texts. This "Vietnam-era oppositional politics of corporeality," as Michael Bibby calls it (5), imagined agency existentially. "[B]odies were imagined as 'sites' of ideological struggle," where integral agents opposed the state (14). But Duncan's work compels us to ask a different question: if one's embodied life is the very *subject* of struggle (rather than the site from which one struggled), and if poetry is an extension of that strife, could one rebuild the terms of universal communality not only more effectively but also much more *affectively*? Rather than asking his readers to sympathize or identify with him, Duncan wars with his own and readers' sensibilities. To will such a war, one must recognize how linguistic and embodied experience is desirous. Perversely, this kind of war—wherein the author's and the reader's bodies are on the line, read in the lyric's own lines—is a queer form of political seduction.

Work remains to be done to think through Duncan's resistance to gay-liberation politics, or even their shared anti-imperialist perspectives and suspicions of the heteronormativity of antiwar and other New Left movements.[10] The queerness I associate with Duncan's

---

10. In 1969, activist Allen Young wrote that gay liberation shared with the New Left a "common enemy in U.S. imperialism." However, queers were forced to the sidelines in this battle. "[T]he onus is on the straight movement to deal with its sexism," Young charges (24). Liberationists believed the chief ills of the country were sexism and straightness, which the Gay Liberation Party Manifesto (1970) defines as "the systematic channeling of human expression into various basically static social institutions and roles" (342). Antiwar movements failed to redress the relation between the state's imperialist policies and static gender and sexual norms.

poetic anarchism, then, is related to the emphasis he places on how eroticism facilitates subjects' resistance to the liberalist attitudes promoted by the biopolitical state. Whereas many gay and lesbian thinkers and activists promoted sex and eroticism as a means of resisting the state, Duncan was preoccupied with how language is an erotic vehicle mediating embodied experience and promoting transformative passions. In 1968, the same year Duncan delivered "Man's Fulfillment in Order and Strife," *TriQuarterly* published two installments of his *H.D. Book* that crucially elaborate the queer dimensions of his anarchistic resistance to biopolitics. To conduct his chief enterprise of narrating "the fiction of what Man is," "the would-be poet stands like Psyche *in the dark*, taken up in a marriage with a genius, possessed by a spirit outside the ken of those about him" (*H.D.* 1.3: 67, 68). Alienated from his "ken," the male poet cross-identifies with his gendered mythic other and imagines himself as "possessed" and "married" to a force that dispossesses him of himself. As in the classic myth, Eros is that husband:

> We are drawn to Him, but we must also gather Him to be. We cannot, in the early stages, locate Him; but He finds us out. Seized by His orders, we "fall in love," in order that He be; and in His duration the powers of Eros are boundless. We are struck by His presence, and in becoming lovers we become something other than ourselves, subjects of a daemonic force previous to our humanity.
>
> (69)

Through eroticism, liberalist fictions of personhood are undone. Vulnerability, becoming undone by an otherness that augments us, is necessary, though risky, for telling the tale of the human differently.

Duncan's erotic scenario posits a bifurcated schema: one facet of desire is resolutely heteronormative in its structure (though it can be homosexual in its content), and one is more resolutely queer. Duncan narrates desire's dual nature through the myth of Eros's birth from the Titan Kronos's castration of his father, the demiurge Uranus. With this "act," a "transformation" occurs. The sign of "the Father" becomes a triumvirate: "the goddess Aphrodite or Beauty where his penis was, and the attendant gods, Eros and Himeros, where his testicles were" (*H.D.* 1.3: 70). Duncan uses myth to imagine the birth of eroticism, Venusian beauty, and what he terms "desire" as the transformative forces simultaneously unleashed by aesthetic production. In his reckoning, this helps us understand the artist's duty differently. If we read the Titans' insurrection against nature's primordial forces as the primeval introduction of strife into life, this revolutionary moment—which generates art alongside love and desire—is also the beginning of politics. That is to say, the *polis* is born in the act of rescripting masculinity so that it no longer embodies the patriarchal state. Thereafter, poets have been obliged to repeat this act, to be transformed by marrying Eros, as Psyche had done. But when they surrender to life's erotic forces, they actually submit to "Eros *and his other* [Himeros]," to the twins of a love we can know and a desire described as "the unknowing" (*H.D.* 1.3: 71, 72; emphasis added).

Poets thus engage a political imaginary by resuscitating desire's twin face through a double marriage to homoerotic "love" and allo-erotic (or himerotic) "desire." Such engagement is predicated upon passion, an affect and passivity akin to Psyche's surrender to the temptation to look at her husband's body. Because politics is born from an irresistible seduction, Duncan does not speak of writers as Romantic agents realizing their will through authorship; instead, writers are, first and foremost, readers. In reading we are most vulnerable, or open, to desire's unknowing nature and thus to language's politically transformative force. Repeating themes from "Man's Fulfillment," Duncan insists: "We have begun to find our identity not in a personality but in a concept of Man, so that all the variety of persons Man has been may be inhabitants of what we are as we impersonate us. In Poetry,... the mask comes to reveal the poet's inner self..." (*H.D.* 1.4: 85). Our own identities are matters of approximation, "impersonat[ing]" others' images of who we are, not as individuals but as representatives of human commonality. To become human, we first must opt to become inhuman, to lose our selves and give ourselves over to language's agency by donning poetry's estranging masks.

Poetry therefore obliquely restores human agency to politics, which Duncan reconceives as politicized passion: "What we follow is enacting the role of Isis in reading or writing, for we must search and gather what we are searching for as we do so" ("Two Parts" 98). Just as Isis must collect and reassemble her husband Osiris's dismembered body, readers are charged with collecting and re-membering a desire deemed irreconcilably other. This process has implications for the relation between the citizen and the state. Duncan writes that once "[w]e had seen, pure and simple, our Osiris or Christos or resurrection, in the vision of a communist soci-ety that was also the vision of a free society—'a voluntary state,' Vanzetti called it." But that vision of a life that gives equal attention to individualism and commonality—a vision Duncan significantly associates with Bartolomeo Vanzetti, an anarchist martyr—has been disrupted by the ideological dogmas of the cold war: "In the dark-ness of communist doctrine, the individual volition is denied, and the Communist Party is substituted for the commune; in the dark-ness of capitalist-democratic doctrine, the communal goods are denied, and the mass-man is substituted for the individual" (98). It is here that queer life has political work to do: "And those of us who saw and acknowledged came into a work or quest: to gather up out of the darkness of democracy and communism the thing we saw. It was the new Adam. It was the new Eros that Psyche saw" (98). The mythopoetic strains of Duncan's queer vitalism evince his own search for past texts, past stories, to narrate an impersonal political possibility. That impersonal, eroticized appeal to other narratives does not forget the state or the writer's present political conditions.

Duncan struggles with the state's definition of life, which—as in the "Empire" of early Christendom—had banished the himerotic to "the margins where things mix" (H.D. 1.3: 77). By opening himself to the possibilities of impersonality offered by language through others' writing, he seeks to reintroduce love's banished twin, desire, into the American Empire so as to make it more of a Queer Nation. This dynamic does more than invite the outside in, more than liber-ally give a place at the proverbial table to the excluded and margin-alized. Rather, it rewrites the life of the community by shifting the whole into that marginal space of difference. To write is "to recall the Palace of Eros," Duncan writes elsewhere in The H.D. Book (1.6: 132). Recalling or remembering is not simply a mnemonic act: it calls into being a lost space or, as in the myth of Isis and Osiris, it reconstitutes bodies. In this material space or body of the queerly re-called national communality, we overcome what Duncan terms the "intense solitude" reinforced by liberalism's flattened ideologies of individualism, entering instead a "communal consciousness" grounded in disidentification (131). This queer nationalism is a process of establishing cosmopolitanism that begins when we set pen to paper or pick up a book, those acts through which we find ourselves "leaving the mother-land or father-land of the national state and entering a Mother-land of an international dream" (132). In sum, poetry's political act begins when we let the written word we have gathered seduce us, when we let the page lure us into a global, communal life that has not yet come to pass. Such beginnings are endings, too; for when we accept them, we also embrace the termination of our fealty to the state, at least for the duration of reading and writing, and instead think in terms of the life of the world. To embrace such an attitude is always painful. Finding one's self necessitates declaring war on the only life, on the only nation and self, one has ever known.

The order of life toward which language impels us pushes us beyond the human, as that entity is defined by the liberal state, as *bios*. The subject then can be treated ecologically, as tied bodily to her setting's human and nonhuman objects. Such a rethinking of subjectivity goes against the grain of received notions, so much so that Rosi Braidotti argues that "[t]he potency of [understanding] *zoē* as the defining trait of the subject displaces the unitary vision of consciousness and the sovereignty of the 'I'" (265). Robert Duncan's poetics makes us more aware of the points of contact between the two sides of life, *zoē* and *bios*. Language and discourse—too frequently believed to be on the side of the "human," of *bios*—are not just expressive tools. They are subject to evolution, and thus they participate in the *inhuman* universe, in *zoē*. Language, conveying the forces of a disruptive himerotic desire rather than a humanitarian erotic love, opens the zone wherein humanity is both human and inhuman. When subjects live in that zone, they can become *homo sacer*, a condition of expendable animality that Giorgio Agamben has described as resulting in victimization and sacrifice. However, Duncan's Vietnam-era writings exemplify that when human life shades over into the realm of *zoē*, a death sentence doesn't necessarily result; rather, such moments also can change how the world is ordered. Living in an intimate, conflict-laden fashion with language, surroundings, and neighbors can serve as a means of letting ourselves be led outside biopolitical "realities," into new pluralities via our desires. Certainly, Duncan's anarchistic project does have its limits: it causes him to attend too much to his own freedom and to insist too forcefully on strife; it costs him friendships and so threatens to alienate him from commonality. Notwithstanding these limits, though, his project also demands a promising revaluation of literature's political agency and its ability to contribute to the imagining and creation of new ways of life.

State University of New York at Albany

WORKS CITED

Agamben, Giorgio. *Homo Sacer: Sovereign Power and Bare Life.* 1995. Trans. Daniel Heller-Roazen. Stanford, CA: Stanford UP, 1998.

Allen, Donald, ed. *The New American Poetry, 1945–1960.* 1960. Berkeley: U of California P, 1999.

Althusser, Louis. "Ideology and Ideological State Apparatuses (Notes towards an Investigation)." 1969. *Lenin and Philosophy and Other Essays.* Trans. Ben Brewster. New York: Monthly Review, 1971. 127–86.

Antliff, Allan. *Anarchy and Art: From the Paris Commune to the Fall of the Berlin Wall.* Vancouver: Arsenal Pulp, 2007.

Badiou, Alain. *Ethics: An Essay on the Understanding of Evil.* 1993. Trans. Peter Hallward. New York: Verso, 2001.

———. *Metapolitics.* 1998. Trans. Jason Barker. New York: Verso, 2005.

Bertholf, Robert J. "Decision at the Apogee: Robert Duncan's Anarchist Critique of Denise Levertov." *Robert Duncan and Denise Levertov: The Poetry of Politics, the Politics of Poetry.* Ed. Albert Gelpi and Robert J. Bertholf. Stanford, CA: Stanford UP, 2006. 1–17.

Bibby, Michael. *Hearts and Minds: Bodies, Poetry, and Resistance in the Vietnam Era.* New Brunswick, NJ: Rutgers UP, 1996.

Bourg, Julian. *From Revolution to Ethics: May 1968 and Contemporary French Thought.* Montreal: McGill-Queen's UP, 2007.

Braidotti, Rosi. *Transpositions.* Malden, MA: Polity, 2006.

Collis, Stephen. *Phyllis Webb and the Common Good: Poetry, Anarchy, Abstraction.* Vancouver: Talonbooks, 2007.

———. *Through Words of Others: Susan Howe and Anarcho-Scholasticism.* Victoria, BC: English Literary Studies Editions, 2007.

Debord, Guy. *Society of the Spectacle.* 1967. Trans. Donald Nicholson-Smith. New York: Zone, 1995.

Dewey, John. "The Crisis in Human History: The Danger of the Retreat to Individualism." 1946. *The Later Works, 1925–1953, Vol. 15: 1942–1948.* Ed. Jo Ann Boydston. Carbondale: Southern Illinois UP, 1989. 210–23.

————. *Liberalism and Social Action*. 1935. Amherst, NY: Prometheus, 2000.

Duncan, Robert. *Bending the Bow*. New York: New Directions, 1968.

————. *The H.D. Book*:

    Part 1, chapter 1. *Coyote's Journal* 5/6 (1966): 8–31.

    Part 1, chapters 3 and 4. *TriQuarterly* 12 (Spring 1968): 67–98.

    Part 1, chapter 6. Duncan, *A Selected Prose* 97–137.

    Part 2, chapter 3. *Io* 6 (Summer 1969): 117–40.

    Part 2, chapter 4. *Caterpillar* 7 (April 1969): 27–60.

    Part 2, chapter 5. *Sagetrieb* 4.2/3 (Fall/Winter 1985): 39–85.

————. "The Homosexual in Society." 1944. Rev. ed. 1959. *A Selected Prose*. Ed. Robert J. Bertholf. New York: New Directions, 1995. 38–50.

————. "Man's Fulfillment in Order and Strife." 1969. *Fictive Certainties: Essays*. New York: New Directions, 1985. 111–41.

————. *Of the War: Passages 22–27*. Berkeley, CA: Oyez, 1966.

————. "Returning to *Les Chimères* of Gérard de Nerval." *Audit/Poetry, Featuring Robert Duncan* 4.3 (1967): 42–62.

————. "The Self in Postmodern Poetry." 1979. *Fictive Certainties: Essays*. New York: New Directions, 1985. 219–34.

Duncan, Robert, and Denise Levertov. *The Letters of Robert Duncan and Denise Levertov*. Ed. Robert J. Bertholf and Albert Gelpi. Stanford, CA: Stanford UP, 2004.

Foucault, Michel. *The History of Sexuality, Volume 1: An Introduction*. 1976. Trans. Robert Hurley. New York: Vintage, 1990.

————. *Naissance de la biopolitique: Cours au Collège de France, 1978–1979*. Ed. Michel Senellart et al. Paris: Seuil, 2004.

————. *Security, Territory, Population: Lectures at the Collège de France, 1977–1978*. Ed. Michel Senellart et al. Trans. Graham Burchell. New York: Palgrave-Macmillan, 2007.

————. *"Society Must Be Defended": Lectures at the Collège de France, 1975–1976*. Ed. Mauro Bertani and Alessandro Fontana. Trans. David Macey. New York: Picador, 2003.

Gay Revolution Party. "Gay Revolution Party Manifesto." 1970. *Out of the Closets: Voices of Gay Liberation*. Ed. Allen Young and Karla Jay. 20th Anniversary ed. New York: New York UP, 1992. 342–45.

Goldman, Emma. *Anarchism and Other Essays*. 1917. New York: Dover, 1969.

Guérin, Daniel. *Anarchism*. 1965; 1969. Trans. Mary Klopper. New York: Monthly Review, 1970.

James, William. *Pragmatism, and The Meaning of Truth*. 1907; 1909. Cambridge, MA: Harvard UP, 1978.

Kaufman, Robert. "Poetry's Ethics? Theodor W. Adorno and Robert Duncan on Aesthetic Illusion and Sociopolitical Delusion." *New German Critique* 33.1 (2006): 73–118.

Kropotkin, Peter. *Mutual Aid: A Factor of Evolution*. 1902. Mineola, NY: Dover, 2006.

Laing, Alexander. "*The Nation* and Its Poets." *Nation* 20 Sept. 1965: 212–18.

Mackey, Nathaniel. "Gassire's Lute: Robert Duncan's Vietnam War Poems." *Paracritical Hinge: Essays, Talks, Notes, Interviews.* Contemporary North American Poetry ser. Madison: U of Wisconsin P, 2005. 71–178.

Paul, Sherman. *The Lost America of Love: Rereading Robert Creeley, Edward Dorn, and Robert Duncan.* Baton Rouge: Louisiana State UP, 1981.

Read, Herbert. "Poetry and Anarchism." 1938. *Anarchy and Order: Essays in Politics.* Boston: Beacon, 1971. 33–125.

Tait, Charles W. "Whatever Happened to the State Department?" *Nation* 13 Sept. 1965: 137–41.

Tomes, Robert R. *Apocalypse Then: American Intellectuals and the Vietnam War, 1954–1975.* New York: New York UP, 1998.

Whitehead, Alfred North. *Process and Reality: An Essay in Cosmology.* 1929. Corrected ed. Ed. David Ray Griffin and Donald W. Sherburne. New York: Free, 1978.

Young, Allen. "Out of the Closets, into the Streets." 1969. *Out of the Closets: Voices of Gay Liberation.* Ed. Allen Young and Karla Jay. 20th Anniversary ed. New York: New York UP, 1992. 6–34.

Žižek, Slavoj. "From Politics to Biopolitics…and Back." *South Atlantic Quarterly* 103 (2004): 501–21.

JIM HANSEN

Samuel Beckett's *Catastrophe* and the Theater of Pure Means

> Identification, in fact, is ambivalent from the first; it can turn into an expression of tenderness as easily as into a wish for someone's removal.
>
> Sigmund Freud, *Group Psychology and the Analysis of the Ego*

Samuel Beckett's work has never been particularly amenable to the maneuvers of political criticism. In fact, in his seminal 1963 essay "Trying to Understand *Endgame*," Theodor W. Adorno goes so far as to claim that "it would be ridiculous to put Beckett on the stand as a star political witness" (248). By reading Beckett alongside retheorized conceptions of the political and the theatrical, this essay proposes that we actually stop asking questions about the various political commitments of Beckett's work.[1] Instead, as I'll suggest, we should begin to ask how his work very consciously stages "theatricality" in order to draw attention to the failings and omissions of modern notions of the political itself.

Catastrophe and the Poetics of Sympathy

At the concluding instant of Samuel Beckett's very brief 1982 play *Catastrophe*, the audience becomes witness to what appears as an

---

1. In particular, I will be using "the political" in the sense defined by Carl Schmitt in *The Concept of the Political*. In the end, I will counter some of these arguments via Walter Benjamin's "Critique of Violence."

Contemporary Literature XLIX, 4   0010-7484; E-ISSN 1548-9949/08/0004-0660

entirely unheralded—if not to say exceptional—moment in the
Beckett canon. Throughout the play, we've witnessed an *auteur*
stage director, noted in the text as (D), chomp incessantly on a cigar
and wear a fur coat and matching toque as he manipulates, critiques, and even redefines his mute, ragged, and debased protagonist, (P). As D continually attempts to represent P as the universal
figure of the human *par excellence*, the audience watches a frail,
unspeaking protagonist, a classic Beckettian figure, laid bare by the
workings of the apparently absolute and sovereign power that
D comes to embody. What's more, the entire action mediates the
problem of political identity by staging it, as Beckett's work so often
does, in terms of the supposedly mythic power, the authority to create *ex nihilo*, that modernity wants to grant the autonomous artist.
Because artists in the modern period have come to symbolize both
the freedom to create and the revolutionary power of the imagination, we tend to give them a great deal of leeway, and in a play like
Krapp's Last Tape or *Catastrophe*, Beckett forces us to watch an artist
whose self-indulgent behavior we would usually prefer to ignore.
The exceptional moment at the end of *Catastrophe* occurs when P, as
Beckett's stage directions explain, "*raises his head, fixes the audience.
The applause falters, dies,*" and the lights fade, leaving the stage in
utter, silent darkness (301).

The critical literature depicts this moment as a curiously un-
Beckettian moment of resistance. When P raises his head and fixes us
and the play's fictive audience in his rather intense gaze, as Anthony
O'Brien tells us, P's action breaks the "bonds of domination" that
hold him in thrall to D (47). One of the minimalist pieces written during Beckett's final decade, *Catastrophe* was dedicated to the political
dissident and writer Vaclav Havel and, as such, has become the
exemplar of precisely the resistant, romantic politics that many critics want to find in Beckett's postwar work. I'm not convinced that we
can discuss the politics of Beckett's work by using terms as overt as
"resistance," however, and it occurs to me that we have yet to
develop a scholarly language or critical vocabulary that catches the
precise nuances and difficulties that Beckett presents for those interested in ideology critique. Nonetheless, every few years, a critic or
philosopher comes along with a new approach that promises to
demonstrate once and for all that Beckett's work is and has always

been inescapably political. For what it's worth, Terry Eagleton's "Political Beckett?" (published in the July-August 2006 issue of *New Left Review*), Alain Badiou's 2003 collection of essays, *On Beckett*, and Pascale Casanova's 2007 *Samuel Beckett: Anatomy of a Literary Revolution* represent only the most recent attempts at just such a critical maneuver. Why is it that even though Beckett was born and raised in a decolonizing country, aided the French Resistance during World War II, clearly despised all totalizing forms of thought and governance, and wrote works that inveighed against masculine forms of cultural domination, many Beckett scholars still feel obliged to begin nearly every essay by arguing that it is imperative that we all finally agree that Beckett's literary output can be read as a kind of ideology critique?[2] The critical obsession itself is an interesting phenomenon, and it points to the fact that in spite of all of our very determined work, Beckett's writing—in all of its pallid ambiguity, its minimalist abstraction, and its stripping down of what his earliest, existentialist critics would have doubtless called "the human condition"—remains impervious to even the most basic techniques of political criticism.

The approach that dubs the concluding gaze of *Catastrophe* as a moment of resistance may be taken as a case in point. This approach, whatever its ends might be, invariably imagines that Beckett's work reconstitutes the space of liberal subjectivity by affirming, in tones that resonate with the work of a Richard Rorty, that liberalism can be satisfied simply to hate and eschew cruelty. From this perspective, P resists, and we—along with the fictive audience who, Beckett reminds us, falter in their applause—are to sympathize with his resistance. The logic of this kind of liberal subjectivity is by now quite commonplace, and it relies on the poetics of

---

2. See specifically David Weisberg's *Chronicles of Disorder*, which argues that Beckett's fiction occupies a space between modernist autonomy and postwar commitment by reading Beckett's work in light of European and literary history. Likewise, Tyrus Miller's "Dismantling Authenticity" reads Beckett in a similarly political, Adorno-inflected fashion. Of course, both Weisberg and Miller largely ignore Beckett's rethinking of experience in light of his Irish background. For a postcolonial reading, see David Lloyd's "Writing in the Shit." A volume of essays edited by Henry Sussman and Christopher Devenney, *Engagement and Indifference: Beckett and the Political*, demonstrates the difficulties of reading for Beckett's politics.

sympathetic identification, which Rorty recommends as a practical, albeit limited method for healing a society's or a global order's various ills.[3] This particular method of sympathetic identification requires both philosophical thought—the ability to reflect on a social or ethical problem on a conscious, reasonable, and intellectual rather than just emotional level—and the poetic capacity to imagine that the world might be different, and that, but for some strange twist of fate, I myself might be the sufferer. I also deploy the term in order to suggest that although this personalizing approach certainly provides us with a very immediate (or in the Hegelian sense, unmediated) poetic identification, it finally fails to mediate our concept of the political itself.[4]

This method of transferential identification offers us a particularly enlightened version of politics. What's more, this same method remains at the heart of nearly any liberal-humanist critique of the sociopolitical world and, to some extent, follows very directly from arguments set out so powerfully by Adam Smith's *Theory of Moral Sentiments* in 1759. Simply put, for thinkers like Smith, the politics of sympathetic identification invites me to imagine myself as an impartial spectator who judges the actions of two opposing agents in order to determine which agent is in the right.[5] Moreover, in his *Theory*, Smith claims, "In every passion of which the mind of man is susceptible, the emotions of the by-stander correspond to what, by bringing the case home to himself, he imagines should be the sentiments of the sufferer" (3). He goes on to assert that sympathy may be "made use of to denote our fellow-feeling with any passion whatever" (3). In Smith's proto-liberal thinking, a kind of imaginative, narcissistic identification with the more injured party will always lead the impartial spectator to a correct moral judgment concerning the situation. The relation that Smith lays out here becomes

---

3. Rorty's version is more Nietzschean in that it imagines sympathetic identification as a version of self re-creation; see in particular *Contingency, Irony, Solidarity*.

4. For a full explanation of the work of "overcoming," see Hegel's "Sublation of Becoming" (106–8).

5. Again, it's important to note that a liberal pragmatist like Rorty would differ here: Rorty would certainly never argue that an objective or impartial position can be occupied by any human subject.

one of proximity, and by "bringing the case home" to myself, by feeling close to the situation or context in question, I inevitably generate a correct moral decision.[6] This form of identification places me at a comfortable distance from the emphatically aggressive, inappropriate, and potentially unethical actions of the more villainous party in any disagreement as well. I relate to the victim and so decry, and distance myself from, the victimizer. Whether we'd like to admit it or not, this type of formula provides the basic assumption of most politically motivated literature, which attempts to get us to recognize our "fellow-feeling" with those who suffer, to help us to imagine a relationship of sympathy between ourselves and an injured, downtrodden, or disenfranchised party.

Think of a more recent play, like Tony Kushner's *Angels in America*, or a much older novel, like Charles Dickens's *Hard Times*. Though they differ quite profoundly in structure and form, both invite us to imagine ourselves in another sociopolitical position, world view, or, as Rorty himself might say, context of practice. These texts invite us to imagine the world differently and so to hope for a more egalitarian, less prejudiced society. After all, both politically motivated art and political criticism tend to look for practical ways to alter the social world. We want to figure out how to move from an unequal to an equal global community, from a structurally racist logic to a logic that understands the nuances of racial difference, from a hetero-normative to a hetero-topian society. Of course, the simple ingenuity of liberal sympathy actually lies in its capacity to manipulate an individual's narcissism. We identify through our own egotism with an injured party. A poetics of sympathetic identification provides me with a way to project myself into different social contexts, to imagine the world differently, and, finally, to work on changing my perceptions about cultural difference. From this perspective, I use literature and literary criticism to create the conditions through which I can imagine myself in someone else's shoes.

---

6. Of course, Smith tends to admit many of the limitations inherent in his conception of sympathy. In part 3 of *The Theory of Moral Sentiments*, he remains particularly critical of the ways that sympathy can be misplaced or disrupted by "self-deceit" and "self-love" (158, 160).

So when we return to the singular moment at the conclusion of Beckett's *Catastrophe*, we might invoke the method of sympathetic identification to argue that Beckett's play allows us to side with the bare, defeated, seemingly dehumanized P and against the careless, dehumanizing power wielded by D. But just how does the poetics of sympathetic identification fit with the general and overarching logic of dehumanized and detemporalized necessity articulated throughout Beckett's work? Another way of putting this would be to ask, yet again, how P's act of resistance jibes with the standard Beckettian line, with the impotent cry of the paradoxically Cartesian yet painfully embodied narrator of *The Unnamable*, who tells us, "I can't go on, I'll go on" (414). The answer to this question is quite simple: it doesn't. P's silence—as opposed to his resistance— remains at the center of this sequence. Beckett's theater, with all of its ragged, impersonal, and vague universality, refuses the condition of proximity, the capacity to bring the situation home to myself, that is demanded by liberalism's system of benevolent and narcissistic moral judgment. P's silence, then, leaves us with a moment of overwhelming ambiguity.

Beckett's *Catastrophe* is not about correct—or practical—moral and ethical judgment so much as it is about the staging of a scene that invites the audience to imagine itself as moral and ethical. Remember, the stage directions at the end of the play indicate that once the audience is fixed in the gaze of P, the applause *"falters, dies."* In the play, we witness not only the image of power exerted upon a helpless protagonist, but also the aesthetic theatricality of violence and domination. Whenever we follow the poetics of sympathetic identification, we separate things out, we identify with a singular figure and against another figure or host of other figures. Hence the binary that Smith begins with, the observer's constitutive "fellow-feeling," which separates an injured party from an injuring party, circumscribes the boundaries of the transferential model of identification. Freud himself provides us with a fairly complex and usefully reflective inversion of this basic transferential model in *Group Psychology and the Analysis of the Ego*. In particular, Freud draws attention to those moments in which one individual identifies with another without the possibility of what he calls "an object-relation to the person who is being copied" (49). In such a case, the subject doesn't identify with someone he/she desires—or even with someone who possesses or controls access to the desired object—but rather with the possibility of putting one's self in the position to have an experience that imitates the experience of another. As Freud claims, the crucial reversal flows from the fact that the sympathizer does not really take on "the symptom out of sympathy. On the contrary, the sympathy only arises out of the identification." Though Freud would undoubtedly maintain that this structure would provide a point of identification that is easily repressed by the subject-sympathizer, it occurs to me that the identificatory experience itself meets both a psychic and an ideological need for the subject as well.

Generally speaking, we don't really think in collectivities when we think in terms of sympathy. Simply put, I sympathize with an other, in the singular sense. But Beckett's play presents us with a peculiar scene in which, by imagining P as the arch-representation of humanity, D himself has already made the narcissistic identification with the protagonist invited by Smith's *Theory of Moral Sentiments*. The play depicts a forceful *auteur* setting up a scene, the power of which will rely on the poetics of sympathetic identification. But D and P are bound together in this scene by the workings of power, by D's capacity to reshape and rethink P. Perhaps this incident points back to the problem with liberal humanism's method of sympathetic identification. Although the Adam Smith version of sympathy invites us to separate individuals out and to identify with one of them, Beckett's play binds two figures together by focusing on the theatricality, on the staging of the scene itself. Following Freud's claims (47), Beckett's play demonstrates the structural ambivalence involved in any act of identification. One of these figures speaks his power, while the other remains silent. One has an appropriate vision of the world's suffering, while the other is appropriated by that vision. D is a symbol-maker who imagines himself in sympathy with P. P's body becomes the symbol writ large on the stage and in front of an audience. Beckett invites us to ask precisely what psychic and ideological needs are met through the act of identification. In fact, *Catastrophe* leads us to ask a series of questions: what is D willing to sacrifice in order to achieve the theatrical effects (and affects) he seeks? What political power structures are concealed within the aesthetic theatricality of sympathetic identification? Finally, when P looks up and the applause fades, we are left to ask, How is the audience itself complicit with these political power structures?

Catastrophe situates the audience in a position to think about how a particular human life is manipulated by aesthetic representation and, reflexively, how mass presumption and social consciousness are molded and manipulated by aesthetic staging. The language of sympathetic identification developed in Aristotle's *Poetics* or Smith's *Theory of Moral Sentiments* and recommended by Rorty is simply not adequate to the experience of Beckett's theater, which very often offers us figures devoid of any real-world context, figures who are confined by narrative structures that they have neither made nor fully discerned, figures who seem to have been born into a world that never comprehended the word "sympathy." In essence, the argument that I'm making here shares elements of Bertolt Brecht's critique of bourgeois theater. For Brecht, the "alienation effect" that his own "epic theater" aimed to achieve would break the bonds of simple identification. He notes in "Alienation Effects in Chinese Acting" that the effect he aspires to in his own work would move acceptance and rejection to a conscious plane, where theatergoers would be forced to think through and judge a character's actions in a deliberate fashion (91). Brecht remains the theater's great debunker of the poetics of sympathetic identification, finally claiming in "A Short Organum for the Theatre" that, at best, sympathetic and empathetic responses have to be treated as simply one of a number of methods of observation (195). But Brecht does not deploy the alienation effect merely in order to break with the Aristotelian conception of dramatic empathy. He also intends his theater to solve certain political problems by allowing the audience to think on the social as opposed to the individual level. That is, via a theater based on alienation rather than sympathy, we are to see problems rationally, clearly, and, most of all, systemically, and we are to remodel society accordingly. Beckett provides us with no such comfort. *Catastrophe* doesn't offer a new way to think about society so much as it demonstrates how an enlightened politics of sympathy miscarries. To grasp the political valence of the play more fully, we need to reposition the conclusion of *Catastrophe* not only as a singular moment in the Beckett canon, but also as a direct attempt to situate the techniques of biopower—the dialectic of dominant sovereign power embodied by D and mute political objectification and bare life signified by P—in the context of the problem of theatrical mediation. The play is not just about protagonist (P) and artist-director (D) but also about theatricality itself.

If Beckett's *Catastrophe* thematizes the theatricality of violence, then it also pushes us to avoid thinking of the audience, of ourselves, as simply witnesses to the inhumane semiotic representation of P's body presided over by D. Perhaps we should instead think of P as the voiceless witness and of ourselves as the implicated viewers who partake of what J. M. Bernstein has elsewhere called the "pornography of horror" offered by an aestheticized violence (2).[7] When we leave our theater seats claiming that D is a horror and P a victim with whom we can sympathize and identify, we have entirely missed the point of *Catastrophe* and the point of Beckett's oeuvre. We have, in other words, missed the dialectical critique implicit in our own aesthetic experience and pleasure. For all of the horrors that it may hold for us, violence also provides us with a spectacle that we find compelling and captivating. As much as Beckett's play is concerned with the power of violence, however, it is more concerned about the aesthetic theatricality of violence, about an audience's capacity to somehow find its morality, its ethics, and its social world affirmed by the spectacle of violence. I don't mean to imply that we all crave violence in an overtly sadistic way. In fact, in a contemporary liberal democracy, we claim to detest nothing so much as we do violence. But in those same liberal democracies, we certainly enjoy the spectacle of violence when it gives us a chance to affirm our humane social values, to feel that we have sided with the victims of history and against their oppressors. Even the violence that we abhor seems to serve an instrumental and structural function for us.

Let me pose the actual problem of *Catastrophe*'s conclusion in a different, but perhaps more direct, way: I do not bear witness to P's

---

7. For Bernstein, pornography carries within itself a critique of the ways in which domination, objectification, and aggression become inscribed in and realized by human sexuality only as the curiously dialectical pornographic image itself attempts to deny and conceal the very presence of its own critique by embracing the taboos that contravene normative and civil society.

shame so much as P bears witness to mine. However, P, like the God of Robert Browning's "Porphyria's Lover," cautiously inverted and profanized here by Beckett, "has not said a word," in fact, cannot say a word. By representing P as humanity-*qua*-catastrophe, D has, at once, erased the space of P's being and slowly pared away the qualities that separate the human from the inhuman. P has, in some sense, been reshaped as an automaton, exposed to the erasure of his own instinct for self-assertion and self-preservation, and his disempowered yet silent gaze signifies a passing out of existence, a cessation of being that calls our ethics, our politics, and the instrumental reason that animates our society into question. At such a moment, an audience should feel discomfited, not affirmed. P is the instance of unrefined particularity that disrupts our universalizing rationality and our desire for what Italian philosopher Giorgio Agamben, following Aristotle, calls our *bios* or, for lack of a better term, our "good life," the political and social life that human beings come together in order to maintain. For Aristotle, a civil or social *bios* remains separate from basic, physiological animal existence, referred to in Greek philosophy as *zoē*. If P represents something like a mere animal existence (*zoē*) subjected to the workings of a legal and social biopower that can define someone (or something) as outside of the civil entirely, then his life cannot be properly understood or even acknowledged by liberal conceptions of sympathy. If the poetics of sympathetic identification cannot provide us with the vocabulary to articulate the political and aesthetic problems that bind D, P, and the audience together, then perhaps Agamben's interrogation of the category of the political might. Agamben's is an ethico-political language much like the liberal vocabulary of sympathetic identification, but Agamben's approach reads relationships as structurally determined precisely in order to bind together those figures that liberal sympathy tears asunder.

Sovereign Violence and Aesthetic Pleasure

Up until now, I have continually appropriated several of the terms that I've used, terms such as "sovereignty" and "bare life," from the vocabulary made fashionable in recent years by the work of Agamben, whose 1995 book, *Homo Sacer: Sovereign Power and Bare*

Life, and its 2005 sequel, *The State of Exception*, connect many of the discursive and ethical strategies of European poststructuralism to the political concerns about sovereignty and state power confronted by the twentieth-century German juridical theorist Carl Schmitt. At its most basic level, I suppose that Agamben's work aspires to move philosophical and political thinking beyond the moment of sovereign governance in which they seem bogged down. Agamben wants to reveal that the very rationale behind social-contract theories of government—theories that cede power over the body politic to a sovereign who can act on behalf of all of the citizens, influence the rights of masses and individuals, and, most importantly, decide on exceptions to the constitution—merely justifies state-sponsored, governmental violence. According to Agamben, we find this justification, a kind of untruth that most of the citizens in a democratic society blithely accept, embodied most clearly in the work of Schmitt, who holds that the link between the law and violence is an indispensable—in fact the fundamental—one, that without violence, the law, and subsequently civil society itself, would cease to exist. For the Schmittian conception of the political, violence quite literally constitutes the foundation of all governmentality. Violence is the threat behind the law that makes the law possible, the threat that both gives the law its force and keeps the law in force. Of course, Schmitt doesn't say it in quite that way. Instead, in his 1922 study entitled *Political Theology*, he says, "Sovereign is he who decides on the exception" (1). Schmitt argues not only that the law is maintained by a sovereign who can declare a state of emergency or martial law in which the military may act with violence upon the citizenry it is enjoined to defend, but also that the law finds its identity, its foundation, on the very site of the sovereign's violence. For Schmitt, the sovereign may act with strategic, focused violence in order to put a halt to what he considers chaotic, unfocused violence. The sovereign may declare, in other words: "This is an exception. This problem cannot be handled within the bounds of the law." Such logic might seem quite familiar to anyone who has read *Leviathan* and encountered Thomas Hobbes's horrified account of the anarchic "state of nature" and the war of "all against all," or, for that matter, to anyone who heard President George W. Bush declare that "when we talk about war, we're really talking about peace." In such cases, he who appears sovereign certainly decides on the exception.

Setting aside the obvious point that Schmitt's theory is thoroughly ahistorical, Agamben instead challenges Schmitt by claiming that the sovereign finally comes to embody a "zone of indistinction," or as Agamben says, "an exclusive inclusion," an agent included in the law by its exclusion from that law (*Homo Sacer* 19). Democratic and social-contract theorists place a great deal of faith in the political systems that they've built up precisely because the sovereign, whether a president or a prime minister, does not make law but rather helps to enforce law and, at most, to guide social and military policy. A president or a prime minister, after all, is not a dictator.[8] We would like to imagine that revolutions constitute power and that a president merely maintains an already-constituted power. But Agamben reminds us that whenever the sovereign declares a state of exception, whenever he/she can invoke emergency powers and suspend the constitution, then the sovereign acquires legislative power, acquires the capacity to make law via his/her sheer, decisive political power (48). That political position, which is meant to enforce an already constituted power, also takes on the capacity to constitute power, to legislate, and the social world changes irrevocably as a result. Schmitt himself finally wants to claim that even when the sovereign suspends the law and introduces overt violence into the sociopolitical sphere, he/she nonetheless remains in the sphere of legality, because proclaiming the state of exception appears to be one of the powers allowed to the sovereign by constitutional law.[9] Agamben counters by arguing that, in placing him/herself in this zone of "indistinction," the sovereign, as Walter Benjamin once warned ("Theses" 259), makes the state of exception into the rule.

At this point we might be led to ask, What does sovereign violence act upon during the state of exception? Agamben follows Benjamin here in referring to the acted-upon object as bare life

---

8. Agamben is very quick to point out, however, that through the lens of sovereignty we can begin to see a historico-philosophical homology between totalitarianism and democratic theories of government (*Homo Sacer* 10).

9. Schmitt lays this out most clearly and provocatively in *Political Theology: Four Chapters on the Concept of Sovereignty.*

(*blosses Leben*). The trick here, as Agamben is anxious to point out, consists in the fact that the sovereign and the bare life upon which he acts both end up existing in zones of indistinction. In the simplest terms, then, the sovereign can kill without being accused of committing homicide, and the representative of bare life, referred to by Agamben as the *homo sacer*, or sacred man, may be killed without being considered sacrificed.[10] The *homo sacer* is an "inclusive exclusion," excluded from the law by means of his own inclusion in it. For Agamben, this means that human life itself—not the actions that take place in or the rules that govern a society or a so-called good life—but the bare, mere, naked fact of living becomes politicized. If the sovereign constitutes the law through his exclusive inclusion, then the sacred man constitutes law through his inclusive exclusion. He is only included in the political sphere as that which is outside, as that which can be denied life. As the two poles of the civil world, the sovereign and the *homo sacer* define the boundaries of that world by providing it with the concept of an outside. The sovereign's power to decide on the exception—to define something as outside the law, is included within the purview of the law. That which he/she defines as outside of the law, as *blosses Leben*, is determined either as a violation of the civil itself, as what Immanuel Kant once called an "unjust enemy," or as that which represents and embodies the other of the civil.[11] Agamben's work finally points to the structural binary that binds sovereign power to bare life. Presumably, Agamben aims to reveal that the relationship between law and violence need not be a fundamental one, and so he hopes to separate *nomos* (law) from violence and anomie.

When we return to Beckett's play, we must ask what we have witnessed in our encounter with the artist-director (D) who holds the right to reshape and revise his mute, ragged protagonist (P). At first glance, it seems like an overtly political scene, one in which a kind

---

10. As Agamben recounts, the *homo sacer* is "an obscure figure of archaic Roman law, in which human life is included in the juridical order [*ordinamento*] solely in the form of its exclusion (that is, of its capacity to be killed)" (*Homo Sacer* 8). In essence, as Agamben explains, the *homo sacer* is someone "who *may be killed and yet not sacrificed*" (8).

11. See the discussion of the "unjust enemy" in Kant's "The Metaphysics of Morals" (170).

of sovereign power exercises its right to act upon and define an other as *blosses Leben*, as bare life. By reducing P to bare life, D declares something about life itself, about the way that we are to imagine the boundaries of the social. But we do not really see power or bare life *an-sich*, in-itself, when we see *Catastrophe*. Instead, these issues come to us mediated by the play's overt attempt to represent the aesthetic theatricality of violent domination. As I've said, despite all of the fear that it may hold for us, violence tends to provide us with a rather compelling spectacle. Beckett's play seems concerned about the aesthetic theatricality of violence, about the audience's desire to use the spectacle of violence to affirm its moral and social world views. When we feel that we have sided with the victims of history and against the victimizers, we feel pleased with ourselves, and we feel our world view reaffirmed. The zone of anomie is for us also the zone of a certain kind of aesthetic pleasure, then. In Beckett's play, the stage becomes just such a zone of anomie. The stage, in other words, constitutes the theater of mass politics.

In *Catastrophe*, we encounter in the metarepresentation of P's body an aesthetic pleasure that manifests itself as a highly politicized zone of indistinction. We could argue that P reveals to us something about bare or mere life, the Aristotelian *zoē* that can only be included in the social and political realms as structurally outside, as that which remains included by means of its exclusion. When bare life can be read as the "natural" background upon which a "good," conscious, and civil life (*bios*) builds its cultures or paints its pictures, then even modernity's autonomous artist, that archfigure of dissidence, remains caught up in the will to dominate the natural world. If the dialectic works in this way, if mere or bare life as *zoē* is that which always remains acted upon, then mere life is granted no real qualities, no substance. We force *zoē*—the physiological body—to take on whatever shape we demand. We put mere life to instrumental use, and we do it precisely by holding life itself in a zone of indistinction. It is always already an inclusive exclusion, included in society only by means of its own exclusion from the social and civil world, the world of *bios*. We may claim to represent *zoē* in all of its truth, but, in fact, as we seek to dominate it, we fail to recognize it as the very condition of possibility for each and every human endeavor.

When an artist builds an aesthetic upon mere life, that artist uses mere life as background material, as the site upon which to establish something more meaningful. In *Stage Fright: Modernism, Anti-Theatricality, and Drama*, Martin Puchner claims that the artist's capacity to manipulate and control life is one of the driving obsessions of Beckett's drama. In fact, Puchner goes on to argue that for Beckett's theater, the "task of turning objects and gestures into signifying entities can only be accomplished if the objects and gestures begin to represent more than just themselves" (161). The figure on stage is converted into a symbol by the workings of the artist's power and control. Such action occurs throughout Beckett's drama, but in *Catastrophe*, the action itself is hypostatized. It constitutes both the structure and the subject of the play as it unfolds onstage.[12] What we see in *Catastrophe*, then, appears as a kind of originary aesthetic violence enacted by the civil upon mere life. As with the poetics of sympathetic identification, in such instances we get an approach that wants to separate things out. In this case, the approach wants to separate the civil and cultural from the natural and physiological. The natural and the physiological appear vulgar, bestial, undignified, and, very often, pathetic, so the civil and the cultural end up trumping the natural and physiological every time. If we were more civil, more cultured, so we are told, we would also be less vulgar and more humane. In fact, the civil and the cultural—those things that the artist makes some pretense to represent—often go so far as to imagine themselves as life, as the world, in its entirety. Paradoxically, that which can be codified as humane somehow gets separated from the condition of mere human life. Following the logic of Agamben's *Homo Sacer*, we might say that D embodies a kind of *lex poetica*, a poetic law that seeks to transform into and realize itself as life in its entirety while simultaneously confronting a particular life that is absolutely indistinguishable from the law (185). D has a vision of the human as victim. Through the force of

---

12. From this perspective, we must also remember that P's final gaze as the applause falters and dies never really marks a potential act of resistance to D because the action itself has been scripted by the playwright, by Beckett himself. The apparent act of resistance remains part of a theatrical plot and, as such, always already constitutes an act of compliance.

imagination, D depicts a world that embodies his perception and communicates his vision. As with Benjamin's discussion of the "great criminal" in his "Critique of Violence," the artist's violence here has a lawmaking quality to it (283–84). The *auteur* becomes a creating poetic law, an autonomous artist who shows us truth by imagining and creating a world. If the imaginative force of a *lex poetica* can be seen as an analogue to revolutionary force, to the "mythic violence" that Benjamin discusses or the "constituting violence" mentioned by Agamben, it also remains true that the artist's force bears an unmistakable similarity to something like sovereign power, to he who decides upon the exception. The problems of the artist and the sovereign become analogous in that both can appropriate and erase that which they pretend to represent. At this point we would do well to recall that it was in the pages of Søren Kierkegaard's *Repetition* that Carl Schmitt, the legal scholar whose writings provoked Agamben's analysis, first learned that "a poet is ordinarily an exception" (228). We are left, then, with a dilemma in which the autonomous artist, the modern poetic law, whose death Beckett presides over as agnostic minister and experiences as literary corpus, looks very similar to both the revolutionary idealist and the sovereign who decides upon the exception. In other words, as Benjamin himself has said: "[I]n the exercise of violence over life and death more than in any other legal act, law reaffirms itself. But in this very violence something rotten in the law is revealed" (286).

At this point, we must remember that D's power in *Catastrophe* always appears mitigated by several factors. For one, the cigar that he chomps on throughout the play goes out constantly, so that its ashen tip continually needs relighting. When we add the ashes of the cigar to the fact that D desires to see P's skin whitened, or as he says in the text, more "ashen," a pattern begins to emerge that binds D's apparently waning, insufficient artistic powers, symbolized by the failing cigar, to the impotent representation embodied by P himself.[13] D and P seem bound together in a way that elaborates P's suffering and the failure of D's artistic power and vision.

---

13. See Anthony O'Brien's "Staging Whiteness: Beckett, Havel, Maponya" for a deft analysis of the often very self-conscious failings of Beckett's play.

They seem drawn into a zone of indistinction, and each figure begins, in some fashion, to resemble the other. Lest we forget, D's orders about P's appearance must be carried out by his assistant, noted in the text as A, so in order to act on P, D seems to need an assistant who will assent to his demands, as well as an audience that will acquiesce to and applaud his world view. The assistant (A) appears to have some fellow-feeling with P—at least she notes his shivering—but she clearly remains in the service of D. What keeps her bound to D when she feels, or at the very least notes, the suffering of P? Perhaps in following the logic of the sovereign artist through to its realization in *Catastrophe*, Beckett collapses the possibility of a poetic law that can imagine itself as the singular realization of humanity. Poetic law relies not only on the lawmaker or law-keeper, but also on those who observe the law. Beckett shows us in the paired figures of D and P art's inability to ameliorate the violent master/slave dialectic that has long characterized the human political sphere. When the artist, like the sovereign, appropriates and dominates that which he/she seeks to represent, he/she also fails to provide us with anything like a politically liberatory or collectivizing and activist work of art. Beckett's revolutionary insight is to realize a world where the word "revolution" itself no longer seems to make any sense. In the figure of A, and with the faltering applause of the audience, however, Beckett imagines an aesthetic and political scenario that is not merely about the extremes and the zones of exclusion. When we imagine the play as only about D (sovereign artist) and P (*blosses Leben*), we are still looking at the spectacle of violence itself rather than at that which makes the theater possible: the audience.

Silence as Mediation, or the Theater of Pure Means

I find Agamben's thesis about the structural binary that connects the sovereign exception to bare life provocative. And I'd like to see in his attempt to distinguish his own project from both the structural undecidability of deconstructive politics and the relentless decisionism of Schmitt's thought a rigorously philosophized and courageously realistic new way, a collectivizing politics that Benjamin himself might recognize as one of "pure means."

In his "Critique of Violence," an essay written in response to the rising popularity in Europe of Georges Sorel's 1908 work *Réflexions sur la violence*, Benjamin claimed: "[I]f violence is a means, a criterion for criticizing it might seem immediately available. It imposes itself in the question whether violence, in a given case, is a means to a just or an unjust end" (277). Of course, he goes on to problematize this distinction by asserting that "the question would remain open whether violence, as a principle, could be a moral means even to just ends." Benjamin was attempting to determine whether a universal proletarian general strike was a violent action that merely accommodated means-ends rationality, or whether it achieved something more. As he saw it, a strictly political general strike simply accomplished an end. It set out to establish better working conditions for its workers alone, and it used the potentially violent means of a work stoppage to achieve this end. Finally, for Benjamin:

> While the first form [political general strike] of interruption of work is violent since it causes only an external modification of labor conditions, the second [proletarian general strike], as a pure means, is nonviolent. For it takes place not in readiness to resume work following external concession and this or that modification to working conditions, but in the determination to resume only a wholly transformed work, no longer enforced by the state, an upheaval that this kind of strike not so much causes as consummates.
>
> (291–92)

That is to say that a "pure means" works through the figure of collectivity not for its own ends but, rather, for a wholly transformed social world. There is, then, in the Hegelian sense, no immediate (or unmediated) end attached to this politics of pure means. It hopes to transform the world, and it arrests all action until that transformation has been achieved. It also refuses to posit what, precisely, the ends of such means would be. Pure means, then, constitutes the arrest rather than the flow of social time.

In this Hegelian sense, an approach via pure means is an act of sublation (*Aufhebung*), and as Hegel claims in the *Science of Logic*, sublation, often translated as "overcoming," is the result of "*mediation*" (107). In a sense, to mediate an object—or a state of consciousness—is to remove it from its immediacy. In the terms laid out by Hegel, "to sublate" means both "to maintain" and "to cause to cease" (107). As

Adorno claims in *History and Freedom*, the only way to grasp the complexity of modern society is to go "beyond the immediate givens of experience" (30). Through the Hegelian concept of mediation, thinking maintains its focus on the determinateness of a problem or object, while refusing the immediacy demanded by that object's social world. A political theory based on "pure means" would give up the compulsion to have an immediate end in mind.

Though Agamben's thesis aims at producing a politics of "pure means," I wonder whether his intervention, which Thomas Carl Wall refers to as Agamben's "radical passivity" (1), provides us with anything more than the mere recognition of the structural binary that links sovereignty to bare life or, for that matter, following my own thesis, to the poetic law embodied by the autonomous artist.[14] Moreover, does it provide us with a satisfactory response to the ethico-political dilemma posed by *Catastrophe*? In moving directly from the structural binary to the political decision (whether it be on the exception or the enemy), we may be occluding the space of the social—that is, of mediation itself—much as liberal social consciousness would like to occlude the mediating power that aesthetic theatricality signifies in Beckett's play. Our relationships to the characters in Beckett's play, to P and to D, are never individualized, one-on-one relationships. We encounter them through the theatricality of a play directed not at a single subject but at an audience that has come to the theater to experience something together, and Beckett foregrounds this fact by making the applause of the audience into part of the play itself. By invoking the idea of the sovereign and the bare life upon which he/she acts, we may be falling back yet again into the private, individualizing metaphors that circumscribe liberal humanism. Perhaps the focus on the exception, derived by Schmitt from Kierkegaard's theories of existence and interiority, still bears the distinctive marks of Kierkegaard's orientation toward privacy, toward the individual, toward the personal, albeit rethought, politicized, and directed toward the potency of community via Schmitt's friend/enemy distinction. In following

---

14. Agamben's *Means without End* presents his attempt to think through the conception of politically pure means.

this Kierkegaardian genealogy, we might actually fail to think the social or the collective in any real sense. We might be forsaking the social, just as Kierkegaard himself does when he warns us to forsake all irremediably conformist collectivities and masses.[15]

By invoking the avatar of the aesthetic performance, Beckett, on the other hand, has set up a scene of domination for our delectation while stigmatizing, precisely, the delight and self-affirmation that our egos enjoy when we come to identify something as morally repugnant. We feel affirmed, in some sense, by siding against the powerful and with the apparently disempowered. But in such a case, the play simply becomes a kind of fantasy-projection for us, an ego trip through which we imagine ourselves as heroic because, at least from the safety of our theater seats, we are on the side of the victim. The theater merely transforms into a reifying spectacle, a theater of affirming violence. We would do well to remember that Beckett has only brought us close to a violence that we have not experienced. By enfolding aesthetic pleasure itself—not just the creative force of the artist, but also the specular satisfaction of the audience—into the dialectic of domination, Beckett has made himself and his various audiences into part of the problem that his play confronts. Through this movement, the artist is bound not only to the mute, bare life of the protagonist but also to the complicit voyeurism of the audience. The audience constitutes the condition of possibility for the scene of domination itself. Mass politics needs more than just a sovereign and a *homo sacer*. It also requires a mass that sometimes willingly and sometimes tacitly supports and reifies the social structure. In *Catastrophe*, the effect that Beckett achieves should force us to ask, as we leave the theater sharing uncomfortable and knowing nods with one another, might we have participated as fully in the stripping away of P's humanity as has D?

What separates Beckett's dramatic effects here from Brecht's alienation effect is the mere fact that Beckett's play openly acknowledges and foregrounds our inability to think the collective. Where Brecht hopes to remodel society by obliging us to rethink its sys-

---

15. Of course, Kierkegaard works to separate the subject from the social world in order to challenge conformity; see in particular *Concluding Unscientific Postscript* 318.

temic architecture, the metatheatricality of Beckett's play points out our failure to do so. Beckett points to the audience as the factor that binds the sovereign to bare life. Brecht's, then, for all of its ethical, social, and political attractions, is still a theater that ascribes to means-ends rationality. Beckett's is a theater of pure means, a theater that hopes for nothing less than a wholly transformed social world, while at the same time demonstrating that the means we currently have at our disposal—even the aesthetic ones—are all impure, all tainted by the logic of individual metaphor and instrumental reason. When P looks up and the fictive audience's applause falters and dies, Beckett does not offer us political solutions but, rather, only silence. But what, precisely, is the implication of this kind of silence on the theatrical stage?

At this point, after gazing at the horrors of a power that always appropriates that which it pretends to represent, after participating as audience in a play that makes the artist into an analogue for repressive state power, we must be reminded that Beckett's play is dedicated to Vaclav Havel, who had been arrested in 1979 and sentenced to prison in Czechoslovakia for "subverting the republic." If the silent protagonist (P) allegorizes Havel's enforced silence, then the figure of P seems as much an analogue for the artist as D. This rather unpoetic *blosses Leben*, the pure means that P represents at the play's conclusion, is one of silence. If the theater is the realm of the performed script, then it always appears governed by the laws of gesture and dialogue. Silence, precisely because it is so uncanny and antitheatrical, wakes us to the theatricality that holds us in sway. In silence, as in unseen violence, significance reigns over spectacle. As P, the so-called protagonist of Beckett's play, gazes silently at us, we should recall that as an audience we sometimes willingly and sometimes tacitly support and reify the social structure. The theater of pure means that Beckett generates in this moment, then, uses silence as its mode of mediation. By removing the action from its immediacy, by interrupting theatricality with silence, Beckett's *Catastrophe* maintains a determinate critique of the theatrical violence of our social world, while also wishing, in the Hegelian sense, to negate that violence. If P is an alternate analogue for the artist, then in a catastrophic world, the artist who can no longer realize life in its entirety in him- or herself, the artist who can no longer represent the multitude of all that can be said, comes to embody precisely the critical potential of what cannot.

University of Illinois, Urbana-Champaign

WORKS CITED

Adorno, Theodor W. *History and Freedom: Lectures 1964–1965*. Ed. Rolf Tiedemann. Trans. Rodney Livingstone. Cambridge: Polity, 2006.

———. "Trying to Understand *Endgame*." 1963. *Notes to Literature*. Vol. 1. Ed. Rolf Tiedemann. Trans. Shierry Weber Nicholson. New York: Columbia UP, 1991.

Agamben, Giorgio. *Homo Sacer: Sovereign Power and Bare Life*. Trans. Daniel Heller-Roazen. Stanford, CA: Stanford UP, 1998.

———. *Means without End: Notes on Politics*. Trans. Vincenzo Binetti and Cesare Casarino. Minneapolis: U of Minnesota P, 2000.

———. *The State of Exception*. Trans. Kevin Atall. Chicago: U of Chicago P, 2005.

Badiou, Alain. *On Beckett*. Ed. Alberto Toscana and Nina Power. Manchester, Eng.: Clinamen, 2003.

Beckett, Samuel. *Catastrophe*. 1982. *Collected Shorter Plays of Samuel Beckett*. New York: Grove, 1984. 295–301.

Benjamin, Walter. "Critique of Violence." *Reflections: Essays, Aphorisms, Autobiographical Writings*. Ed. Peter Demetz. New York: Schocken, 1978. 277–300.

———. "Theses on the Philosophy of History." *Illuminations*. Trans. Harry Zohn. New York: Schocken, 1968. 253–64.

Bernstein, J. M. "Bare Life, Bearing Witness: Auschwitz and the Pornography of Horror." *Parallax* 10.1 (2004): 2–16.

Brecht, Bertolt. "Alienation Effects in Chinese Acting." *Brecht on Theater*. Trans. John Willett. London: Methuen, 1978. 91–99.

———. "A Short Organum for the Theatre." *Brecht on Theater*. Trans. John Willett. London: Methuen, 1978. 179–205.

Casanova, Pascale. *Samuel Beckett: Anatomy of a Literary Revolution*. Trans. Gregory Elliott. London: Verso, 2007.

Eagleton, Terry. "Political Beckett?" *New Left Review* July-Aug. 2006: 67–74.

Freud, Sigmund. *Group Psychology and the Analysis of the Ego*. Trans. James Strachey. New York: Bantam–Matrix, 1965.

Hegel, G. W. F. "The Sublation of Becoming." *Hegel's Science of Logic*. Trans. A. V. Miller. New York: Prometheus, 1969.

Hobbes, Thomas. *Leviathan*. New York: Penguin, 1982.

Kant, Immanuel. "The Metaphysics of Morals." Trans. H. B. Nisbet. *Kant: Political Writings*. Ed. Hans Reiss. London: Cambridge UP, 1991. 131–75.

Kierkegaard, Søren. *Concluding Unscientific Postscript*. Trans. David F. Swenson and Walter Lowrie. Princeton, NJ: Princeton UP, 1968.

Lloyd, David. "Writing in the Shit: Beckett, Nationalism, and the Colonial Subject." *Anomalous States: Irish Writing and the Post-Colonial Moment.* Durham, NC: Duke UP, 1993. 41–58.

Miller, Tyrus. "Dismantling Authenticity: Beckett, Adorno and the 'Post-War.'" *Textual Practice* 8 (1994): 43–57.

O'Brien, Anthony. "Staging Whiteness: Beckett, Havel, Maponya." *Theater Journal* 46.1 (1994): 45–62.

Pattie, David. *Samuel Beckett: A Sourcebook.* New York: Routledge, 2001.

Puchner, Martin. *Stage Fright: Modernism, Anti-Theatricality, and Drama.* Baltimore, MD: Johns Hopkins UP, 2002.

Rorty, Richard. *Contingency, Irony, Solidarity.* New York: Cambridge UP, 1989.

Schmitt, Carl. *The Concept of the Political.* Trans. George Schwab. Chicago: U of Chicago P, 1996.

———. *Political Theology: Four Chapters on the Concept of Sovereignty.* 1922. Trans. George Schwab. Chicago: U of Chicago P, 2005.

Smith, Adam. *The Theory of Moral Sentiments.* London: Waking Lion, 2006.

Sussman, Henry, and Christopher Devenney, eds. *Engagement and Indifference: Beckett and the Political.* New York: State U of New York P, 2001.

Wall, Thomas Carl. *Radical Passivity: Levinas, Blanchot, and Agamben.* Albany: State U of New York P, 1999.

Weisberg, David. *Chronicles of Disorder: Samuel Beckett and the Cultural Politics of the Novel.* New York: State U of New York P, 2000.

JINI KIM WATSON

The Way Ahead: The Politics and Poetics of Singapore's Developmental Landscape

> The objective of national liberation is, therefore, to reclaim the right, usurped by imperialist domination, namely: the liberation of the process of development of national productive forces.
>
> Amilcar Cabral, "National Liberation and Culture"

State and Poetic Narratives of Postcolonial Modernity

In January 1964, Senior Minister Lee Kuan Yew undertook a whirlwind tour of independent African states in order to win support for his new country, Malaysia, which had incorporated Singapore, Sabah (British North Borneo), and Sarawak into the Federation of Malaya in 1963. In this period of emerging postcolonial statehood, recognition of Malaysia by African states was an essential international PR exercise in the face of suspicion and aggression from Sukarno's Indonesia. In Lee's memoir *The Singapore Story*, Lee relates the experience of visiting seventeen African countries in thirty-five days; the varied levels of welcome given to the Malaysian contingent reflected the complicated national ideologies in currency at the time.[1] Although Lee's diplomatic exercise was made moot by the effective ejection of Singapore from Malaysia in 1965, just two years

---

1. On the one hand, because of its defense and economic ties with Britain and the pro-Western attitude of the Malaysian leader, the Tunku Abdul Rahman, some interpreted the new Malaysia as betraying the spirit of independence struggles and the nonalignment movement. On the other hand, Indonesia's "Konfrontasi," a low-level war against Malaysia, could be viewed as a large country attempting to absorb another sovereign state, bringing sympathy for the latter.

Contemporary Literature XLIX, 4   0010-7484; E-ISSN 1548-9949/08/0004-0683
© 2008 by the Board of Regents of the University of Wisconsin System

after their merger, the trip was nevertheless important training for this leader of the fledgling postcolonial city-state of Singapore. More than the varying levels of support garnered at the meetings with African heads of state, Lee's memoirs describe his own reactions to the physical and spatial environments of these encounters. His brief and metonymic descriptions read as a comparative architectural tour of Africa's new seats of postcolonial power, where the presidential personage, the built environment, and the well-being of the nation are strictly correlative. For Edwin Thumboo, the father-figure of Singaporean poetry, such a correlation between built form and nationalist ideology would also be crucial. Approximately ten years after Lee's trip—the experience of which would deeply influence Singaporean national space—Thumboo published the landmark collection *The Second Tongue: An Anthology of Poetry from Malaysia and Singapore*, and the images most useful to his project have to do with the modernizing physical landscape. This essay explores the way forms of a statist, developmental landscape are taken up in both political and poetic discourses. I examine the relationship of poetry to nation-statehood through the work of Thumboo and Arthur Yap, two prominent Anglophone poets early awarded literary Cultural Medallions by the Singapore government.

Before returning to the question of poetry, I will briefly trace the genesis of Lee's understanding of rationalized, national space. For Lee, his African experience is most instructive regarding the varying material environments of different nations. In order to meet Ghana's Kwame Nkrumah at his refurbished Danish slave-trading post, for example, Lee is forced to "walk[] between Indian-style oil lamps, wicks floating in small brass bowls lining both sides of a red carpet" (531). This is only to be outdone by his encounter with Emperor Haile Selassie of Ethiopia, who is dressed in British-style military uniform and flanked by "two cheetahs lightly chained to posts" (536). Here, Lee points out that "[i]n contrast to the sometimes handsome buildings around them, [the people] looked shabby and poor" (536).[2] But in Northern Rhodesia, soon to

---

2. We find that Lee most favorably judges the postcolonial leaders perceived to be most "British" in manner—that is, with a taste for quality and propriety rather than ostentation. Thus Nigeria is praised over Ghana because there "[t]he ceremony was totally

become Zambia, Lee notes approvingly, "[w]e were put up at the Livingstone Hotel, an attractive, single-storey, rambling building, like a large inn in an English provincial town" (532). The governor's mansion of Lukasa, moreover, deserves praise for its well-maintained—but not luxurious—condition, evidence of the "one well-run system" put in place by the British.

Recalling later visits to the Zambian capital, Lee remarks on the dilapidation of the once beautifully kept city:

> I remembered the flowers, shrubs, trees and greenery at the side of the roads and at the roundabouts when I was driven in from the airport in 1964. Roses grew in abundance. Six years later, the roses had gone and weeds had taken over. Nine years after that, even the weeds had given up; the roundabouts were covered with tarmac.
>
> (*Singapore Story* 538)

The disappearance of the "well-run" British system is visibly evident in the physical deterioration of the landscape. Lee is clear about the insights that this trip afforded him:

> I had received an unforgettable lesson in decolonisation, on how crucial it was to have social cohesion and capable, effective government to take power from the colonial authority, especially in Africa.... [W]hen misguided policies based on half-digested theories of socialism and redistribution of wealth were compounded by less than competent government, societies formerly held together by colonial power splintered, with appalling consequences.
>
> (538–39)

One can read Lee's experience, of course, as justifying his own selective rejection of socialist and democratic principles, and as retrospectively casting doom on all those postcolonial states which took that path. The origins of Lee's own thirty-one-year (1959–1990) authoritarian-style rule through the People's Action Party (PAP) may be discerned in his emphasis on "competent government" and "social cohesion." The strongest impression, however, is the

---

British" and "[m]any of the public buildings [in Lagos] looked identical with those in Malaya and Singapore" (*Singapore Story* 532). Julius Nyerere of Tanzania (then Tanganyika) hosts the entourage in the presidential mansion formerly used by both the British governor and the German administrator, but Nyerere himself displays British restraint in "prefer[ing] to live in a small house nearby" (533).

recognition that the control and care of national space, from the presidential mansion down to the roundabouts, is intimately tied to the nation's success—a recognition that would be embodied in the massive urban-renewal programs undertaken by Lee's PAP government. No opulent mansions, red carpets, or cheetahs, but a national order built on the rational and efficient order of its structures.

The impact that Lee's lessons from Africa would have on Singaporean space would also be reflected in Singaporean poetry. As many critics have noted, Anglophone poetry in Singapore has occupied a peculiarly privileged place with regard to state-building. Rajeev S. Patke writes, "the poet in Singapore bears an over-determined relation to the development of the state into nation, especially during the first few decades of the history of poetry in Singapore" ("Voice" 90). Similarly, Robbie B. H. Goh notes, "[i]n a variety of ways... this [Anglophone] poetry echoed and in many cases articulated the macro-narratives of nationhood" (38). While these correspondences take several forms, I am most interested in how these parallels operate through representations of space. Goh accurately observes:

> The poetic treatment of space often becomes foregrounded... taking on a central symbolic role as the means of constructing a shared communal and ultimately national space. In this sense Singapore's poetry of emergent nationalism once again reinforces, and is reinforced by, a kind of national ideology, in this instance the *symbolic control of space* enacted by the government's Housing Development Board (HDB) and similar agencies.
>
> (Goh 34; emphasis added)

To be sure, both "symbolic" and actual control of space was effected under Lee's PAP. After being expelled from Malaysia in 1965, Singapore's most immediate problem was the question of a new "hinterland," as well as the problem of the association of its majority Chinese population with Communist China.[3] Eliminating union power, arresting leaders of the previously allied Barisan Socialists,

---

3. Singapore had been careful to maintain a military alliance with Britain after its withdrawal and forged new strategic partnerships with Australia, New Zealand, and the U.S. Lee secured military expertise and advice from Israel (another nation with troubled boundaries) and, thanks to a quiet agreement made with Chiang Kai Shek's son Chiang Ching-kuo in 1974, gained space to train Singapore's troops in Taiwan. For a history of Singapore's postindependence politics, see Chan.

and being ruthless toward anti-PAP (or "antinational") opposition were all crucial to ensuring social stability and the construction of an internationally oriented modernity. The government modeled its Economic and Development Board after Japan's Ministry of International Trade and Industry and reshaped the nation space to attract foreign manufacturing companies; Singapore eventually found its new economic "hinterland" in the large first-world markets of the U.S., Japan, and Europe. This required the construction of massive state-of-the-art industrial estates like the nine-thousand-acre one at Jurong, complete with "roads, sewers, drainage, power, gas, and water all laid out" (Lee, *From Third World* 61), as well as Housing and Development Board–built complexes that would eventually fill in most of the island. With the Economic and Development Board acting as a "one-stop shop" for foreign investors, the importance of *presenting* Singapore's modern infrastructure became the PAP's number one concern, to the delight of companies like General Electric and Hewlett Packard. Retrospectively describing the remarkable ability of Singapore to attract major international investment and manufacturers, Lee confirms that the modernization of Singapore's space was the defining factor:

> I thought that the best way to convince [visiting CEOs to invest in Singapore] was to ensure that the roads from the airport to their hotel and to my office were neat and spruce, lined with shrubs and trees. When they drive into the Istana domain, they would see right into the heart of the city a green oasis, 90 acres of immaculate rolling lawns and woodland.... Without a word being said, they would know that Singaporeans were competent, disciplined, and reliable, a people who would learn the skills they required soon enough. American manufacturing investments soon overtook those of the British, Dutch and Japanese.
>
> (*From Third World* 62)

The new cityscape, rather than simply being incorporated into poetry, became the impetus for new poetic images and, I argue, for thinking about, reflecting, and critiquing the very logic of productive postcolonial states. In the exemplary national poetry of Edwin Thumboo, we will see how a poetic aesthetic might be forged in terms of the new cityscape's productive demands. That is, if Lee ensured that the country's essence could be read from its architecture and built environment, Thumboo's poetry attempts to distill and present a nationalist essence through a poetic rendering of those same built forms. In contrast, for Arthur Yap, who has been called the "most complex and intricate poet of the Singaporean city" (Haskell 245), an equal investment in poetically reworking urban forms will show us other possibilities for thinking the Singapore nation.

Between graduating from the University of Singapore in 1955 and returning to do a Ph.D. in African literature in 1966, Thumboo (born in 1933) worked for the Department of Inland Revenue and the Central Provident Fund Board for seven years. His early proximity to bureaucratic structures of the state may account for what Dudley De Souza calls a "transition from the poetry of powerlessness to... the poetry of power" (302), seen in the shift from the personal mode of his early poetry to the explicitly public poetry of his collections *Gods Can Die* and *Ulysses by the Merlion*, from 1977 and 1979, respectively. While Thumboo's mature poems are an attempt to come to terms with uneven societal power under the PAP and the smallness of Singapore, they undoubtedly also work to forge a national, literary identity based on the government's developmental path. These poems have often been considered ideologically at one with the PAP development described above.[4] Shirley Geok-lin Lim writes, "much of Thumboo's later poetry comes from an explicit desire to explain the ways of the Singaporean state to his readers, to participate in converting 'cultural tolerance to active cultural acceptance'" (118).

We see such a desire in the poem "Island," from *Ulysses by the Merlion*, which narrates succinctly—almost simplistically— Singapore's startling transformation from tropical island to economic wonder. Initially, the virgin purity of the island's past is revealed through the frame of the speaker's memory, which is at once personal and mythic:

---

4. There have been many studies of Thumboo's poetry, as well as several comparisons between his work and Yap's. Significant works in addition to those of Lim, Patke, and Goh include Kirpal Singh and Ooi Boo Eng's study of Thumboo's early to mature poetic stages and Anne Brewster's monograph on the early experiments of Anglophone Singaporean and Malayan writers.

Once
There was a quiet island,
With a name.
You must believe me
When I say that sunlight,
Impure but beautiful,
Broke upon the bay, silvered
The unrepentant, burning noon.

(*Ulysses* 16)

The inhabitants of this paradise are generic Malay children, Aminah and Harun, "too young to know the sea," "who followed crab and tide." The idyllic image is elaborated by the requisite "Mangrove and palm" and "Houses on stilts, boats drawn up," until these fanciful illustrations are brought to a halt with the accusing lines "Romantic. Nostalgic. / But images change." The remainder of the poem narrates the replacement of every physical trace of the former way of life:

Nearby hills are pushed into the sea.
Tractors roar, lorries thrive
Till the ochre of the land
Scooped out day and night,
Crept upon the sand.
Aminah, Harun now reside in flats,
Go to school while father
Learns a trade.

Along Shipyard Road,
Not far from Bird Park,
A new song in the air:
Cranes and gantries rise;
Dynamo and diesel hum.
Men in overalls and helmets
Wield machines, consulting plans.

A welder's torch explodes
Into a rush of stars;
Rivets are hammered home till
Hulls of steel emerge.
Sophisticated, self-propelled,

> The towering drillers look attractive:
> This one bound for Norway;
> The one before works by Antarctica.
>
> (16–17)

In contrast to the sleepy island and unworldly inhabitants, tractors, lorries, cranes, drills, and boats testify to the immensely increased productive power of mechanized society. The previously unlocated island, floating alone as the word "Once" does, is now the mediating point between places as far off as Norway and Antarctica, marking not just a recognizable geography but the beginning of its history. The inhabitants, docile in comparison to the exploding torches and drills, now dutifully "reside in flats," attend schools, and learn trades. Women, unmentioned and presumably still limited to the domestic sphere, are apparently the only ones untouched by the modernizing process.[5]

Yet even as this is presented as a world dominated by machines, Thumboo suggests that after a necessary time lag, the liberation of these productive powers will give rise to the formation of a new, collective identity:

> In time images of power,
> Our emergent selves,
> Will be familiar
> As, first, the body learns
> This other song.
>
> (17)

For Thumboo, the potentially fearsome power of industrialized society is tempered by its status as simply "This other song" or, perhaps, the very song of poetry. In accordance with the developmental state's drive to modernization, top-down industrialization—the reshaping of the nation as "hills are pushed into the sea"—is simply necessary. At the same time, the people adapt to this new world and "the body learns," producing the first stage of Singaporean national identity. In his astute study on the links between the modernization

---

5. For a seminal account of the gender politics of the Singaporean state, see Geraldine Heng and Janadas Devan's analysis of state discourse surrounding desirable and undesirable forms of reproduction.

of urban space and government power, Beng-huat Chua has described how the left-leaning People's Action Party was first elected in 1959 by "a society craving for a new future" and a population that "strongly support[ed] a development-oriented government" (160). Although material development was actively desired by Singaporeans, what Thumboo's poetry provides is the necessary monumentalizing of its new forms into a national landscape. The very process of material development sees the poetic production of "images of power," with which its citizens can identify.

Although Yap, whose work is often pitted against Thumboo's, is less interested in national identities, he is no less interested in collectivities.[6] Born in 1943 and therefore of a slightly younger generation than Thumboo, Yap received an elite education at the National University of Singapore and the University of Leeds. In contrast to Thumboo's explicitly public poetry, his work is paradigmatic of the kind of Singaporean poetry that deals with the everyday, the commonplace, and the local. Regarding this literary strand of "emergent nationalism," Goh notes, "Apart from the sheer preponderance of poems directly or indirectly concerned with local places, the poetics of place involves a creation of 'commonplace' (to use the play on words which forms the title of Yap's 1977 volume)—and idiom of references, experiences, personages and topics which might plausibly form the common currency of the Singapore people" (36). If for Thumboo grand spatial transformations become poetic material in the service of national history, Yap's poetry heads in the opposite direction by taking on a small-scale but clear-eyed view of the changing industrial landscape. In "there is no future in nostalgia," from *Commonplace*, Yap reworks the same narrative of urban transformation that was the subject of Thumboo's "Island." Whereas Thumboo's task was to harness the energies and forms of the developmental project toward an official, national past, we can read Yap as trading in terms of what Anne Brewster describes as the "additive and iterative nature of memory" (Introduction xiii). Here, the replacement of human workers with machines is methodically recounted:

6. Another important poet often read in relation to Thumboo is Lee Tzu Pheng, whose 1976 "My Country and My People" reads something like a counternationalist poem and includes this memorable description of HDB flats: "They built milli-mini-flats / for a multi-mini-society" (162).

& certainly no nostalgia in the future of the past.
now, the corner cigarette-seller is gone, is perhaps dead.
no, definitely dead, he would not otherwise have gone.
he is replaced by a stamp-machine,
the old cook by a pressure-cooker,
the old trishaw-rider's stand by a fire hydrant,
the washer-woman by a spin-dryer

(*Space* 59)

Note two major contrasts to Thumboo's "Island." First, instead of the awe-inspiring technologies of modernization—roaring tractors and exploding torches—Yap chooses decidedly less impressive modern gadgets as poetic material: the stamp machine, the pressure cooker, and the spin dryer. The replacement of former human characters— "the corner cigarette-seller" or "the old cook"—by such technologies renders the moment of modernity anticlimactic and bathetic rather than momentous or historical. Second, Yap's poem diverges from Thumboo's nationalist aesthetic in its refusal to attempt any unifying consciousness that would wrap around and make nationalist sense of such changes. The poem ends simply and undramatically: "& it goes on / in various variations & permutations. / there is no future in nostalgia" (59). Yap neither aestheticizes the state-led modernization nor rues it for a previous time of authentic plenitude; his level-headed observer is simply content to note the changes and move on. Lim concludes that by "focusing on the particular situations of his community, [Yap] mocks them from an antagonistic position" (156) and defines his main poetic device as irony. Yet the distinction is not explained by a simple opposition between Thumboo as propagandist and Yap as ironist of state rhetoric. By understanding the complicated play of nationalist rhetoric, modernist developmental landscapes, and poetic form, we can address deeper assumptions and possibilities concerning literature and the constitution of subjects, citizens, and collectivities within a certain kind of postcolonial state.

The Developmental Revolution

Lee's—and relatedly, Thumboo's—nationalist rhetoric taps into and reveals the deeper logic of the modernizing Singaporean landscape, a logic that might be contrasted to the more familiar culturally nationalist positions articulated in other areas of the third world.[7] On closer examination, however, the PAP's apparently straightforward, pragmatist program of development has more in common with other, more typically revolutionary and liberatory postcolonial goals than first appears. Considering the case of Singapore, we need to ask, How is the production of a modernized national space—arguably *the* preoccupation of many postcolonial regimes—narrated by such regimes as the country's future path to national freedom? Such a narration, it seems, posits a statist version of Amilcar Cabral's theorization of national culture in terms of "the liberation of the process of development of national productive forces" (56). Cabral writes of the armed revolution against colonialism creating "a veritable forced march along the road to cultural progress" (64), wherein he assumes cultural progress to be a corollary of nationalized industrial development. With a slightly different emphasis, we might think of certain Pacific Rim postcolonies as evincing a *developmental* revolution that creates a forced march along the road to *material* progress.

Along the same lines as Cabral, Frantz Fanon famously diagnosed the postcolonial problem as the historical and ongoing weakness of the "national bourgeoisie," who become profiteering intermediaries between the nation and global capitalism. For Fanon, facilitating this "transmission line" (152) excludes the masses, inhibits the development of productive forces, and results in the stagnation of modern industry. In other words, without the intellectual—and not just muscular—participation of the masses, the "national bourgeoisie ... reveals itself incapable of simply bringing national unity into being, or of building up the nation on a stable and productive basis" (159). He illustrates this nicely:

> If the building of a bridge does not enrich the awareness of those who work on it, then that bridge ought not to be built and the citizens can go on swimming across the river or going by boat. The bridge should not be "parachuted down" from above; ... on the contrary it should come from the muscles and the brains of the citizens.
>
> (200–201)

---

7. Singapore's developmental logic, however, has much in common with other newly industrializing countries of the Asian Pacific, such as South Korea, Taiwan, and Hong Kong.

In arguing that under no circumstances should development be "para-chuted down" by the state, Fanon stresses the productive *and* political activity required of all members of the independent nation. Pheng Cheah has more recently posed a related question regarding the organic nation and the alien, externalizing mechanism of the state, the latter of which he refers to as *techne,* an Aristotelian term he views through the lens of Immanuel Kant's moral philosophy. "Can the social or political body," Cheah asks, "transcend finitude and assimi-late the artificial prostheses [the state] that threaten to contaminate it, or is it irreducibly exposed to an inhuman and nonorganicizable *techne*?" (224). Yet in contrast to Fanon's and Cheah's pessimism regarding the nation and the corrupting technologies of state that work against it, the material operations of *techne* may not always oppose the emergence of a postcolonial nationalism but actually constitute it. Thumboo has written of Singapore that unlike postcolonial African states, "the anti-colonial movement had been mainly intellectual in ori-gin and drive," such that the "dialectics of nationalism lacked a back-ground of intense mass suffering" (Introduction xiv); the explosive theories of Cabral and Fanon would therefore seem unsuited to a population simply craving "a development-oriented government" (Chua 160) and therefore accepting of statist *techne.* To complicate this, I argue that even in such conditions, state apparatuses must tacitly draw on revolutionary articulations of postcolonial nationalism and freedom in order to effect the "transmission line" and direct develop-ment toward international markets in a neocolonial manner.

Let us return to the remarkable physical form that political power has taken under the modernizing regime of Singapore's Lee. The physical trappings of political power associated with grand archi-tectural monuments or luxurious lifestyles were clearly not his goal; indeed, this may be one way of understanding the differences between certain African and Asian postcolonial modalities of sover-eignty.[8] Lee remarks how he and his colleagues had no intention of

---

8. Achille Mbembe describes Cameroon in terms of its "aesthetics of vulgarity," as a political power defined by the grotesque, obscene, and "phallocratic" (103, 110). In his account, postcolonial rule "must be extravagant . . . ; it must furnish public proof of its prestige and glory by a sumptuous (yet burdensome) presentation of its symbols of sta-tus, displaying the heights of luxury in dress and lifestyle, turning prodigal acts of generosity into grand theatre" (109).

memorializing their power in the usual manner of "renaming streets or buildings or putting our faces on postage stamps or currency notes" (*From Third World* 50). Rather, in Singapore, political power attains a more far-reaching physical imprint in the highways, housing complexes, industrial zones, bridges, and airports. Indeed, we can see the postcolonial leader's desire to transform space as akin to the modernist desire to apply the revolutionary power of technology to all realms of life. In Fredric Jameson's terms, the latter finds expression in Le Corbusier's minimalist architecture, which would replace the "diseased city fabric: the insalubrious, reeking, airless, sodden alleys of a dead inherited medieval city, the industrial slums of a modern agglomeration—best to do away with those streets altogether, to open all that to sun and fresh air by an act of joyous destruction, and to erect…exhilarating high-rises rearing off their ground on *pilotis* that stood as a symbol of defiance and refusal of, escape from, the old world, the old Europe, the nineteenth century" (Jameson 142). We might view developmental political policies and documents as akin to that modernist genre of the manifesto; what both genres share is a desire for the new, where a change in the aesthetic form engineers a change in the social. Lee's disgust with the slums of Singapore, which he encounters while canvassing for the 1955 domestic election, seems entirely congruent with the attempt to escape from the rotting nineteenth century and open up—in Le Corbusian fashion—to sun and fresh air. Lee writes:

> Another scene of filth and dilapidation was presented by the rows of mean, broken-down shophouses in Narcis Street and the roads leading to it on the site where Tanjong Pagar Plaza now stands. They had not been repaired for many years, and the drains were clogged with rubbish left by roadside hawkers, so that there was always a stink of decaying food. Enormous rats ran fearlessly in and out of these drains, ignoring the cats around….I retched.
>
> (*Singapore Story* 185)

Under Lee's direction, the Housing and Development Board did indeed decide it was "best to do away with those streets altogether" in the massive urban renewal projects that would eventually house almost 90 percent of the population and replace nearly all of Singapore's original building stock. Yet the impetus for this "joyous destruction" (Jameson 142) arises not from a desire to escape "the old Europe" and its congested industrialism but rather to correct the backward conditions of the Asian colony and its *lack* of industrial capabilities. Moreover, the modernity and freedom envisioned here is directed not by any ideal of nonaligned independent development, as articulated at the 1955 Bandung Conference, but by the nation's very willingness to link to the international market. National culture is thus not the mass struggle to achieve independent modernity but the by-product of the latter's *forms*.

Having imbibed the importance of first impressions from his trips to foreign states, Lee's first priority as prime minister was the presentation of a functioning and orderly Singapore. On his many official visits elsewhere, "[w]hat impressed me was not the size of the buildings but the standard of their maintenance. I knew when a country and its administrators were demoralized from the way the buildings had been neglected—washbasins cracked, taps leaking, water closets not functioning properly, a general dilapidation, and, inevitably, unkempt gardens. VIPs would judge Singapore the same way" (*From Third World* 175). Lee therefore envisions the modernity of Singapore against the background of other third-world locations also competing for investments of transnational capital. His comments indicate the paradoxical position of forging a new economy for *national* survival by means of creating a comparative regional advantage which best serves the *international* interest. In contrast to other postcolonies that may have followed the dire pronouncements of Fanon, Singaporean popular nationalist sentiment is reworked into economic nationalism, and physical infrastructural improvements and export levels themselves become the very symbolic terms of the national project: to produce or perish. The national scale of the built environment's reconstruction allows the PAP's commitment to the national project to be read symbolically and internalized by the population. Such "powerful signs" also signify the path of Singapore's future through the assumption of consent, that is, the population's desire for freedom through material improvement. The road to Singapore's national future is thus not just the one from the airport, but the one that leads the population into its new factories, processing plants, and hotels.

In his article on the rapid development of the Asian Pacific "tiger" economies, Manuel Castells offers a definition of the developmental state: "A state is developmental when it establishes as its principle of legitimacy its ability to promote and sustain development, understanding by development the combination of steady high rates of economic growth and structural change in the productive system...." (56). He continues: "The historical expression of such a societal project generally takes the form...of the building or rebuilding of national identity, affirming the national presence of a given society or a given culture in the world...." (57). What we see in Singapore and similarly developed Pacific Rim countries is an "economic and structural change" in the *productive system*—and not the social system—which is legitimized and most clearly inscribed in the concrete forms of the "building or rebuilding of national identity." The success of Singapore's manufactured products, shipped and consumed all over the world, effectively constitutes its "national presence" on the international scene.[9] Complicating narratives of simple authoritarian repression or the blind desire for material improvement, Castells observes that "the fundamental element in the ability of developmental states to fulfill their project was their political capacity to impose *and internalize* their logic on the civil societies" (64; emphasis added). Despite the fact that the forms of development promoted usually replace local building methods and structures with generic layers of concrete or asphalt, when combined with a rhetoric of crisis and survival, they confirm that the revolutionary national task is none other than accelerated economic development.

We thus arrive back at a strange reformulation of Cabral's notion of national liberation as the liberation of productive forces: here, the subject of postcolonial national freedom or independence is shifted away from a national people to the "setting-free" of its productive powers. The subject of freedom moves from living societies to the

---

9. Such forms are able to signify future success to the outside or become objects of national competitive development (South Korea's Park Chung Hee and competition with North Korea); or they can showcase the operation of a model provincial economy in the face of political exclusion (Taiwan and the Kuomintang). In such cases, the shift to a modern, built environment is the leap into the future that legitimizes the national project of future development.

dead labor of commodity production, and the mediating links between them become the nationalized housing developments, factories, and ports. National culture may then be defined as that *in the name of which* the shift in mode of production is undertaken. The nation is produced, paradoxically, as the unchanging term that organizes and directs the transformation of the rest of society. By returning to the poetry of Thumboo and Yap, we can now trace different responses to this developmentalist landscape.

Poetic Reinscriptions and Productions

Thumboo and Yap have been described by Lim as "both construct[ing] an imagined community called Singapore," one speaking for "social harmony," the other speaking against "social hypocrisies" (156). More specifically, we can understand the differences between Thumboo and Yap in terms of their respective relationships to language, technology, and the national landscape. As noted above, independence for Singapore was not characterized by a violent anticolonial struggle: although the Malayan Emergency was significant, the island passed relatively peacefully into home rule in 1959. This, Thumboo recalls, along with the mixed racial makeup of colonial Singapore, made the forging of a nativist oppositional voice difficult. The brief effort to "assemble a synthetic language using English as a base with importations from Mandarin and Malay"—"Engmalchin"—was short-lived, rendering the language of colonial bureaucracy and postcolonial development the only available national literary language (Thumboo, Introduction xvi).[10]

According to Thumboo, who is himself of mixed Chinese and Indian heritage, because the language that poets are "obliged" to use is no one's native language but everyone's "second tongue," English carries less of an anticolonial national identity than Chinese, Tamil, or Malay. The solution to forging a national literature in English therefore relies heavily on remaking the language "by adjusting the interior landscape of words in order to explore and mediate the

---

10. We should note, however, that before 1987, English was the language of instruction for only about 10 percent of the population, and a dialect of Chinese (and not the "official" Chinese language of Mandarin) was the mother tongue of most Singaporeans.

permutations of another culture and environment" (Introduction ix). That is, the task is to map the interior poetic and linguistic landscape on to an external one, differing from much other postcolonial writing in English which marks specificity of place through nonstandard syntax or dialect. Thumboo admits that he has chosen the public form of poetry to carry the "pro-nationalist feeling" that was a natural sentiment for Singaporeans of his generation ("Interview" 269). The 1965 separation from Malaysia meant that whereas for Lee the task was to find an economic hinterland, the proper task for Singapore's poets was to construct a "psychic hinterland." Thumboo explains, "We are busy constructing a common, shared culture out of the very diverse elements we have inherited, and therefore the creation of this hinterland is important because it really is the base, upon which all writing ought to rest" ("Interview" 272). Thumboo's lyric poetry, therefore, attempts to narrativize a people's relationship to this hinterland in a way precisely determined by the developmental revolution described above. If Lee saw the ability of the landscape to narrate the nation's future, Thumboo uses it to invoke the nation's past. As evidenced in "Island," Thumboo must refigure the nation diachronically through a narrative history of the city-state's development.

The consequence is that in his less reflective poems, Thumboo's voice is almost at one with PAP national rhetoric. In "Catering for the People," Thumboo admonishes those responsible for the "delinquent days" of Singapore's 1960s race riots with the appropriate government reminder of the common task of national arrival:

> *Bring the hill to the valley, level the place and build,*
> *And generally cater for the people . . .*
> Set all neatly down into Economy.
> There is little choice—
> We must make a people.
>
> (*Gods Can Die* 56)

It is difficult to tell whether these lines are ironic parodies of PAP rhetoric or not. Thumboo goes on to list, in Lee style, the marketable strengths of the emerging city-state: "We have a promising amalgam— / Youth, anger, a kind of will, a style of politics, / And bargain hard, sell common and unlikely things." The final stanza, moreover, reminds the reader of Singapore's geopolitical precariousness, the most concrete of shared political motivations:

> We are flexible, small, a boil
> On the Melanesian face.
> If it grin or growl, we move—
> To corresponding place,
> Keeping sensitive to trends, adapting,
> To these delinquent days.
>
> (57)

Thumboo's free-verse poems, with their succinct, pragmatic language, thus align neatly with official national ideology, or, in Patke's words, "Thumboo…adopts the persona of a friend to the post-independence nation" (*Postcolonial Poetry* 75). In the logic of "Catering for the People," insecurity over Singapore's immediate and potentially hostile neighbors (Malaysia and Indonesia) is countered by a general education and a complete spatial reorganization of the domestic sphere—"*level the place and build.*" If Thumboo does not quite celebrate the political and economic direction of the nation, he accepts it out of his rational understanding of the nation's tenuous viability. In such poems, the sense of "the national" comes from an understanding of the *Realpolitik* project of building (economic/political) stability.[11] The personal, poetic "I" thus slides seamlessly into the nationalistic "we."

This is not to say that Thumboo's poems are always simply mouthpieces for the developmental state and its official historical narratives. His poem "The Way Ahead" questions the already-decidedness of the use of the city. Appropriately for Singapore's premier poet, this poem is nothing less than a poetic rendition of a bureaucratic planning meeting:

> We were to speak, to chat,
> Involve our several minds on how
> To frame a City.
> We were asked, judiciously, to talk of beauty
> In a town, how the town would change,
> Turn supple, rugged, yet acceptable.
>
> (*Gods Can Die* 58)

---

11. Such a desire is reflected in overtly national/political poems in *Gods Can Die*, including "9th of August–I" and "9th of August–II," which deal with the day Singapore was thrown out of Malaysia and uneasily embarked on independence; "the Exile"; "The Interview"; and "A Quiet Evening" (which seems to be about a dinner with Lee Kuan Yew).

The speaker/poet is an interloper among the technocrats. Next to a "Professor," a "Senior Civil Servant who knew the way ahead," and "The Town Planner"—all with capitalized occupations—the poet is "The average man, the man-in-the-street / Feeling nervous." Invited to this think tank on the future of the city, the professor and town planner argue over competing visions: a congested Chinatown—"The teeming interchange of word and gesture"—versus the Corbusian ideal of "A flat in the sun" and "regiments of flats." Despite their apparent differences, both versions actually rest on the same assumption that the city can be rationally determined by "the right perspective" or correct "principles." Instead of advocating another competing "view," our poet-turned-bureaucrat balks: "What could I say? Or think?" His tactic is to change the language of the discussion from rational town-planning precepts to a poetics based on lived spatial experience:

> A City smiles the way its people smile.
> When you spit, that is the city too.
> A City is for people, for living,
> For walking between shadows of tall buildings
> That leave some room, for living.
> And though we rush to work, appointments,
> To many other ends, there must be time to pause,
> Loosen the grip of each working day,
> To make amends, to hear the inner self
> And keep our spirits solvent.
> A City should be the reception we give ourselves,
> What we prepare for our posterity.
>
> (59)

Thumboo affirms the nonrational aspect of the urban environment as the backdrop to the everyday and as the material counterpart to the collective "people's heart." Unlike the modernist emphasis on sun and fresh air as natural rights, he emphasizes the need "For walking between *shadows* of tall buildings." Instead of presenting a city teeming with life, Thumboo reminds us it is also what we leave behind on our deaths, "What we prepare for our posterity"; it is the very image of national heritage to be passed on. The "way ahead," Thumboo indicates, cannot be exhausted by the technocrat's national vision. At the same time that Thumboo recognizes, in many of his poems, the lack of choice for developing states, he seems unsatisfied to leave the defining of the nation entirely to the state. He thus both participates in the language of the state (English, bureaucratic) and shows how it has set up immovable terms of debate (where the nation equals economy, education, plus town planning). The question remains as to whether Thumboo, by bringing in the poetic, lived, and unquantifiable elements to the experience of the city, actually challenges PAP developmental logic or is merely the "voice of a propagandist mediating for 'active cultural acceptance'" (Lim 118). Rather, we can see Thumboo's poetry as offering the appropriate nationalist structure of feeling corresponding to the facts of political and economic developmentalism: poetic renderings naturalize and aestheticize the city as the *proper image* of "our emergent selves."

More interesting, however, is the way that Thumboo accedes to a model of poetry that sees its role simply as mediating or reconciling the existing realities of the nation to its people. While the formal tone, public nature, and influence of canonical English poets have all been identified in his poetry, what remains unsaid is Thumboo's remarkable fidelity to the objects of the Singaporean landscape as his poetic material. The relevant theory of reading here is Pierre Macherey's insight that literature is not merely a reflection of some other reality but "is an authentic *production* rather than a reproduction" (qtd. in Kavanagh 36) that nevertheless uses existing social realities as its raw material. In terms of this theory, we see how Thumboo's poetry assumes that the only way to use those "raw materials" is as pregiven, self-evident social objects, which results aesthetically in the "effect of deliberate arrangement" and "expository constructions" (Lim 114). Although the added contours of mythic history or daily lived experiences add another dimension to the imposing forms of Singapore's new landscape, they do not, in the end, challenge their fundamental status as something to be accommodated. By accepting both the forms and terms of "development," Thumboo's poetry thus participates precisely in the reinscription of material progress into cultural-national progress and history.

By contrast, Yap's poetry invokes what we might term "small-*m*" memory (Yap's general aversion to capital letters will be discussed further) and is often characterized by a limited, singular perspective. In explicit opposition to Thumboo's wide-lensed, nationalist perspective, Brewster notes that "many of [Yap's] scenes are framed by a window" (Introduction xvi); the preferred point of view is often from within the narrow and intimate Housing and Development Board flat. The effect is to reverse the top-down view of the cityscape and undermine those official discourses of development. In "sunny day," for example, the window frame thoroughly domesticates even the sun's actions—"sunny day / comes through the window / and sits on the table" (5). In "june morning," originally published in Yap's 1974 collection *Five Takes*, the mundane viewpoint of an anonymous inhabitant actually seems to precede the existence of the landscape:

> think sharp:
> this scene is also very brittle,
> copes with the problem of the accidental
> to make it come more fully to life.
> you look up from your thick black diary,
> frowning, lines fragile as little bones
>
> and it is you who structure this scenery.
>
> (37)

What is given substantial reality in this poem is not the observed exterior world from any perspective—the "brittle" scene—but the reader's internal thought: "your thick black diary." Such a shift in scale and hierarchy is echoed at the linguistic level, where Yap differs starkly from Thumboo's standard, at times formal, English. Patke notes, "Yap at his best excels at projecting a voice that is uniquely personal, but capable of absorbing Singlish [Singapore's English dialect] into the dramatization of a wide range of local sensibilities and speech habits" (*Postcolonial Poetry* 75). As Yap himself has stated, however, it is not merely a choice between standard English and the development of a local literary language:

> [I]t is certainly not merely a question of "standardness" nor is it, on the other hand, a set of quaint terms and idiosyncratic structures....It is the use of language where the notions of "standardness" and "non-standardness" are not external prescriptions and where, internal in the situation, the two terms are perhaps not so crucial at all.
>
> (qtd. in Patke, "Voice" 92)

Yap's poetry, then, does more than simply narrate an oppositional, personalized experience "from below" in vernacular and local idiom. It involves "a bigger clutch of parameters" (Yap, qtd. in Patke, "Voice" 92) that questions the poet's very "fidelity" or responsibility to the raw materials of his or her society. I have described how the new technological landscapes of statist development—the prosthesis of *techne*, to recall Cheah's analysis—may be poetically inscribed through a coherent, mediating nationalist poetic voice (Thumboo) and, in reverse, challenged by a local, "bottom-up" perspective (Yap). While on one level Yap's work does offer an alternate, grass-roots version of Singaporean experience, more radically, it *reveals and goes beyond* the material logic and ideology of the new productive landscape, undermining poetry's ontological dependence on those very forms of modernization. Let me work through this claim in two parts. As noted above, for Macherey, the available materials and social conditions do not fully determine the form of the work: "A condition is not that which is initially given, a cause in the empirical sense; it is the principle of rationality which makes the work accessible to thought" (55–56). As James H. Kavanagh puts it, the special nature of literature's transformative labor is that it "'resumes,' elaborates, and displays the ideological in a peculiar way, endowing it with a *visibility* that it did not have before the literary work" (36).

Yap's poem "& the tide" (1977) performs precisely this labor that makes visible the rationality—and not merely the material forms— of urban renewal.

> & the tide which is being urban-renewed
> at bedok must go on its own tidy ways
> without too much of a fuss,
> coming in as riprap waves
> met by the breakwaters
> or going out sufficiently
> for undisturbed analysis.
> & the sum of their margin:
> a littoral of slightly raised damp sand
> & carefully arrayed litter.
> out there where the waves curl,
> the liquid is greenly uneven
> in the sun's rays & the sky's
> layers of noon darkness.

(58)

The ostensible theme of the poem is nature, where the tide, waves, sand, and sun's rays compose something like a beach scene. Yet these untamable natural forces all succumb to the calculus of a Housing and Development Board bureaucrat. The tide becomes another controllable feature of the landscape, "going out sufficiently / for undisturbed analysis," showcasing Yap's ironic ear for "the formal bureaucratic English used by the civil-service class" (Lim 152). From the perspective of the productivity-driven planning tenets, curving waves and liquid are found lacking as "greenly uneven," the double-stressed syllables of the phrase ironically demonstrating the equilibrium and measure demanded. Yap's originality lies precisely in the absurd application of the logic of urban renewal to that most romantic of poetic material, the natural landscape, such that every inch of sand and water is now subject to the tidy imperatives of the productive state. By taking this logic, which pushes "tide" into "tidy" and "littoral" into "litter," to its illogical extreme, the poem distills the peculiar ideology of the developmentalist landscape—its indiscriminate and constant renewal—offering a deeply parodic materialist critique. Commenting on the enigmatic final lines of the poem, "the renewal of a large imagination / may be rare, in a seascape" (58), Dennis Haskell comments, "Yap's poem may suggest that curtailment of nature means curtailment of the imagination also" (246).

The second part of my claim—that Yap moves beyond a materialist ideology—deals with just this "renewal of a large imagination," and how his work simultaneously offers an alternative image of expansion. A striking feature of Yap's urban poetry is its anthropomorphization of the landscape and lack of poetic agents. In the early poem "expansion" (1971), for example, the poet contemplates how

> the skyline of houses
> grows with the sky
> and who can tell
> what is this completion;
>
> (10)

The poem progresses by way of loose chiasmus, putting the sky and houses into a reversed relation with "sponginess":

> the line of sponge houses
> soaks in the sky

> as the sponge sky
> seeps into the houses.
> where once houses hung from sky
> they now are clutches.
> so one urban expansion
> has to lean on another
> or they die.
>
> while the tree of night grows and grows
>
> (10)

Mysteriously, the expanding stretch of new dwellings is absorbed, spongelike, into the darkening sky, where they take on a life-form of their own. Existing as hybrid creatures in "clutches," they must "lean on another" in order to survive. We might think of the poetic impulse here as the reverse of that in "& the tide." Instead of nature being controlled and directed by an absurdly rationalist logic of development, here, the very principle of "expansion" is what gives life to usually inanimate objects. In this case, the logic of the natural world—the symbiotic connection between life-forms, the tendency for creatures to huddle together—takes over the man-made environment. The result is an oddly antihumanist but living landscape; not quite devoid of human evidence, it is still firmly rooted in the organic world.

We can understand Yap's reworking of nature/technology/ humanity in terms of Walter Benjamin's well-known study of the Paris arcades. Recall that for Benjamin, the new architectural technologies inaugurated in the nineteenth-century arcades (iron and glass construction and mass production) function as something like a text in which competing images are reflected. The shift from traditional masonry columns to iron-strut construction, for example, elicits "images in the collective consciousness in which the old and the new interpenetrate" (4). Benjamin explains:

> These images are wish images; in them the collective seeks both to overcome and to transfigure the immaturity of the social product and the inadequacies in the social organization of production. At the same time, what emerges in these wish images is the resolute effort to distance oneself from all that is antiquated—which includes, however, the recent past. These tendencies deflect the imagination (which is given impetus by the new) back upon the primal past.

In the most provocative of Yap's poems, we see both the critiquing of the "inadequacies" of the developmentalist logic—or the revealing of its absurd logic—and the "deflect[ing of] the imagination" which intertwines the new and the "primal past." Yap reveals how these new urban technologies give rise not only to the urge to historicize and order them into a national image à la Thumboo, but also to the impetus for radically reimagining a social landscape where buildings and sky are organically connected, animate houses huddle together, and large-scale renewal applies to the imagination. Thus at the moment of the actual wiping out of communal kampongs (Malay villages) under the processes of urban renewal, the new landscape also enables emergent images of a primal, mythic collectivity. In other words, Yap's poems do not merely narrate a localized, culturally specific viewpoint to counter the top-down, parachuted *techne* of roads, urban redevelopment, or bridges. His poetry also offers us a way beyond both Lee's statist projects and Fanon and Cabral's commitment to the release of people's productive powers for the authentic national project. Most radically, Yap's poetry delinks the forms of production from the productive landscape itself. To put it in Benjaminian terms, his work reflects on the inadequacy of "immaturity of the social product"—on the forms of the developmental landscape—in order to liberate the forces of *thinking* and the reimagining of a collective project.

To look more carefully at the formal means by which Yap achieves this, let us turn again to one of Thumboo's poems. Recall "The Way Ahead" and Thumboo's re-creation of a bureaucratic planning meeting. Despite his acknowledgment of the spaces and moments that escape rationalist planning principles, the "City" retains it capitalization and stability as object throughout the poem. Similarly, despite the free-verse form, for much of the poem the line length and rhythm are roughly uniform, with each capitalized line corresponding to a natural breath or phrasal unit. In contrast, a poem like Yap's "would it have been" from *Down the Line* (1980) relishes in breaking as many poetic conventions as possible. The first part of the poem reads:

> would it have been different if it were not an apple
> but a bomb which bit the world into being
>
> &, whatever the conditionals, would it be different
> after the bite, the lingua franca of the world

were sign language, metalanguage, antilanguage,
argot, braille, ipso facto esperanto...

(82)

First, as with all of Yap's poems, uppercase letters are completely eschewed, giving all words the same (lack of) formality. Second, the poem seems less interested in mediating a world out there than in playing with a grammatical structure, the conditional tense: "would it have been different. . . ." The structure of each line, moreover, demonstrates the extent to which Yap rejects phrase- or breath-based poetic form. The second stanza starts abruptly with two typographical symbols—"&,"—and continues with two instances of interruptive enjambment: "different / after the bite" and "world / were sign language." The poem concludes:

> houses were nests & people prefabricated
> soyabean sculptures,
>
> sunlight falling on a field burnt grass
> into terminal rainbows,
>
> cities held to ransom by their own devils
> or collective dream sequences
>
> : would it be very different if all these things
> have had being been untrue?

(82)

Even in the three stanzas where the poem settles into a regular formal pattern of three discrete scenic images—"houses," "sunlight," and "cities"—the *content* of these images moves us firmly into the world of unreality. As in the previous poems discussed, Yap disrupts or confuses our idea of natural versus man-made logic by proffering nest-houses, "prefabricated / soyabean sculptures," and cities plagued by "collective dream sequences." What is most striking is the poetic challenging of their status as unreality. We expect the final stanza to read "would it be very different if all these things / *had been true*?" only to discover that the question imagines the poem's content being *untrue*; or—better—it describes the very problem of constructing an appropriate grammatical tense ("have had being been") for their unstable ontological status. What Yap does, therefore, is offer a powerful way to reread what otherwise would merely be the signifying forms, or *techne*, of state power—those pre-fab houses, planned cities, and reclaimed tracts of land. Like the moment of Benjamin's Paris arcades, the gleaming new forms of Singapore's modernity are *also* an opportunity to deflect the imagi-nation into previously unthought "collective dream sequences."

Many analyses of Asian Pacific modernity define it only in terms of the economic and have had little to say about culture or national-ism prior to the political liberalization of the late 1980s and 1990s. An examination of the politics and poetics of Singapore's develop-mental landscape reveals a more complicated understanding of sta-tist versus popular nationalist aesthetics and points to the need to look further at how literature that reflects on new roads, housing complexes, or factories—the very *techne* that fills in and connects the developmental state to the rest of the world—might offer other ways of thinking about nationalism. As demonstrated in the Singaporean case, a postcolonial nationalism might arise where dis-continuities between peoples, languages, and states (the results of colonial histories) find symbolic cohesion in the very "parachuted-down" forms of material development that Fanon warned against. The liberation and development of productive forces becomes mir-rored in the changing landscape, and its symbolic representation may gesture toward both a national past and a geographical or eco-nomic future. On the other hand, these very objects of *techne* may also give rise to wholly new ways of conceiving the social land-scape, in which developmentalism, communal forms, and futurity are themselves open to debate. Either way, we shall have to trace further trajectories of this development, its struggles and achieve-ments, in order to avoid the simple judgment of an inherently nar-row and conformist Asian form of modernity.

New York University

WORKS CITED

Benjamin, Walter. *Arcades Project*. Trans. Howard Eiland and Kevin McLaughlin. Cambridge, MA: Belknap-Harvard, 1999.

Brewster, Anne. Introduction. *The Space of City Trees: Selected Poems*. By Arthur Yap. London: Skoob, 1999. xi–xxii.

———. *Towards a Semiotic of Post-colonial Discourse: University Writing in Singapore and Malaysia, 1949–1965*. Singapore: National U of Singapore/Heinemann Asia, 1989.

Cabral, Amilcar. "National Liberation and Culture." *Colonial Discourse and Post-colonial Theory*. Ed. Patrick Williams and Laura Chrisman. New York: Columbia UP, 1994. 53–65.

Castells, Manuel. "Four Asian Tigers with a Dragon Head: A Comparative Analysis of the State, Economy, and Society in the Asian Pacific Rim." *States and Development in the Pacific Rim*. Ed. Richard P. Appelbaum and Jeffrey Henderson. Newbury Park, CA: Sage, 1992. 30–70.

Chan, Heng Chee. "Political Developments, 1965–1979." *A History of Singapore*. Ed. Ernest C. T. Chew and Edwin Lee. Oxford: Oxford UP, 1991. 157–81.

Cheah, Pheng. *Spectral Nationality: Passages of Freedom from Kant to Postcolonial Literatures of Liberation*. New York: Columbia UP, 2003.

Chua, Beng-huat. *Political Legitimacy and Housing: Stakeholding in Singapore*. New York: Routledge, 1997.

De Souza, Dudley. "*Gods Can Die*: The Writer and Moral or Social Responsibility." *Singaporean Literature in English: A Critical Reader*. Ed. Mohammad A. Quayum and Peter Wicks. Serdang: U Putra Malaysia P, 2002. 299–307.

Fanon, Frantz. *The Wretched of the Earth*. Trans. Constance Farrington. New York: Grove, 1963.

Goh, Robbie B. H. "Imagining the Nation: The Role of Singapore Poetry in English in 'Emergent Nationalism.'" *Journal of Commonwealth Literature* 41.2 (2006): 21–41.

Haskell, Dennis. "'People, Traffic and Concrete': Perceptions of the City in Modern Singaporean Poetry." *Perceiving Other Worlds*. Ed. Edwin Thumboo. Singapore: Times Academic, 1991. 237–49.

Heng, Geraldine, and Janadas Devan. "State Fatherhood: The Politics of Nationalism, Sexuality, and Race in Singapore." *Nationalisms and Sexualities*. Ed. Andrew Parker et al. London: Routledge, 1996. 343–64.

Jameson, Fredric. *The Seeds of Time*. New York: Columbia UP, 1994.

Kavanagh, James H. "Marxism's Althusser: Toward a Politics of Literary Theory." *Diacritics* 12.1 (1982): 25–45.

Lee, Kuan Yew. *From Third World to First: The Singapore Story, 1965–2000*. New York: HarperCollins, 2000.

———. *The Singapore Story: Memoirs of Lee Kuan Yew*. Singapore: Prentice-Hall, 1998.

Lee, Tzu Pheng. "My Country and My People." *The Second Tongue: An Anthology of Poetry from Malaysia and Singapore*. Ed. Edwin Thumboo. Singapore: Heinemann Educational, 1976. 162.

Lim, Shirley Geok-lin. *Nationalism and Literature: English-Language Writing from the Philippines and Singapore*. Quezon City, Philippines: New Day, 1993.

Macherey, Pierre. *A Theory of Literary Production*. Trans. Geoffrey Wall. New York: Routledge, 2006.

Mbembe, Achille. *On the Postcolony*. Trans. A. M. Berret et al. Berkeley: U of California P, 2001.

Patke, Rajeev S. *Postcolonial Poetry in English*. Oxford: Oxford UP, 2006.

———. "Voice and Authority in English Poetry from Singapore." *Interlogue II: Studies in Singapore Literature, Vol 2: Poetry*. Ed. Kirpal Singh. Singapore: Ethos, 1998: 85–103.

Singh, Kirpal, and Ooi Boo Eng. "The Poetry of Edwin Thumboo: A Study in Development." *World Literature Written in English* 24 (1985): 454–59.

Thumboo, Edwin. *Gods Can Die*. Singapore: Heinemann Educational, 1977.

———. "An Interview with Edwin Thumboo." Conducted by Peter Nazareth. *Singaporean Literature in English: A Critical Reader*. Ed. Mohammad A. Quayum and Peter Wicks. Serdang: U Putra Malaysia P, 2002. 266–81.

———. Introduction. *The Second Tongue: An Anthology of Poetry from Malaysia and Singapore*. Ed. Edwin Thumboo. Singapore: Heinemann Educational, 1976. vii–xxxv.

———. *Ulysses by the Merlion*. Singapore: Heinemann Educational, 1979.

Yap, Arthur. *The Space of City Trees: Selected Poems*. London: Skoob, 1999.

IAN BAUCOM

Afterword: States of Time

e know no time when we were not as now,"
Satan raises his proud boast to Abdiel in book
5 of John Milton's *Paradise Lost*, "Know none
before us, self-begot, self rais'd / By our own
quick'ning power..." (859–61). Thus at one end of the spectrum of
the modern drama of the subject and the state, a rebellious claim to
the priority of the time of nonsubordinated collective life (the life of
the "we," the life of "us") *over* and *before* and *simultaneous* with the
time of sovereignty: a claim that the Hobbesian political theory
beginning to assert its hegemony at the moment of Milton's writing
can be understood—then, as now—to have charged itself with rendering not merely "outlaw" but, in a term Rita Barnard's superb
contribution to this collection renders newly resonant, "unimaginable." As Barnard, citing J. M. Coetzee's *Diary of a Bad Year*, notes:
"[I]t is characteristic of the novelist that the temporality—the plot
structure, if you will—of our subjection should be of interest. When
exactly did we voluntarily accede to the rule of the state? Can we
imagine an alternative to it? The safest answer is to say that we cannot: we are, as Coetzee declares, 'born subject.'" If, as Barnard thus
indicates, the capacity to render "the origins of the state...*sensu
stricto* unimaginable" may be taken as integral to the grammar of
that Hobbesian political theory whose enduring power Coetzee's
narrator unhappily acknowledges, then so too should the corollary
imperative be taken as crucial to the state's *arcana imperii*: the imperative to hold equally unimaginable and equally outlaw what Satan
asserts to be true—that in the contest with the sovereignty of the
state, there *is* a time outside sovereignty, and that that time is, and
always has been, "now."

Contemporary Literature XLIX, 4   0010-7484; E-ISSN 1548-9949/08/0004-0712
© 2008 by the Board of Regents of the University of Wisconsin System

I begin with Satan's boast and its Hobbesian rejoinder because it strikes me that between the bad angel's assertion of a self-begetting, self-raising, quickening time (a time, perhaps, in Walter Benjamin's terms, of "constituting power"), temporally coincident with the time of sovereignty (the time of "constituted power"), and the Hobbesian will to figure such an order of time dually unlawful and unimaginable—to outlaw it as epistemologically ungraspable and historically catastrophic—lie many of the issues raised in this special issue. We are accustomed to thinking of the nation, and to posing questions regarding the relation between literature and nation, in temporal terms. Nationalism—following Benedict Anderson, Benjamin, Frantz Fanon, Ernest Renan, and countless others—has become legible as a phenomenon of (at least) two distinct and overlapping registers of time: the time of the simultaneous and the time of the messianic, the time of the meanwhile and the time of a looming anteriority, the time of the performative and the time of the pedagogical. As such, the relations of the literary (and the aesthetic more broadly) to the nation, nationalism, and national culture are, in a certain sense, broadly evident (while in all of their particulars endlessly complex). Time finds meaning as narrative or in the lyric moment, through gothic haunting, along the grid-works of epic, or through countless other stylized forms. Whatever the case, time has its genres, and the nation, as a figure of time, thus also possesses its generic codes of interpretation and critique. The state, however, has yielded a thinner grammar of time, in significant part because it has seemed to succeed in putting the question of time outside itself or, at most, in producing a simple binary code of before and after. There was an "unimaginable" time *before* the state and then there *was* the state, which may progress through its various Hegelian, or Kantian, or Scottish Enlightenment "stadial" phases, but which inevitably marks its advent as coincident with the advent of true historical time—before which is the time of myth; time, in Hobbes's words of "no account" (76); time "unimaginable."

Or almost so. For as the rhetorical ambivalence of the "unimaginable" suggests, the time that cannot be imagined is also a time one would not wish to imagine, and which the prosodists of the state then promptly proceed to image, as threat, invoking the unimaginable as what Hobbes calls "a tract of time" (76): the dystopic time of the state of nature, the time of the war of all against all, the time of brigandage, the native time (not only for Hobbes but for Locke and for Kant) of America. With that second, savage figure of the unimaginable in place, the dominant time-scheme of the state is largely complete: in the present there is nothing but the state, no other order can be imagined; the properly historical past admits of no time without the state, except the unimaginable time of war from which the state delivers us; the future similarly contains nothing but the state, other than the nightmare of the return of the unimaginable. In this sense, the temporal grammar of the state mirrors by reversing the temporal code of the nation. In either case, present time is, finally, informed by the "deep" time of a looming anteriority. But where the promise of the nation is to model the present and the future on that mythic, utopian past ("we are what you were, we will be what you are" [19], as Renan's Spartan ode puts it), the temporal contract the state purports to sign with its "born subjects" is to guarantee that the unimaginable past will not invade the present and has been banished from the future. As negative homologies of one another, the time of the nation and the time of the state thus both diverge (where one finds its utopic source, the other locates its savage *raison d'état*) and complement one another, at least in Hobbes's account. Emerging "as if" by the consent of all its subjects, the state, Hobbes insists, gives birth not only to its own "over-aw[ing] power" but to a set of conditions that become culture's (including a national culture's) conditions of possibility—above all the conditions necessary for the cultivation of "arts," "letters," and "society" (75–76). The full time of the nation (past, present, and future) is thus bracketed *within* and contained *by* the present time of the state, and what had appeared to be two competing versions of the relations between the now, the what-has-been, and the what-is-to-come are subsumed within one dominant and over-awing order of time: the now time of the state, which sets itself off as guarantor of national culture and the sole measure of imaginable time.

That, at least, is how one might schematize what I have been calling the Hobbesian rejoinder to Satan's boast, a rejoinder that haunts not only Coetzee's *Diary of a Bad Year* but the long history of political and literary thought that lies between the publication of *Leviathan* and Coetzee's novel, and which thus, unsurprisingly, crowds its ghostly shadow over much of the recent critical theory (whether developed along Foucauldian lines or within a nexus of work by Walter Benjamin, Carl Schmitt, Giorgio Agamben, and Judith Butler) which in taking up the problem of state power and sovereignty has found Hobbes's shade unslippable. It is among the virtues of this special edition of *Contemporary Literature*, as I indicated above, not only to further the articulation of that ongoing critical project but to do so by providing a more complex account (or set of accounts) of the temporal orders of the state (and thus also of its "plot structures") than the Hobbesian scheme would allow. In my reading of these essays, that labor of complication takes at least three forms, the first of which Matthew Hart and Jim Hansen firmly articulate in their introductory essay. The problem of the state within the present moment, as they remind us, is not exclusively one of its hegemony, of its temporal unassailability, but one of its uncanniness, of its uncanny capacity to persist into the contemporary beyond the apparently waning conditions of its historical possibility. The end of the state, certain strands of globalization theory have suggested, inheres not in a fall "back" into a state of nature but in a supercession of the form of the nation-state by the form(s) of the global. And yet the state persists, now, perhaps, as its own figure of the unimaginable, of the anterior, the un-overcome; or as Hart and Hansen alternatively suggest, not as the archaic (national) opposite of the global but in a relationship of "mutual production" with the global, as the instrument which, once having licensed the triumph of the national, now enables and facilitates the flow of bodies, commodities, images, war machines, and laws across world space.

Whatever the case, whether viewed as an anachronism within globalization or as a predicate condition for "the agonistic interrelation" of global (including global literary) "parts," the purchase of the state on the imagination clearly shifts in a moment in which rather than being taken for granted as the *a priori* form-giving agent for one or another national culture's canon of "arts," "letters," and "society," the state's belated (uncanny, form-shifting) pertinacity up and down the global scale must, instead, be accounted for. And, certainly, one way to account for that persistence is to conceive of the state in Jamesonian terms, as, precisely, a genre: as an

epistemologico-aesthetic solution, that is, to a set of concrete historical problems, originally (in the fifteenth through seventeenth centuries) the problems of intracontinental European religious and civil
war and extracontinental imperial war-making. As Jameson, via
Ernst Bloch, has further argued, the problem of genres is not, however, only that of the first historical dilemmas they are called on to
resolve but of their portability into subsequent historical moments,
the problem of their use and reuse, the problem of their noncontem-
poraneity within the contemporaneous (141). As a genre of sovereignty within the present, the question of the state, this collection
thus powerfully implies, emerges as a dilemma of the untimely, of
the uncanny return not only of a *form* but of the crises (preeminently,
I would suggest, the crises of war) which that form of power was
first fashioned to resolve.

In our own war-haunted moment, however, the state persists not
only as a machine of world-making and remaking but alongside
(and perhaps *as*) a global mechanism for the production of stateless-
ness or, as John Marx powerfully demonstrates, for the management
of "failed" stateness. Two broad critical paradigms, he argues, present themselves for a reading of the failed-state/stateless zones of
the contemporary: one (via Agamben) that in reading the camp or
the terrain of national or global civil war (or as Hart indicates, "the
strike") as a space *of* exception and a space *for* the exceptional production of sovereignty again figures the persistence of the state in the
registers of the anachronistic and the uncanny; and the other
(Foucauldian) paradigm that in noting a "governmental" reason's
capacity to shade the distinction between the plenitude and the
absence of the state, and so normalize camp, war zone, and strike as
but another set of tasks for an administrative biopolitics, recodes the
state/failed-state dyad within a teleological narrative of the governmental end-of-politics. Whether read through the critical optic provided by Agamben or by Foucault, however, the topographic
simultaneity of thick-state and failed-state (or stateless) being within
the global expanses of the contemporary strikes me as posing a second temporal challenge to the Hobbesian account, the challenge of
what classical republican theory calls mixed-constitutionalism, the
challenge, alternately put, of the heterochronicity of a present
marked not by its full "afterwardness" to the unimaginable

time-without-the state but by the (now dystopically) Satanic simultaneity within the now of constituted and constituting power.

If, for Milton's rebel angel, the prospect of a mixed constitution of state-governed and stateless being provided a ground of hope that much contemporary thought reapprehends far more starkly—as, indeed, something akin to a condition of hopelessness in the face of the implacable resilience or expansion of developmental, governmental, or biopolitical reason—then the third significant contribution of this collection's recasting of the temporal codes of the state is, nevertheless, to recover the possibility of hope for life both *in* and *outside* the state and to recover in that hope a project for the future. The forms of such hope are various. In Jini Kim Watson's reading of the developmental and counterdevelopmental poetics of Singapore, they take the shape of a type of Benjaminian dream work of collective life (both human and inhuman) in the neoliberal city. For Jim Hansen, perhaps not precisely "hope" but the possibility of arresting the theater of violence which binds sovereignty to subjectivity emerges from another Benjaminian formulation—in an aesthetic of pure means, of narrative and temporal arrestment and silence (rather than liberal sympathy) before the spectacle of subordination. "Queer anarchism," as present in Robert Duncan's relentless desire for a way of "living differently," provides Eric Keenaghan with a way of imagining this opening to another future. And for Jeremy Cronin, as Andrew van der Vlies's provocative interview indicates, "the struggle for the desirable" need not exclusively imply a flight from the state but a determination (by the poet and the citizen) to shape the state as a "democratic hegemonic power." With that formulation, the collection returns us to one of its other points of departure, to Hart and Hansen's reminder that in our readings of the state, Foucault and Agamben do not serve as our exclusive sources; that Antonio Gramsci provides at least one other; that alongside (and potentially at every point of articulation of) the hegemonic there is the possibility of a counterhegemony; that the challenge of the literary is to expand not only the "archive" of our knowledge of those points of contestation but, in Diana Taylor's terms, the "repertoire" of the "imaginable," not only in the future but "now."

Duke University

WORKS CITED

Benjamin, Walter. "Critique of Violence." *Selected Writings, Vol.1, 1913–1926*. Ed. Marcus Bullock and Michael W. Jennings. Cambridge, MA: Harvard UP, 1996. 236–52.

Coetzee, J. M. *Diary of a Bad Year*. New York: Viking, 2008.

Hobbes, Thomas. *Leviathan*. Ed. Edwin Curley. Indianapolis: Hackett, 1994.

Jameson, Fredric. *The Political Unconscious: Narrative as a Socially Symbolic Act*. Ithaca, NY: Cornell UP, 1981.

Milton, John. *Complete Poems and Major Prose*. Ed. Merritt Y. Hughes. New York: Macmillan, 1957.

Renan, Ernest. "What Is a Nation?" Trans. Martin Thom. *Nation and Narration*. Ed. Homi K. Bhabha. New York: Routledge, 1990. 8–22.

Taylor, Diana. *The Archive and the Repertoire: Performing Cultural Memory in the Americas*. Durham, NC: Duke UP, 2003.

CONTRIBUTORS

MATTHEW HART is assistant professor of English and the Unit for Criticism and Interpretive Theory at the University of Illinois, Urbana-Champaign. His articles and reviews on modern and contemporary Anglophone writing have appeared in *American Literary History, Journal of Modern Literature, Modernism/Modernity,* and *Postmodern Culture.* His first book, *Nations of Nothing but Poetry,* is forthcoming from Oxford University Press in the Modernist Literature and Culture series.

JIM HANSEN is assistant professor of English and critical theory at the University of Illinois, Urbana-Champaign. His first book, *Terror and Irish Modernism: The Gothic Tradition from Burke to Beckett,* is forthcoming from the State University of New York Press. He has published articles on topics ranging from James Joyce and Oscar Wilde to Marxism and postcolonialism in journals such as *New Literary History* and *Studies in Romanticism.*

ANDREW VAN DER VLIES is lecturer in Anglophone postcolonial literature and theory in the school of English literature, language, and linguistics at the University of Sheffield. He is the author of *South African Textual Cultures: Black, White, Read All Over* (Manchester, 2007), the editor of a special issue of *English Studies in Africa* (2005), and co-editor of a special issue of *Scrutiny 2: Issues in English Studies in Southern Africa* (2008). He has published articles on South African authors, literary historiography, print cultures, and publishing history. He is an associate editor of *The Oxford Companion to the Book,* forthcoming in 2010.

RITA BARNARD is professor of English and director of the Alice Paul Center for Research on Women, Gender, and Sexuality at the University of Pennsylvania. In addition, she was recently appointed Professor Extraordinaire at the University of Stellenbosch. Her published work includes *The Great Depression and the Culture of Abundance* (Cambridge, 1995) and *Apartheid and Beyond: South African Writers and the Politics of Place* (Oxford, 2006), as well as numerous articles on twentieth-century literature and culture in journals and edited collections. She is editor-in-chief of *Safundi: South African and American Studies.*

JOHN MARX is associate professor of English at the University of California, Davis. He is the author of *The Modernist Novel and the Decline of Empire* (Cambridge, 2005) and has published articles on the feminization of globalization, postcolonial literature and the Western literary canon, and modernism and picturesque aesthetics. His current project is a book manuscript titled "Fiction after Liberalism."

ERIC KEENAGHAN is assistant professor of English at the State University of New York at Albany. His publications include *Queering Cold War Poetry: Ethics of Vulnerability in Cuba and the United States* (Ohio State, 2009) and several articles and reviews on queer theory and modernist poetry of the Americas. He is writing a book on Robert Duncan's "belated modernist poetics of life, war, and love."

JINI KIM WATSON is assistant professor of English and comparative literature at New York University. She has published articles on postcolonial theory and Asian literature and urbanism. The title of her book manuscript is "The New Asian City: Figuring and Imagining Built Form in Singapore, Seoul, and Taipei."

IAN BAUCOM is professor of English and department chair at Duke University. He is the author of *Out of Place: Englishness, Empire, and the Locations of Identity* (Princeton, 1999) and *Specters of the Atlantic: Finance Capital, Slavery, and the Philosophy of History* (Duke, 2005), and he is co-editor of *Shades of Black: Assembling Black Arts in 1980s Britain* (Duke, 2005). His current book project is tentatively titled "The Disasters of War: On Inimical Life."

◆ COMING IN ◆

CONTEMPORARY LITERATURE

◆ VOL. 50, NO. 1, SPRING 2009 ◆

NEW IN THE MLA SERIES
TEXTS & TRANSLATIONS

An Anthology of Modern Italian Poetry
In English Translation, with Italian Text

NED CONDINI, ed. and trans.
DANA RENGA, introd. and notes

I talian poetry of the last century is far from homogeneous: genres and movements have often been at odds with one another, engaging the economic, political, and social tensions of post-Unification Italy. The thirty-eight poets included in this anthology, some of whose poems are translated here for the first time, represent this literary diversity and competition: there are **symbolists** (Gabriele D'Annunzio), **free-verse satirists** (Gian Pietro Lucini), **hermetic poets** (Salvatore Quasimodo), **feminist poets** (Sibilla Aleramo), **twilight poets** (Sergio Corazzini), **fragmentists** (Camillo Sbarbaro), **new lyricists** (Eugenio Montale), **neo-avant-gardists** (Alfredo Giuliani), and **neorealists** (Pier Paolo Pasolini)—among many others.

Available March 2009

xxxviii + 436 pp.
Paper ISBN 978-1-60329-032-6
$11.95

Modern Language Association
26 Broadway, 3rd floor, New York, NY 10004-1789
646 576-5161 ▪ Fax 646 576-5160 ▪ www.mla.org